KEEPING AUSTRALIA

RIGHT

EDITED BY
JAMES ALLAN & PETER KURTI

CONNOR COURT PUBLISHING

Published in 2020 by Connor Court Publishing Pty Ltd

Connor Court Publishing Pty Ltd
PO Box 7257
Redland Bay QLD 4165
sales@connorcourt.com
www.connorcourt.com
Phone 0497-900-685

Printed in Australia

ISBN: 9781922449160

Front cover design: Maria Giordano

Front cover picture: Johannes Leak

Dedicated to the memory of Bill Leak

CONTENTS

INTRODUCTION

This book is the successor to 2016's *Making Australia Right: Where to from Here?* Back then I was approached by the publisher and asked what I thought of the idea of editing a book that would bring together some of this country's leading right-of-centre writers who would then give readers their take on the title's theme. My job was to find the top class writers, add something of my own, and put it all together in a book for Connor Court Publishing.

That same publisher must have thought the first effort, the 2016 book, was a success because here we are four years later and he wants a follow-up or successor book. Better still, this time I have a co-editor Peter Kurti. So this time it has been a two person job to find the top notch authors to write the chapters and then to agree a topic with each of them. Between us Peter and I came up with this line-up for the successor book, the one you are holding in your hands. Alan Moran (our only holdover from the first book) considers energy policy; Andrew Stone tackles immigration; John Ruddick writes on reform of the Liberal Party itself; Robert Carling surveys economic policy; John Slater examines labour relations; Terry Barnes focuses on health policy; Morgan Begg delves into the thorny topic of constitutional recognition; next comes a chapter on gender dysphoria written under a pen name (for reasons of professional survival); Karina Okotel explores women in politics; Richard Alston examines the ABC and the media more generally; John Lee does the same with foreign policy; Scott Prasser takes on the public service; Denis Dragovic wades into religious freedom; and the last two chapters are then those of your editors. I look at the theme of government bravery, in particular at its record when it comes to appointments. Peter goes more big picture and looks at whether this Morrison government can do what the title of this book posits, keep Australia right. So fifteen chapters in all (where last time there were but fourteen chapters, marking an added bit of value for all purchasers).

As with last time Peter and I looked for top people in their field and then, once again in keeping with the general philosophical approach of many of us on the right side of politics, we gave each author a very laissez-faire and minimal set of instructions. Take this assigned chapter topic of yours, together with the new theme not of making but (if plausible in that topic area) of keeping Australia leaning the way right-of-centre voters wish. Again, as before, there was no one-size-fits-all mandated approach. If authors wished to be highly critical of these past seven years of Coalition governments, fine. If they wished to heap praise on those same Coalition governments that was fine too. As was anything in between. And so readers will find a wide range of approaches. Some are big picture and philosophical. Some are more narrowly and factually focused. Some offer roadmaps for the future. Some don't. What you get is a variety of treatments by top writers on a panoply of the most important issues facing this country. That said, and as with the precursor book, the overall tone is not one of bubbling optimism.

In part that is a function of the Wuhan virus. This book was at first timed to come out a number of months ago. But Peter and I and the publisher decided to hold off and give the authors an opportunity to ponder on the effects this pandemic might have on their chapter's topic. That means this is a timely book on a host of topics written by top people in their fields. As with the 2016 effort, this book gives you something you will not find on the ABC, namely an outlook and an analysis that is something other than the bog-standard left-wing perspective that dominates so much of our airwaves, newspaper columns and social media writings.

As a very special extra treat we approached Johannes Leak to do the cover for this book. His late father, Bill Leak, then cartoonist for *The Australian*, had agreed to do the cover for the earlier 2016 book. When we asked Johannes to repeat the kindness of his dad, Leak Jr – today's cartoonist for *The Australian* – quickly agreed. Peter and I are most grateful to him for this. And if any reader happens to own the earlier book then by buying this one too that reader will have covers by *pere* and *fils*, two of this country's best ever political cartoonists and two friends of free speech.

I finish by noting that the 2016 book appeared almost immediately after Donald Trump's stunning, and for many his surprising, election win. This book will appear just before the 2020 US Presidential election in which Mr. Trump attempts to repeat that winning trick. Whether he succeeds or fails will have wide-ranging effects for Australia and for all western democracies. We will see. Meantime all of the contributors to this fine book hope that you enjoy reading it.

James Allan

July 8th, 2020

1

ENERGY

Alan Moran

Introduction

Policy scope

There are several different dimensions of energy policy. These include:

- exploration and development of coal, gas, petroleum and uranium resources;

- export policies; and

- policies concerning the transformation delivery and sale of these and other energy sources (principally hydro, wind and solar).

It is this third facet that is the prime concern of this chapter. Although exploration and development, and exports are vital to the national wealth (energy comprises over 35 per cent of exports) they will be addressed only in so far as they have a bearing on the supply of electricity and gas to domestic consumers.

Electricity supply has four components: generation, comprising 30-50 per cent of costs; local distribution, with 40-50 per cent; long distance transmission and retail (billing etc) each with about 10 per cent of the costs. Gas has a similar structure.

In the space of 30 years, policy interventions in electricity generation and gas exploration have shifted Australia from world leader to world laggard in the efficiency of its reticulated energy supply industries. The cause of this stands squarely with government. As well as being of considerable direct importance to households, energy prices and reliability are vital to the costs of all activities, hence policies of federal and state governments covering the domestic gas and electricity industries have created an economic tragedy for the nation.

The energy policy journey

With regard to the electricity industry, 25 years ago, the nation was a pioneer in global moves to replace central control of electricity supply with a market-based system based on competitive provision in generation and retailing.

Observing the benefits of electricity provision within a competitive market in several US jurisdictions and in the newly liberalised and privatised UK market, from the early 1990s Australia embarked upon the series of reforms. One catalyst of these reforms was, ironically, the result of the near bankruptcy of Victoria's state government, leading to the election of the Kennett government, which reformed and privatised the state's gas and electricity assets.

Learning from some unwanted effects of inadequate competition that followed Britain's electricity privatisation, the Victorian government tempered its goal of maximising the return from asset sales by a strategy that created sufficient entities to ensure competitive tensions. This was important to prevent undue market power and excessive prices and to drive cost cutting. The disaggregation of the assets into separate entities was accompanied by the adoption of a bidding process for generator scheduling, modelled on those in place in Pennsylvania, New Jersey and Maryland (PJM) and the England and Wales' markets.

Partly as a result of transmission links between the different state systems and partly because of government policy, other states adopted similar reforms to that of Victoria. The previous monopolistic supply by five government entities in the four interconnected states (all except Western Australia, the Northern Territory and Tasmania) was replaced by two dozen independent rival generator businesses. Though several of these were government owned (and this remains the case in Queensland) competition and less direct political control due to the corporatization and disaggregation of the government generators brought about vast improvements in the availability of supply and considerable cost reductions.

The outcome was an upgraded electricity supply that was already relatively cheap because of the nation's abundant, low cost coal reserves that are conveniently located close to major markets. The introduction of competition and profit-oriented private owners brought great changes in generator costs, including a more than fivefold saving in the heavily unionised labour force employed within the industry.

Competitive provision was also introduced in the retail sector with the individual state monopolies being replaced by some thirty rival suppliers. Distribution and transmission, as natural monopolies, were subjected to independent regulation over their prices and connection conditions.

Hence at the turn of the present century Australian electricity supply was cheaper than that of any other major nation and highly reliable. Generation was around 85 per cent coal with the rest split between gas and hydro.

The resurgence of the regulatory state
Electricity power costs

Uniquely throughout the world, and reflecting a governmental penchant for regulating in response to the latest fashionable ideas (in this case anti-war), nuclear power is illegal in Australia. But the high costs of nuclear power, in the context of Australia's low-cost coal, has probably meant Australia's ban amounted to virtue signalling. This may no longer be the case now that smaller modular reactors are becoming available.

However, the Australian regulatory malady soon spread beyond the nuclear psychosis. No sooner had Australia achieved its peerless position in electricity supply, than government regulatory initiatives started to undermine it. By far the most important of these initiatives was the reinvigoration of measures, which were originally put in place in response to ill-conceived fears about resource depletion, to require retailers to assist in reducing demand for fossil fuels.

Commencing in 2002, in a measure which then Prime Minister John Howard has described as his worst political blunder, requirements were introduced mandating an increasing share within generation of renewables (excluding large scale hydro, new supplies of it – then and still now – being banned on environmental grounds). The level of renewables required – the Renewable Energy Target (RET) – was set at 9,500 GWh by 2012, ostensibly two per cent of "additional" energy.

Once in place, there was unrelenting pressure to increase the renewables share and its associated subsidies. The Howard government itself commissioned former Senator Grant Tambling to review the program. His 2006 report, which the government did not accept, recommended a 50 per cent lift in the mandatory renewables level.

The Rudd ALP government, elected in 2007, was intoxicated by climate concerns. Rudd's first major act was the ratification of the Kyoto agreement to limit greenhouse gas emission growth. The Howard government had signed this and, though not having ratified it, was abiding by it with the renewable energy program and measures to prevent land clearing. Rudd expanded the renewables requirements to gradually grow to 41,000 GWh annually together with acceding to an unlimited number of small-scale units (roof top panels), subsidised at a lesser rate; new installations of these are presently running at over 10,000 GWh per year. State governments introduced additional subsidy-dependent renewable energy requirements.

The subsidies that these measures entailed came, via retailer obligations, from consumers, impacting on bills and on the competitiveness of (subsidy-free) fossil fuel generators. For several years, renewable energy subsidies may have contributed to keeping prices low by adding capacity with low marginal costs to an inflexible existing coal-based supply. The price outcome of the renewables' guarantee subsidy varied between $35 and $90 per MWh, far in excess of the $30-50 per MWh electricity wholesale price.[1] This meant renewable generators would automatically run, if available, irrespective of prices offered by other generators.

---

1 The renewables' price advantage is tempered by wind's reduced available during (hot, still) high price events, which brings about a discounted average price on the spot market.

The most reliable estimate of different power source costs was undertaken for the Minerals Council by Solstice/GDH. Table 1 summarises the costs of alternative power supplies.

Table 1: Cost estimates of different sources of generation

	Capacity factor	capex	Fuel	O&M	Tax 30% company	Total
	per cent	$/MWh	$/Mwh	$/MWh	$/MWh	$/MWh
650 MW black coal low	87	17	11	8	4	40
650 MW black coal high	87	22	35	15	6	78
650 MW gas ccgt low	82	9	55	3	2	69
650 MW gas ccgt high	82	14	86	12	3	115
650 MW solar low	20	62		12	16	90
650 MW solar high	20	127		19	26	171
650 MW wind low	37	42		12	14	64
650 MW wind high	37	68		33	12	115
650 MW solar+battery low	96	263		22	44	328
650 MW solar+battery high	96	782		29	102	913
650 MW wind+battery low	96	156		20	36	211
650 MW wind+battery high	96	577		43	73	693

Subsidies have led to an extraordinary growth of new capacity in wind and solar as illustrated in Figure 1.

Figure 1. New capacity installations

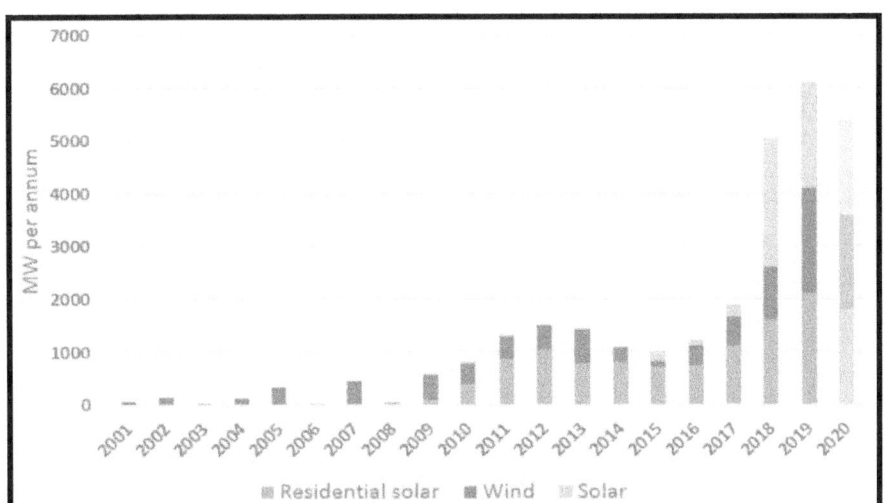

The initial effect of increased renewable supply was reduced incentives for additional commercial supply (the last major coal-fuelled electricity supply source was commissioned in 2006). This injection of subsidised renewable supply impacted upon the profitability of coal plant, both by reducing the hours it could operate and by imposing stop-start operating costs on plant designed for continuous operation. These factors disincentivised major maintenance expenditure.

In 2016, the fermenting effect of subsidies to wind and solar on coal plant profitability brought about the closures of South Australia's Northern and Victoria's Hazelwood power stations.

These closures took out about four per cent of the national electricity capacity from stations that had been supplying around seven per cent of demand. The upshot (see Figure 2) was a two-and-a-half-fold increase in the wholesale price compared with

2008 in a period during which overall inflation was 30 per cent. The COVID-19 crisis has led to prices temporarily failing due to overseas demand for gas collapsing and its diversion to domestic markets.

Figure 2

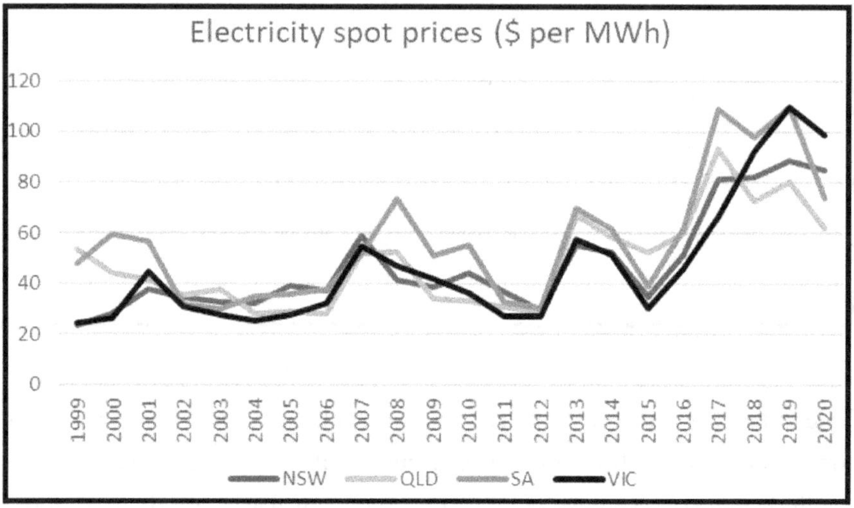

Source: *AEMO*

The increased prices have been accompanied by much greater price volatility as a result of the intermittent nature of wind.

The large share of subsidised wind capacity in South Australia, where wind supplied 44 per cent of the state's energy in 2018, has brought increasingly common negative prices which prevailed for 9.9 per cent of the time in August 2019 in that state. Such events are also seen in other states – on September 4 2019, the electricity spot price in Queensland was stuck at the -$1,000/MWh regulated floor price for several hours.

In addition, the displacement of coal generation by wind and solar has reduced stability and brought a deterioration of reliability.

One result of this was the complete loss of power in South Australia during September 2016. Although it is claimed that new requirements (or the proper application of extant requirements) will prevent a recurrence of that blackout, at a minimum the new supplies have necessitated a considerable intervention (and associated costs – amounting to $44 Million in 2019/20) by the market manager, as illustrated in Figure 3, to shore up system security.

Figure 3

(Source: Energy Security Board.)

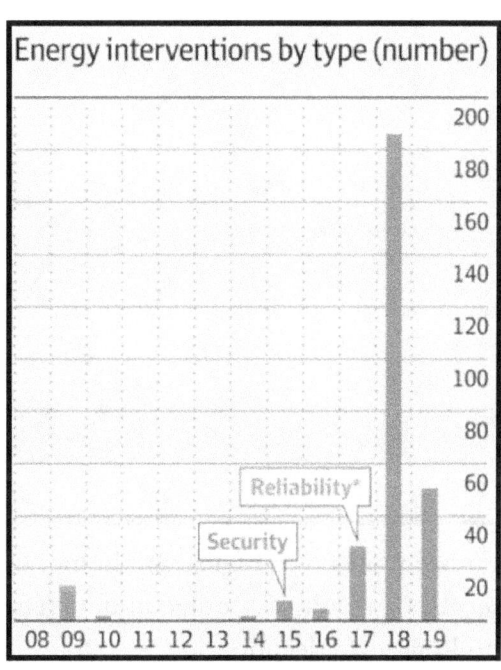

Reliability concerns remain and have spread to Victoria, which on one isolated hot day, Friday December 20th 2019, came close to failure when output from wind farms gradually fell to one third of its earlier levels. This was in spite of the fact that 9 out of the 10 major fossil units were on line, and demand was 15 per cent below previous peaks.

Government commissioned studies have usually shown a high degree of optimism over future renewable costs. This, together with sanguine expectations that the existing generators would continue to run, even with mounting financial losses, led consultants to consistently forecast imminent falls in prices. As indicated in Figure 4, forecasts commissioned by governments failed to pick the doubling of wholesale prices 2015-2018 and they likewise estimated (wrongly, to be clear) that such levels would not be reached even were there an intensification of the regulatory measures then in place.

Figure 4

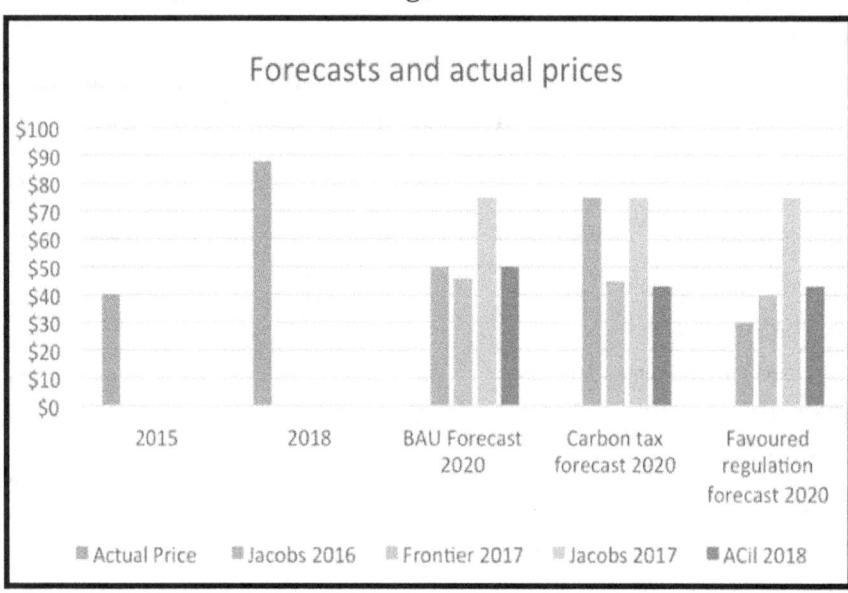

Future prices (see Figure 5), though likely to moderate in the near term as a result of a bulge in new renewable installations, indicate no long term decline.

The higher wholesale prices are reflected in the cost to the final customer, though the increased wholesale and environmental costs are muted by the relatively large share of total costs accounted for by networks, costs which have not shown the price escalation seen with generation. Even so, as evidenced below, Australian electricity prices have increased far more than those of other countries.

Figure 5

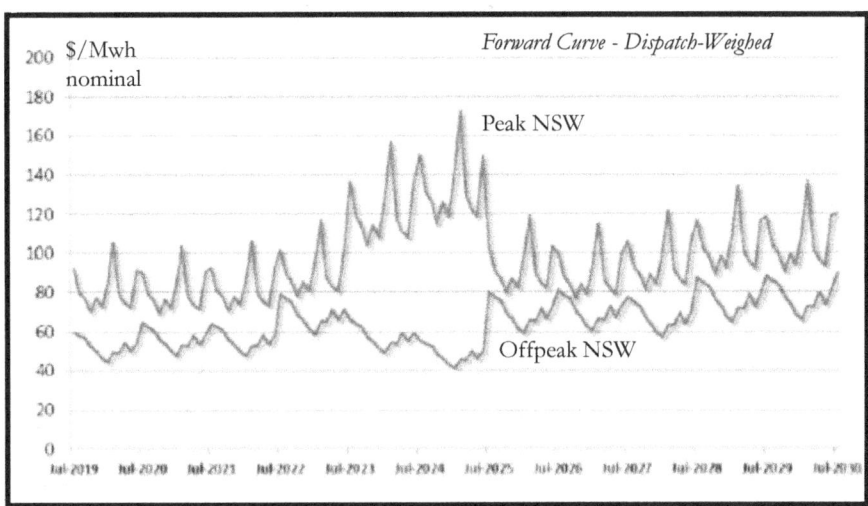

Source: Marsden, Jacobs

Figure 6

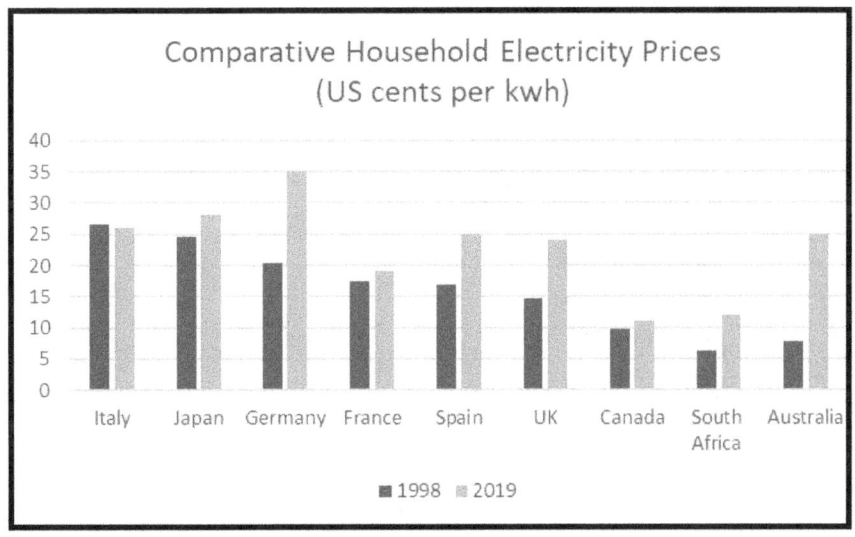

Sources: 1998 ESAA, 2019

Comparative data was not available for the US, China and India in 1998 but average household prices for China and India in 2019 were one third of those in Australia; US average prices were boosted by high prices in some States but averaged a little under one half of those in Australia.

While subsidies to renewables have been a feature of all OECD nations' electricity policies, as well as for some developing economies, Australia is far more indulgent in this regard than anywhere else. Per capita investment in Australia was almost twice that of the next two highest countries, US and Japan); it was fivefold that in China; and it was almost fortyfold that of India. Figure 7 illustrates this.

Figure 7

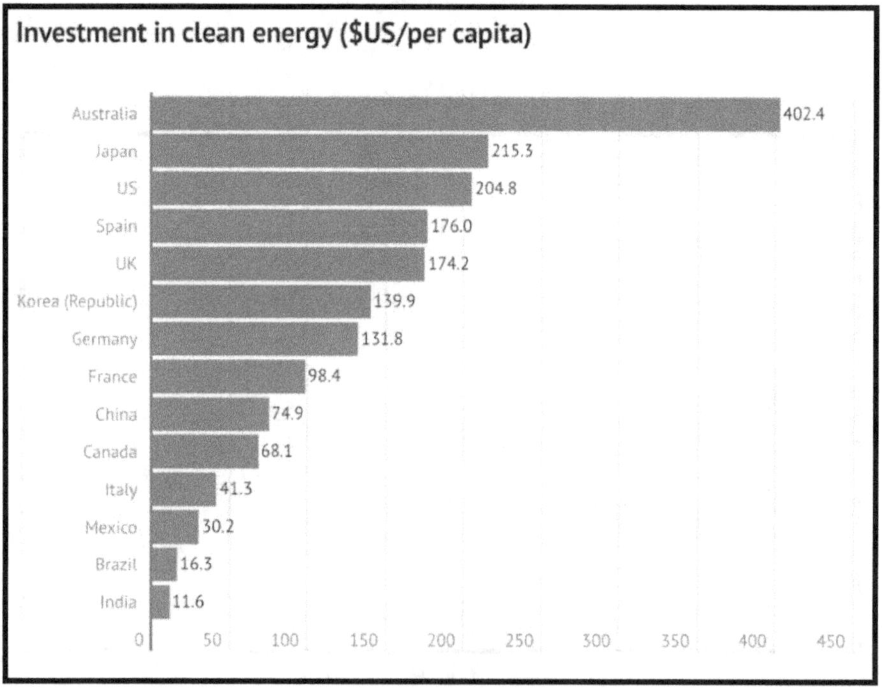

Investment in clean energy ($US/per capita)

Australia	402.4
Japan	215.3
US	204.8
Spain	176.0
UK	174.2
Korea (Republic)	139.9
Germany	131.8
France	98.4
China	74.9
Canada	68.1
Italy	41.3
Mexico	30.2
Brazil	16.3
India	11.6

Supplied by Minister Taylor AFR

Australia also leads the world in rooftop solar, as shown in Figure 8, for which subsidies provide 30-40 per cent of the capital cost. AEMO's draft 2019 Integrated System Plan noted that, "Some 3,700 megawatts (MW) of new capacity has entered the NEM since summer 2018-19. The bulk of this new capacity (some 90%) is rooftop PV and grid-scale solar generation." AEMO's modelling projects that these facilities could provide 13% to 22% of total underlying annual NEM energy consumption by 2040. Rooftop solar is far more prevalent in Australia than in other countries as shown in Figure 8. (Some have suggested this is due to Australian solar radiance but in areas of high population, Australia is not especially rich in sunlight).

Figure 8

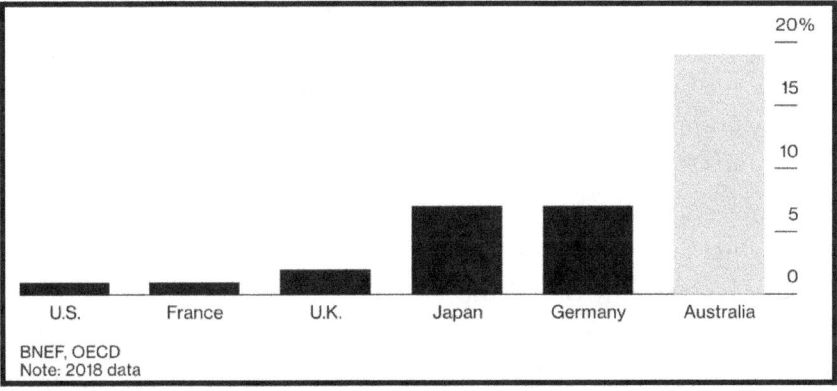

Australia's high take-up of (heavily subsidised) wind and solar energy has not prevented Australian policy being criticised for its inadequacy by The Greens and the Labor Party Opposition and being lampooned with "fossil of the day" awards by activists attending UN Climate Conferences like that in Madrid in December 2019.

But one recent analysis has focussed on the widening gap in prices received in the market between dispatchable and intermittent wind/solar power. In South Australia, where renewables in 2019 comprised half of supply, because wind was not available on hot still days when prices are highest dispatchable power attracted a price premium of 70 per cent. This and the associated costs of firming up the inherent unreliability of wind/solar will offset the subsidy these sources receive.

Electricity network and other costs

The AEMC put the 2019-20 national weighted average electricity bill for the representative household consumer at approximately $1,375 exclusive of GST. This was made up of:

- 44 per cent regulated network component
- 40 per cent wholesale market component
- 6 per cent environmental policy component
- 10 per cent residual component (comprising retailer's operating costs, customer acquisition and retention costs, return for investing in the business, and estimation errors)

(Note: the environmental component includes only the direct expenditures and not the effect of these in boosting wholesale prices two-and-a-half fold.)

Network charges have also increased over recent years but at less than the general rate of inflation in those states where there is long-standing private ownership of networks (Victoria, South Australia). Higher increases have taken place in Queensland, Western Australia and Tasmania, where continued government ownership of the networks remains and in NSW where partial privatisation took place only in December 2015.

This is not coincidental. There are greater disciplines on costs in privately owned networks. All networks will approach the regulator (the AER) with ambit claims for future expenditures and therefore the prices they are permitted to charge. For private investor-owned networks, the shareholders' representatives (the

Board of Directors) will force economies in management's actual expenditures in order to boost profits. This provides a base on which the regulator can determine future permissible expenditures for rate setting purposes. With government ownership, these disciplines are much less forceful: having set a budget based on the allowable expenditures sanctioned by the regulator, government owned businesses face far fewer pressures to economise on these expenditures.

Privatisation, however, remains unpopular based on fallacious notions that it involves the loss of public assets and a replacement of public service by commercial motives.

Depending upon the size of the load, the cost of generation for business customers tends to comprise a larger component – up to 70 per cent for smelters – than is the case for households. The pattern of increased customer costs for electricity is, however, evident with prices to businesses as well as households. Indeed, the uplift in electricity prices has impacted severely upon energy-intensive industries, especially aluminium smelters, which formerly spearheaded the nation's industrial competitiveness. Although the smelters' electricity is largely exempt from the renewable requirements, and is on long term contract, these contracts are facing renewal. Their replacement at threefold former prices is leaving the smelters dependent on government support for their on-going operations.

In this respect, Australia's strong relationship with the Trump Administration may have averted further pressure. Notwithstanding the overt government life-support, Australian aluminium exports to the US have avoided the countervailing tariffs imposed on subsidised aluminium from other nations in spite of having made sales gains.

One aspect of the industry that has boomed is the bureaucracy governing it both at the formal level of control and in the political oversight. The initially relatively small agencies responsible for operational management (AEMO), the legal features of trading (AEMC) and price fixing on the monopoly poles and wires (AER) have all sought and been given expanded resources and responsibilities for policy advice. New agencies have also been created including the Energy Security Board (ESB) and expanded roles have been given to the ACCC and various technical agencies like the CSIRO. Ministerial councils and individual state governments have also assumed considerable controls. Quantifying the costs of increased oversite is difficult because the regulatory agencies, perhaps understandably, do not assemble the material in a way that enables easy comparisons.

Unsurprisingly, the expanded oversight over the industry by bureaucrats and politicians has been inversely corelated to its efficiency.

Gas

For gas, a similar pattern of price increases to that of electricity is evident. Gas is responsible for 10 per cent of electricity generation (coal is 68 per cent, hydro 7 per cent and wind/solar 15 per cent). Its availability has been progressively squeezed by state government policies (in this respect there is little difference between the ALP and the LNP). Responding to fanciful scares about the safety of fracking as a means of tapping gas reserves, exploration (let alone new production) for gas that would require this process has been virtually banned by all governments except that of Queensland (where most new gas is contracted to overseas markets). The Victoria government banned all gas exploration but lifted the ban on exploration for conventional gas from July 2020.

The upshot has seen supplies become progressively scarcer and the price rise from under $3 per Gj to over $8 per Gj. This was more than double the US price where impediments to the exploration and production of "unconventional gas" have not been effective. Prices fell with the COVID-19 restrictions to under $5 per Gj but forward prices are $8 per Gj.

Figure 9

Victorian gas market average daily weighted prices by quarter

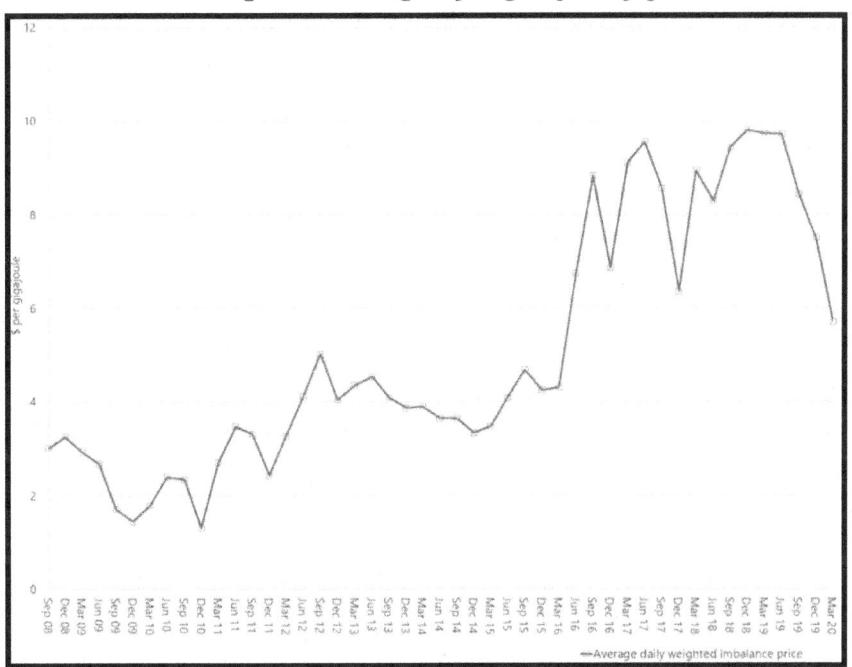

Measures introduced by the LNP government since 2013

The LNP has followed different paths under its three Prime Ministers: Tony Abbott, September 2013-September 2015; Malcolm Turnbull, September 2015 - August 2018; and Scott Morrison since August 2018.

The Abbott Government sought to reduce the renewable subsidies requirements (and abolished a carbon tax introduced in 2012). Businessman Dick Warburton was appointed to recommend future policies; his report sought a *de facto* halving of the 41,000 GWh RET. Without control over the Senate, the government was forced to compromise with the RET being reduced to 33,000 GWh.

The LNP government led by Malcolm Turnbull, supported by his Energy Minister Josh Frydenberg, sought to introduce a version of a carbon tax on electricity, which it disarmingly and inaccurately called the National Energy Guarantee. State governments, the Opposition, the energy bureaucracy and many in industry largely supported this goal. It was however the issue which caused the Liberal Party to replace Turnbull as Prime Minister in 2018. This same issue resulted in the replacement of Turnbull as Leader of the Opposition in 2009.

Many continue to press for new subsidies and/or carbon taxes for renewables – indeed, Josh Frydenberg as Treasurer remains influential in energy policy and has appointed Steven Kennedy, the author of the climate alarmist Garnaut Report (2008), as Treasury Secretary.

The appointment of Angus Taylor as minister for energy under Scott Morrison brought a somewhat greater resolve to extricate the nation from the poisonous effects of almost two decades of subsidies and taxes in support of economically inferior technologies.

Current policy approaches

Subsidies and other regulatory instruments remain the dominant factors in the energy industries' structure and cost. Total annual subsidies in 2016 were estimated at $4.9 billion.

While the different components of the subsidy have changed – especially with the small-scale renewable energy scheme (SRES) having increased to an estimated cost of $1.5 billion this year – the aggregate cost is somewhat higher than the 2016 estimate.

As previously discussed, more important than the direct cost of these subsidies is their effect in lifting prices. With static demand, over the four years since the withdrawal of coal capacity due to the subsidies to renewables, the annual wholesale cost of electricity has increased from $7.5 billion to approaching $20 billion.

Minister Taylor's policy approach is:

- To avoid any further expansion of the requirement on retailers to increase the amount of (subsidised) large scale to wind and solar. Incongruously, however, he is maintaining the (SRES) subsidy to roof top solar, that has resulted in Australia leading the world in these installations and that even interventionist minded bodies like the ACCC have recommended closing
- Trying to prevent further closures of coal generators, including by requiring a three-year notice of closure, and to foster new ones
- Jawboning retailer-generators into lowering prices, partly through ensuring customers are made better aware of lower cost options, requiring retailers to have adequate contract coverage to supply their customers, and setting in train "big stick" laws that can bring asset divestiture
- Promoting Snowy 2, a major expansion of pumped hydro that aims to improve the Snowy scheme's ability to counterbalance the increase in intermittent power
- Encouraging transmission designs that will avoid further subsidies to remotely located renewables
- Requiring a form of domestic gas reservation to keep prices lower/ availability higher than might otherwise occur.

All this is far less harmful than the redoubling of the subsidies to renewables that was the ALP platform taken to the nation in the May 2019 election. It will not however bring lower prices nor markedly greater reliability. Still less will it return Australia to its former world leadership in low price/high reliability. Such an outcome is possible only if action is taken to remove the existing subsidies that are to remain in place for a further 10 years as well as to cease issuing new ones under the SRES scheme for roof-top solar installations.

The government's unwillingness to repeal the SRES scheme is one indicator of a lack of resolve (or political capital) to take even modestly unpopular decisions that are necessary to repair the broken supply system.

Ironically, virtually all parties now consider that there is little alternative but to have further government intervention in the market that has been undermined by such intervention. Many within the energy bureaucracies and the renewables industry call for further support for what they see – or claim to see – as a renewables-dominated energy future. Characteristically, those seeking intervention in that direction often express outrage at interventions that do not support their favoured industries.

The costs imposed on conventional reliable plant by renewables includes the "hollowing out" of demand during the daytime, which wrecks the economics of baseload plant that is designed to amortise capital costs by continuous operations. Even though the government has won a grudging deferral of the next scheduled major plant closure, Liddell owned by AGL, the largest energy company, the market operator's forecast future pattern of closures (Figure 10) shows the difficulties in reversing course.

The difficulties are further exemplified in the outcome of Minister Taylor's plan for a form of government support for "dispatchable" plant, which many saw as code for coal, especially in view of gas supply constraints resulting from state government exploration bans. Part of this has been a plan to require retailers to hold "firming" contracts to provide assurances that power will be available to their customers; wind and solar cannot supply such contracts. But these requirements are unnecessary, as retailers' internal risk management procedures already insist on such contracts to avoid exposure to spot electricity prices of up to $14,000 for a product that is retailed at perhaps $150.

Figure 10. Scheduled coal power station decommissionings

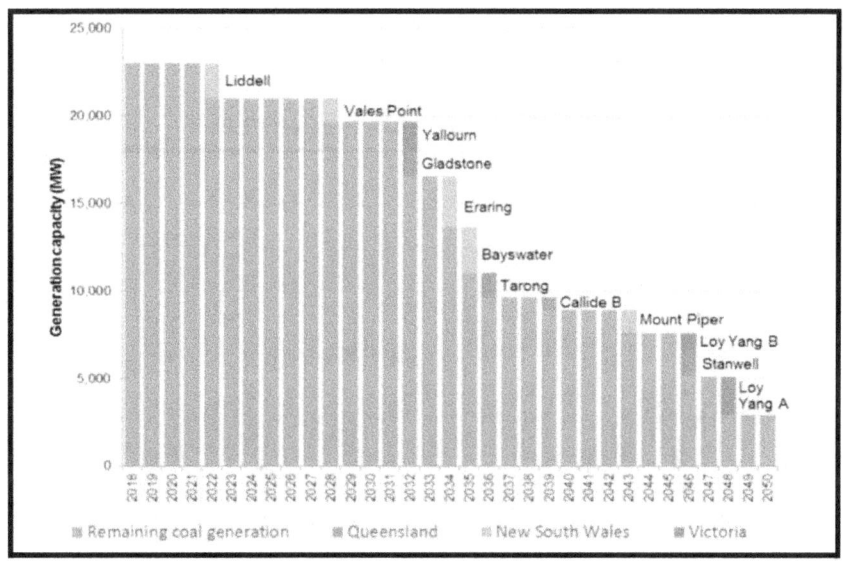

Moreover, the fact is that with existing policy settings favouring wind/solar, any new coal power station would simply expedite the closure of an existing coal station, adding little to the increased security and reliability that is the initiative's immediate goal.

Furthermore, the committee appointed to advise on the best prospects, recommended only one small coal fuelled generator upgrade, which perhaps underlines the difficulties governments now have in obtaining advice that is untarnished by the dominant green paradigm. Indeed, the Commonwealth Government supports the Carbon Market Initiative under which firms are invited to donate up to $12,500 per year in what amounts to an assisted suicide pact involving a "journey towards net zero emissions".

The Department of Environment and Energy, in its *Australia's emissions projections 2019* report, sees an ongoing increase in renewable supplies at the expense of coal and gas. It envisages (Figure 11) the following fuel supply shares, where renewables (with no growth in hydro) lift their share of generation from 27 per cent in 2020 to 48 per cent in 2030.

Figure 11. Projected supply to 2030

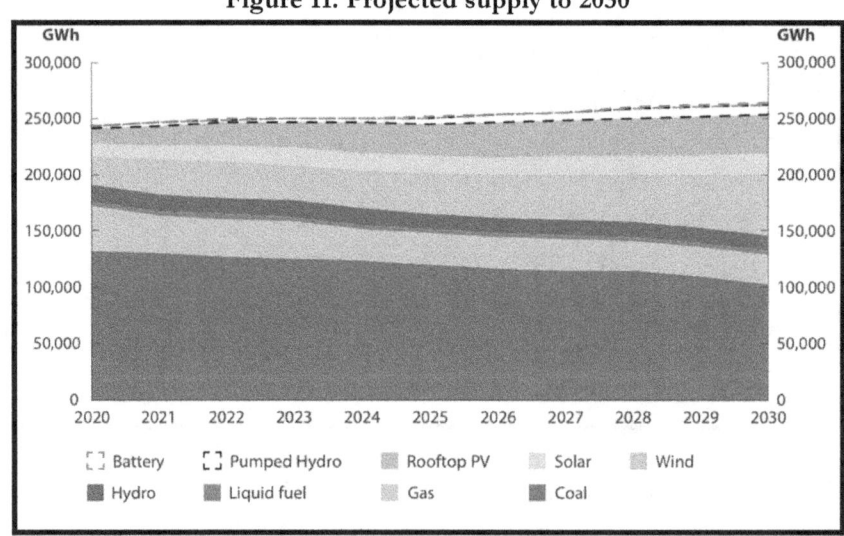

The deep hostility to coal throughout official circles is also illustrated by a decision in February 2019 of the senior judge in the NSW Land and Environment Court, Mr Justice Brian Preston, who rejected the application to operate for a new coal mine because, among other reasons, he said it would be unable "to meet generally agreed climate targets" for a "rapid and deep decrease" in emissions. The case against the mine was run by the activist Environmental Defenders Office NSW, which is funded in part by the state government and at which Preston once served as the founding principal solicitor.

In NSW, there are several gas and coal projects that have been derailed through the planning system where local interests and activists are allowed to dominate. With such views prevalent throughout the judiciary as well as in political circles, it would require some form of government guarantee as indemnification against any new measure that might prejudice fossil fuels in the market.

The "march through the institutions" of green left ideology has resulted in high public approval of green energy, with a September 2019 Omnipoll finding (Figure 12) that 81 per cent of Australians support a role for it. Perhaps more worrisome is the importance younger people attached to reducing carbon emissions compared to reliability or price.

Figure 12

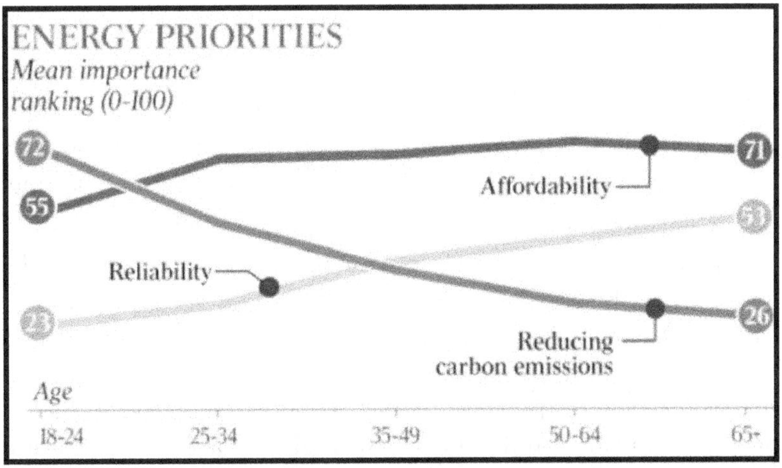

ENERGY PRIORITIES
Mean importance ranking (0-100)

Affordability

Reliability

Reducing carbon emissions

Age

| 18-24 | 25-34 | 35-49 | 50-64 | 65+ |

Many see these considerations and claims by the big four domestic banks that they will not invest in new coal as evidence that global warming psychosis would prevent new mines from obtaining finance. This is untrue. The domestic banks rarely lend for major projects and the hundreds of coal facilities planned or under construction around the world is testimony to the availability of finance. Australia, as illustrated by the nine year long proposal by Adani for a new coal mine (and the aforementioned views of a senior NSW judge) is vulnerable to political and judicial activism.

Australia also is somewhat hostage to labour unions with regard to major programs. For this reason, in assessing the costs entailed in new greenfield coal generators, Solstice in a meticulous report commissioned by the Minerals Council placed a loading of 25 per cent on labour costs compared to those prevailing in the US. Even so, the report still found a new coal generator could profitably operate at an electricity price of \$50 per MWh if operated continuously as a baseload generator.

The government, with support from the Opposition, is seeking to curb what it sees as market power from generator-retailers. This is misplaced in the case of retailing. Though not all are active in every state market, there are 33 different brands among electricity retailers (16 for gas). Even though the big three (AGL, EnergyAustralia, Origin) have a 75 per cent market share this still means there is a very high degree of competition. It was, however, a mistake by the NSW government to prefer an asset sale program in 2014 that left the state market with too few competitors by selling the Bayswater and Liddell stations to the same buyer, AGL. This has left that firm with profitable opportunities in closing Liddell and gaining from the resultant price increase. The government, rightly, is pressuring AGL to on-sell Liddell.

The ACCC has expressed concerns about vertical integration. These are unwarranted. Vertical integration is just a variation of long term contracting and, as with other industries involved in make-or-buy strategies, offers firms different degrees of certainty.

Politicians and regulators alike have also expressed concerns about price insensitive customers, who have remained loyal to their retailers and have accepted uncompetitive price packages. They have done so in spite of an abundance of comparator sites, requirements to facilitate easy switching of retailers and a crescendo of information about how to get a better deal. On spite of sticky customers, the churn rate is very high, typically 30 per cent a year, (see Table 6.1) though misguided policies of the ACCC in restricting aggressive sales campaigns and cold-calling by retailers has tended to mute this.

Other issues being debated largely surround measures that might prevent a further deterioration in reliability. The renewable sector makes considerable noise about breakdowns of "archaic" fossil fuel plant. This is unfounded. Although, as Figure 13 shows, there has been an increase in fossil fuel plants' forced outage levels in NSW, this has not been substantial and is not seen in other states.

Figure 13

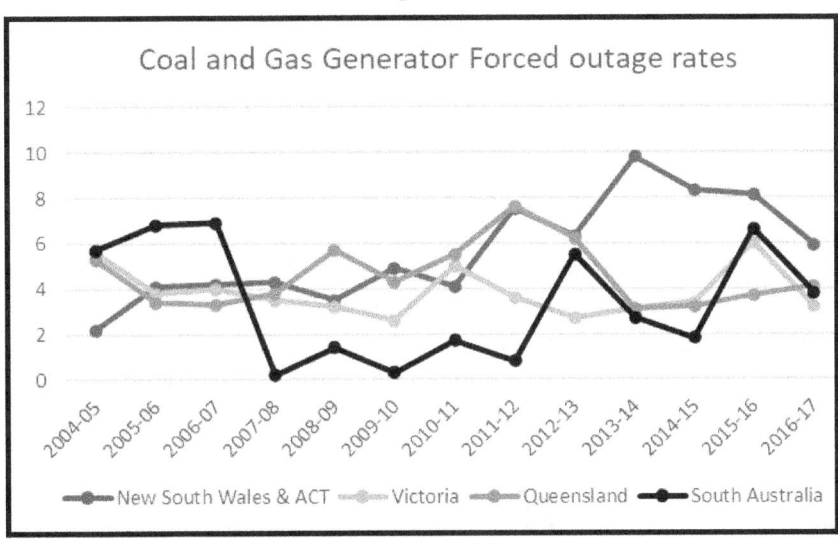

Source: EGA, Australian Energy Council

The market operator, AEMO, is calling for new expenditures to offset the deleterious effects on grid reliability caused by household and other small-scale weather-dependent generating facilities as well as by dispersed and remotely located wind. It, like the remotely located renewable facilities, favours the costs to this being incurred directly by customers rather than by the generators themselves. This would be a new form of subsidy for renewables and large scale solar and would provide little incentive for new facilities to choose locations that take the costs of transmission into account.

The AEMC, the rule-making body, had taken a different view and was calling for a policy change which would see new generators which choose to locate away from established transmission (or on transmission lines where their presence might cause congestion) to incur the costs. This latter view is preferable but faced with opposition from an industry and other regulators which prefer to have central direction and socialised cost, this position has been largely abandoned.

In addition, there is the plan to change the nature of the Snowy and the Tasmanian hydro-electricity systems. These have assumed greater importance in a network with far greater price volatility. Snowy is to be redesigned as a pumped storage facility to allow better balancing of the intermittent renewable supplies, even though this will reduce gross output by 40 per cent. Initiated by Prime Minister Turnbull (under whom the Commonwealth bought out the NSW and Victorian governments' shares of Snowy Hydro) the government speaks of the Snowy scheme becoming "the battery of the nation".

Like so many government schemes, the cost of the pumped storage initiative has blown out and its claimed effectiveness has been questioned, especially by competitive solutions, including those involving actual batteries. Originally foreshadowed at $2 billion, costs including for beefed up transmission are now credibly estimated to be some $10 billion.

The Marinus Link with Tasmania is another transmission plan, which is to add an additional 1200MW of capacity to the existing 400MW of constrained generation to the mainland.

The Prime Minister has announced a new one billion dollar fund for the Clean Energy Finance Corporation to "future proof the electricity grid". While such power sharing vehicles may help prevent regional blackouts, they also deter new private investment and therefore further raise prices.

It is doubtful that such expenditures would pass a test of commerciality under any circumstances and they can only approach such a standard because of the price volatility subsidies to renewables have created.

Concluding Comments

The bottom line of policies under consideration is that none of them is going to restore the former low-cost electricity and gas supply. Unless the Commonwealth government finds a way to renege on the subsidies to renewables, stops all new ones immediately, and can pressure state governments to cease impeding gas exploration and production, the present tragedy of high energy prices amidst an abundance of supply potential will continue.

Australia will certainly be the poorer for destroying its energy advantages. It is only the nation's vast natural wealth that has enabled a steady increase in living standards, an increase achieved despite government energy policies.

The bushfires in late 2019 and early 2020, though due to inadequate cold season burning, have illogically (or opportunistically) been blamed by activists and vested interests on Australia not doing enough to replace fossil fuels by renewables. The resultant media pile-on has made for further difficulties in the government's ability to pursue sensible polices.

While consumer prices are the most visible and publicised aspect of the deterioration in electricity supply costs and reliability, it is the effect on commercial customers that is most serious. Mention has already been made of the aluminium plants, standing for many years at the apex of the nation's world class manufacturing facilities. The three major facilities in Victoria (Portland), NSW (Tomago) and Queensland (Boyne Island) account for 10 per cent of electricity demand. All face difficult contract negotiations for this supply, which comprises some 30 per cent of their costs. These plants cannot rely on government subsidies over the long-term and, in any event, this leaves them vulnerable to countervailing trade measures of the sort that the Trump Administration has already imposed on some exporters.

Moreover, electricity and to a lesser degree gas is ubiquitous in all commercial activities. In addition to its vital importance to aluminium smelting, it comprises over five per cent of costs in other smelting, iron and steel, wood and paper, glass and ceramics. And while these industries might see a silver lining in the power price collapse that would accompany the closure of an aluminium smelter, that closure would undermine the economics of baseload coal plants. What would follow is the closure of one of them and the return of high prices, accompanied by a further diminution of reliability across the system.

Similarly, government, judicial and activists' opposition to new gas has also seen its prices increase two and a half fold compared to those in the US. Five years ago, they were similar. Industries highly dependent on gas include pulp and paper, metals, chemicals, stone, clay and glass, plastic, and food processing.

Present energy policies will therefore, at best, mean a serious underperformance of the economy. The core determinant of this, the attack on fossil fuels and uses of other resources including water and land itself has been boosted by activists' populist slogans like "climate emergency" and "extinction rebellion". The wider tacit support for such highly inaccurate refrains, even within the LNP, make it difficult to assemble the political will to reverse course. And government planning documents, like *Australia's emissions projections 2019*, are predicated on a continued increase in wind/solar displacing coal and increasing the overall renewables share from 27 per cent in 2020 to over 48 per cent of supply in 2030.

The feasibility of such increases will come under scrutiny as wind/solar gain market share. Already evident in South Australia are price discounts for these generation sources (24 per cent in 2018/19), discounts that recognise the lower value of intermittent and unreliable sources of electricity.

Finally, we have the coronavirus effect. The new reality of a world facing increased cost pressures surely calls for deregulatory cost reducing measures. Aside from the $16.5 billion Adani coal mine, which took 9 years to clear regulatory barriers, the Institute of Public Affairs finds activist groups have delayed 28 projects between 2000 and 2019, with an estimated value of over $65bn.

Oblivious to the increased need to reduce costs, some with an ideological antipathy to fossil fuels, like the IEA's Fatih Birol and Australia's Ross Garnaut, advocate using the coronavirus crisis to expedite the transition to renewables.

2

IMMIGRATION

ANDREW STONE

Australia has long had a large annual immigration intake, and this has generally served us well. As a relatively isolated nation, we were very exposed strategically when our population was only a few million. At the start of World War II there were just 7 million Australians. Eighty years later that figure exceeds 25 million, in large part due to strong immigration.

This does not mean, however, that more immigration is automatically good. Many factors influence the success of an immigration program, including the pace of intake, the skills and cultural mix, the policy approach to new migrants (whether it encourages mixing in or separateness), and the efficacy of planning to accommodate the additional needs for infrastructure and housing.

Currently there is strong debate about aspects of the mix of Australia's migration program. Many legitimate questions have been raised – including about the greater security, policing and cultural compatibility challenges which migrants from some parts of the world are generating. Here, however, space limitations mean that I will focus only on the *economic* aspects of Australia's annual migration program – especially its size, how this has changed since the mid-2000s, and how it ought to change again over coming years to best serve the nation's interests.

I will offer specific suggestions for changes that the Morrison government ought to pursue, to start to undo the damage that overly-rapid immigration has been and is causing in relation to jobs, wages growth, community amenity and the housing market.[2] These recommendations pre-date the recent Wuhan virus pandemic, but remain appropriate.

In a brief epilogue, I will also outline some further, separate implications for Australia's immigration policy flowing from the pandemic.

Overall, immigration has generally enriched Australia, culturally and economically. However, the nation has not been served well by either the massive ramping up in immigration since the mid-2000s, or the progressive dilution since the 1970s of the pressures on new arrivals to fit in and become Australian, rather than form ethnic enclaves. Both developments should be reversed.

Background on Net Overseas Migration (NOM)

For the quarter-century to the mid-2000s, Australia's net overseas migration – the net inflow of foreigners to Australia less net outflow of Australians to other countries – fluctuated around 100,000 p.a. as domestic economic conditions varied (Chart 1). This was already a very rapid pace by international standards – faster in per capita terms than every other developed country except Israel (reflecting a mass influx of Russian Jews following the collapse of the Soviet Union) and Luxembourg (a tiny European tax haven).

From 2006 onwards, however, a marked change began. As the mining boom moved into full swing and Australia's unemployment rate declined towards 4 per cent, the lowest level since the early

---

2   These issues are examined at greater length in my recent book, *Restoring Hope – Practical Policies to Revitalise the Australian Economy*, Quadrant Books, 2019. The proposals outlined here form part of a larger, politically achievable economic and fiscal policy agenda set out in that book.

1970s, NOM was ramped up rapidly in the final two years of the Howard government. It then grew even further under the Rudd government – reaching a staggering 300,000 in 2008-09. Following the Global Financial Crisis (GFC), it dropped back below 200,000 in 2009-10 and 2010-11 – demonstrating that a major slowing in immigration can occur without prompting economic or social disruption – but then increased again in Labor's final two years to just over 230,000. Overall, in the 13 years from mid-2006 annual NOM has averaged over 225,000, effectively twice the pace of the preceding 25 years (after allowing for a definitional change by the ABS as to when individuals should be classed as *migrants* to Australia, versus extended but temporary visitors – see footnote 4, Chapter 2 of *Restoring Hope*, available at https://restoringhope.net. au, for further details). NOM is currently running above even this annual pace in the latest ABS data.

Chart 1: Annual Net Overseas Migration to Australia

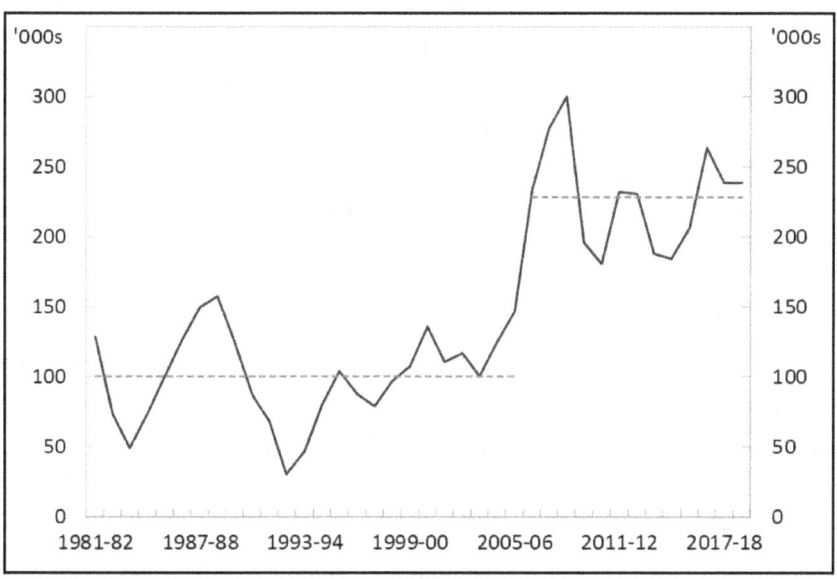

Some of the increase in Australia's average NOM since 2006 is accounted for by factors unrelated to our permanent migration program, such as hugely increased numbers of international students.[3] Extraordinarily, every tenth person currently residing in Australia is not a permanent resident or citizen.

Even so, most of the increase in NOM reflects a discretionary decision to have a higher annual intake of *permanent* migrants – as can be seen from the permanent migration program target set each year by the Commonwealth Government. This target skyrocketed from just 76,000 as recently as 2000-01 to 120,000 in 2004-05, and then 190,000 by 2008-09. It was then lowered only modestly to around 170,000 for the two years after the GFC – and thereafter quickly restored to 190,000 for the six years to 2016-17 (albeit converted, at the end, from a "target" to a "cap").

In 2017-18 the *actual* permanent migration intake was finally reduced noticeably, to just over 160,000, even though the cap remained unaltered at 190,000. This reflected a (probably unilateral) decision by the Minister, Peter Dutton, to significantly tighten the visa approval process, so as to minimise fraud (and, even so, annual NOM remained extremely high). Only in the 2019-20 Budget was the annual intake cap formally reduced to 160,000.

Economic Damage

In terms of employment, job security, wages growth, community amenity and housing affordability for Australians, the doubling of our annual migration intake since 2006 has been damaging and inappropriate.

---

3   Annual NOM is affected by shifts in long-stay temporary migration (especially international students and various temporary worker categories), and in some permanent migration categories that are not part of the permanent migration target (net immigration from New Zealand, and Australia's humanitarian intake).

Prior to the GFC, during the mining investment boom, it made sense to facilitate some increase in annual NOM – although not by as much as was done. It has made no sense, however, to *keep Australia's NOM at these extraordinarily elevated levels, even as unemployment climbed again and the mining investment boom dissipated.*

Employment Growth

In the last decade of the Howard government, 2.1 million new jobs were created while NOM to Australia totalled 1.3 million. With only some of those 1.3 million seeking employment, jobs were plentiful and the unemployment rate declined towards its lowest level in thirty years.

By contrast, in the following decade just 1.85 million new jobs were created, but NOM to Australia almost doubled to 2.25 million. In addition to placing pressure on housing and infrastructure, this huge rampup in immigration meant that jobs felt harder to find for many Australians, and the number of unemployed rose by 220,000 over this period.

Of course, reducing annual immigration would, at the margin, make it more difficult for the Coalition to achieve its recent pledge to create 1¼ million new jobs over the next five years, since high immigration itself creates some jobs servicing all these extra people.

Nonetheless, this jobs target should still be readily achievable, even with lower immigration. After all, it requires annual jobs growth of only 1.9 per cent, whereas the Howard government managed average growth of 2.1 per cent with a much smaller immigration program.

Even more to the point, government's responsibility is to try to maximise the employment opportunities *of Australians*, not achieve a given jobs growth target by bringing in an economically inappropriate number of immigrants, who then compete with existing workers and, as discussed shortly, undercut their wage bargaining power.[4]

With the unemployment rate above 5 per cent, and underemployment separately at almost 9 per cent (for a total "under-utilisation rate" of nearly 14 per cent), NOM should urgently be reduced to a more economically sensible level.

Youth Unemployment

A further consideration, regarding the nexus between immigration and employment, relates to youth unemployment. In mid-2019 the unemployment rate for 15-19 year olds was almost 17 per cent (and not long ago, in 2015, was briefly around 20 per cent, the highest level since mid-1997).

By allowing entry-level jobs that might be filled by young Australians to be taken by foreigners, several components of Australia's immigration arrangements are contributing to elevated youth unemployment. These include: massively ramped-up numbers of foreign students, many of whom fill casual and part-time jobs (including sometimes working more hours than permitted under their visas); and various immigration streams targeted at supplying temporary entrants to do low-skilled jobs in sectors like agriculture and tourism.

Having large numbers of jobs filled by migrants on temporary visas is also making it more difficult to achieve sensible tightening of the conditions on access to the dole for young Australians – whether

---

4   More broadly, an important issue with immigration is: how much of any benefits from migration accrue to the existing population, versus accruing just to the new migrants? Regarding these distributional effects, a 2006 Productivity Commission Research Report noted (with all the customary caveats) that: "Most of the economy-wide gain from migration is likely to accrue to the new immigrants themselves" (see *Economic Impacts of Migration and Population Growth*, p. 123).

"earn or learn" requirements, or even just slightly delayed access to New-start. Many Australians understandably worry that it would be unfair to impose such conditions – designed to discourage welfare-dependency – when youth unemployment is high and jobs may not be readily available even for committed young job-seekers.

To address these concerns, the number of foreign student visas for study at Australian universities should be sharply scaled back (which would also help to stem the erosion of academic standards at these institutions). In addition, the Seasonal Worker and, much more importantly, the Working Holiday Maker (WHM) visa programs – which have been significantly ramped up since the mid-2000s – should be phased down, since holders of these visas particularly compete with young Australian workers. With youth unemployment elevated since the GFC, bringing large numbers of foreigners in to fill low-skilled jobs has made little sense (even allowing that there is a significant foreign aid element to Australia's Seasonal Worker Program, in supporting certain Pacific Island nations).

What of the concern that some jobs being filled by foreign workers, such as fruit-picking, are ones that Australians just don't want to do? The answer is simple: there should be no such thing as a job that young job-seekers are allowed to turn their noses up at – not if they expect to receive support from the taxpayer.

To avoid disruption in particular sectors, such as agriculture, numbers under the relevant immigration programs could be scaled back gradually, with the reduction coordinated with efforts to assist alternative domestic sourcing of labour. In particular, phase-down of WHM numbers could be made conditional on trials of the conversion of New-start Allowance from a direct payment to a HELP-style repayable loan for unemployed young Australians in fruit-picking areas during picking season. Turning the dole into a loan when low-skilled work is widely available would increase the incentive for unemployed locals aged under 30 to take these jobs, rather than incur a debt they'll later have to repay.

Wages

A further implication of ongoing high immigration has been downward pressure on wages, adding to households' cost of living pressures.

Prior to the GFC, annual wage growth (using the ABS's Wage Price Index) was strong, at around 4¼ per cent. After some volatility during the crisis, it slipped to 3¾ per cent over 2010-11 and 2011-12, and then, from mid-2012, underwent a further long and steady decline, to reach just 1.9 per cent over 2016-17 – the slowest pace in the 22 year history of the series.

This deterioration occurred despite the economy continuing to perform tolerably if unspectacularly through this period; and, while wage growth has picked up since then, it remains very subdued (at just 2.3 per cent over 2018-19).

Ongoing high inflows of potential workers while GDP growth was persistently slightly-subtrend will surely have contributed to this situation – notwithstanding that it will also have created some domestic jobs servicing these additional people.

Of course, slower wages growth is an appropriate adjustment mechanism for an economy experiencing modest growth, as Australia has for much of the post-GFC period. Weaker wage growth in such an environment helps to moderate job losses. Nevertheless, the required slowing (and resultant cost-of-living pressures on workers and their families) would have been less, if high immigration had not exacerbated the imbalance between supply and demand in the jobs market.

To the extent that reduced immigration would contribute to stronger wages growth, this would be opposed by many business organisations. In general, businesses (especially big businesses) have been happy to have increased access to global labour markets, precisely because this has helped to undercut workers' bargaining power and so put a lid on wages.

This is not a compelling reason, however, to keep the immigration intake so high — especially since business coped perfectly well during the Howard government with a much lower immigration intake (and much more rapid wages growth).

Skills Shortages

In certain sectors where there are genuine skills shortages, tapping into global labour markets *temporarily* to overcome these can help to preserve and increase Australian jobs (by enabling complex projects to proceed that might otherwise be unviable for want of required expertise for one component). This was exactly the rationale for the 457 visa category.

Over time, however, it became clear that the 457 visa scheme was being rorted, leading the government to replace it in 2017 with two new temporary work visas, with altered entitlements in terms of a pathway to permanent residency. The lists of eligible skilled occupations under the new visas were also tightened. These were sensible changes.

Nevertheless, it is doubtful whether they went far enough. The skills list for the new short-term temporary work visa stream, for instance, still includes occupations such as hairdresser, cook, sign-writer, youth worker and public relations professional, while over 200 occupations remain on the government's Medium and Long-Term Strategic Skills List.

The Housing Market

One area where the impact of immigration has received far too little sustained focus is the housing market. From the mid-1980s there was a large step-up in house prices driven by financial deregulation and, especially, the shift in the early 1990s to low and stable inflation. By the mid-2000s, however, this had largely run its course. Following some correction from the cyclical peak in house prices in 2003, a sustained period of only moderate house price growth finally seemed feasible.

Just at this moment, however net overseas migration began to be massively ramped up – hugely affecting supply-demand balance in the housing market over time (especially in Sydney and Melbourne). Consistent with this, Sydney house prices skyrocketed by 74 per cent over the five years to mid-2017 and, despite a welcome correction over the next two years, remain over 50 per cent above their mid-2012 level (versus a rise in wages of just 17 per cent).

To quantify this supply demand impact note that, for the 25 years to 2013-14, just under 140,000 homes were added each year, on average, to the nation's housing stock. For the first two thirds of this same period, from 1989-90 to 2005-06, annual NOM averaged just under 100,000.

With average household size drifting down from around two and three quarters to two and a half, this plausibly corresponded to demand for a little over 35,000 dwellings p.a. on average. In other words, nationally, NOM was soaking up around one quarter of typical net annual supply of new dwellings through this period, leaving around 100,000 dwellings per year to meet the combination of natural population increase and the trend towards smaller household sizes.

From 2006-07 onwards, however, annual NOM moved

dramatically higher, averaging over 225,000. Even noting the definitional caveat mentioned earlier, the same simple arithmetic suggests that this has represented *additional* housing demand each year of around 40,000 dwellings – or roughly a further 30 per cent of the typical housing supply – bringing net housing demand from migration to well over half of the nation's typical annual supply.

To describe this as a material shift in the supply-demand balance in the housing market, repeated year after year, would be an understatement! Clearly, these demand increases will have exerted sustained upward pressure on national house prices over the past decade.

In short, there is every reason to believe that massively faster immigration, in a market where supply (for a range of reasons) has been notoriously unresponsive, played a large role in giving house prices renewed impetus, driving them even higher relative to domestic incomes through to mid-2017, and further out of the reach of many young Australians.

Indeed, even though supply finally responded vigorously from 2014-15, the large increase in construction since then (with private dwelling completions averaging just over 200,000 for the past five years) has likely only been enough to begin, modestly, to overcome the accumulated boost to demand from still-elevated NOM. And even this modest progress will evaporate unless stronger supply is sustained – yet annual residential building approvals have fallen by around one quarter from their record 2015-16 level. By contrast, annual NOM is still around 140,000 higher than its typical pre-2006 level, *above* even its elevated average of recent years.

This national-level analysis of the impact of migration flows on housing demand and prices can also be extended to the State level – provided allowance is made for net interstate migration, not just net overseas migration. Doing so for the case of New South Wales confirms a picture of migration as a major factor in driving house price developments over the past decade (see Chapter 2 of *Restoring Hope*, A. Stone, Quadrant Books, 2019).

Infrastructure and Community Amenity

A final set of economic/social issues affected by immigration relates to congestion in Australia's major cities, and levels of community amenity more broadly.

Most immigrants settle in major urban centres. Even leaving aside issues of integration and the formation of enclaves (where the *pace* of influx can have a major influence on whether problems develop), States have struggled to keep up with the current rate of inflow, in terms of provision of community infrastructure and services, parking, road capacity, and so forth.

Failure to do so has contributed to significant discontent among existing residents in relation to lack of adequate planning, ever longer commute times, the resort to makeshift facilities to cope with crowding at schools, and so forth.

Counter-arguments – Are there Offsetting Benefits?

These considerations add up to an overwhelming argument, on economic grounds, for annual immigration to be cut – at minimum to a level comparable to that recorded, on average, under the Howard government. Australia's much lower NOM during that period can hardly be said to have held back the economy, which grew more than a full percentage point faster than subsequently and, in per capita terms, at two and a half times the rate (2.4 versus 0.9 per cent p.a.).

Are there any counter-arguments, however, why immigration should not be cut back? Several are frequently raised, but none are compelling.

Population Ageing

One claim often made is that we need higher immigration to offset ageing of the population that would otherwise occur (and that will dramatically affect many European and some Asian countries over coming decades). This reflects the fact that Australia's migrant intake tends to be younger than the existing population, strongly skewed towards people in their twenties and thirties. Over coming decades, such an infusion of younger people will indeed diminish the pace of population ageing.

These young migrants will, however, themselves age (and their fertility rate tends to converge rapidly with that of the underlying population). Whether higher NOM reduces ageing ought therefore to be assessed on a suitably long horizon of 50-100 years, to allow for these effects to flow through. On these horizons, the clear finding is that faster migration does *not* significantly reduce net population ageing – unless the ramp-up is repeated ever more forcefully at regular intervals, in what former Labor MPs Mark Latham and Kelvin Thompson have accurately called a form of multi-generational Ponzi scheme.

Indeed, as long ago as 1999, noted demographer Peter McDonald examined the impact on ageing of various scenarios for faster migration above an annual NOM baseline of 80,000. After observing that this baseline "makes a worthwhile and efficient contribution to the retardation of population ageing", he and co-author Rebecca Kippen concluded (see *The Impact of Immigration on the Ageing of Australia's Population*, p. 21, emphasis added) that:

"Levels of annual net migration above 80,000 become increasingly ineffective and inefficient in the retardation of ageing. *Those who wish to argue for a higher level of immigration must base their argument on the benefits of a larger population, not upon the illusory 'younging power' of high immigration."*

Budget Impact

It is also argued that permanent migration must be kept high because any cut would entail a significant budgetary cost. Among the many ways in which this is absurd, here are some of the main ones.

First, it is highly doubtful that there would even be a fiscal cost from cutting immigration, let alone a serious one. In the 2009-10 Budget, the Rudd government unwound some its huge permanent migration increase of the previous year by lowering the annual intake by 21,600, consisting of a reduction of 25,400 in the skilled program partially offset by an increase of 3,800 in the family reunion stream. The estimated budget cost over the four-year forward estimates period was only a little over $400 million (compared with total Commonwealth spending in those years of over $1,400 billion). On that basis, the cost of a comparable sized cut spread more evenly across the family reunion and skilled streams would have been far less (and hence trivial in a budget context), or possibly even negative, given that family reunion entrants generate less tax revenue and use more government funded services than skilled entrants.

Subsequent budgets have sometimes shown larger fiscal effects for a given change in permanent migration. However, the reasons are unclear, with these larger effects not explained by compositional differences, or by indexation of the outlay and revenue effects over time.

Even more importantly, there is a serious *structural* reason why costings over a four-year budget horizon will always give a misleadingly positive impression of the budget impact of immigration, relative to its true long run impact.

The reason is that Australia has long barred access to welfare payments for most new immigrants for their first two years in the country (recently increased to three or four years for some benefits). For an ongoing increase in permanent migration a *four year* costing will therefore fully capture the expected revenue boost from the change, but will significantly understate the true ongoing cost on the outlays side. Focusing on the budget impact of immigration changes over a four year horizon will therefore always yield a pro-immigration bias in the minds of unwary observers.

Finally, even if there were sizeable near term budget costs from a cut to permanent migration – rather than the trivial impacts the 2009-10 Treasury costing suggests – it would still be absurd for this to be treated as a decisive factor in whether or not to make such a cut. After all, so long as NOM is maintained at its current breakneck pace it will continue to significantly distort the nation's housing and labour markets, with serious short and longrun consequences (including negative demographic effects on family formation and average family size). The idea that we should continue to do that, just for (say) a few hundred million dollars' improvement to the budget each year, is deeply perverse.

Allowing Speedier Family Reunion

Finally, higher NOM since the mid-2000s is also sometimes defended on the grounds that, although weighted towards skilled migration, it has still allowed a substantial increase in the family reunion stream. This is praised as allowing for loved ones to be reunited more rapidly.

A larger overall intake, however, also increases the demand for family reunion places – so it is unclear whether the net effect is to ease or exacerbate delays in reuniting families.

Even more fundamentally, in relation to parents, the whole idea of achieving family reunion outcomes through *permanent* migration – as opposed to long-stay temporary migration that does not impart expensive entitlements such as medical care at taxpayer expense – is counterproductive, both for Australia and for migrant families.

This point was made forcefully by the Productivity Commission in its 2016 report *Migrant Intake into Australia* (which estimated that the average taxpayer cost, over the lifetime of each such entrant, currently runs well into the hundreds of thousands of dollars). It has also been partially taken on board by the government, with the introduction of a new temporary Sponsored Parent Visa. Inexplicably, however, introduction of the new visa does not appear to be occurring in conjunction with any wind down of the two pre-existing permanent parent visa programs.

Specific Policy Proposals

The Morrison government should move swiftly to reduce Australia's permanent and long-stay temporary migrant intakes, so as to start to repair the substantial economic distortions being caused by excessively rapid immigration. Action in this area would generally not require Senate approval, and so could also be put in place without delay.

Sensible options the government could consider, to improve the welfare of the Australian people, include the following.

Proposal (Permanent Migration): Starting in 2020-21, Australia's annual permanent migration program cap should be reduced by two successive increments of 25,000, lowering it to 110,000 from 2021-22 onwards. These annual reductions should be achieved via cuts of 16,000 and 9,000 in the skilled and family reunion streams, respectively, in 2020-21 and 2021-22.

Proposal (Longstay Temporary Visas): To further reduce pressure on housing and infrastructure, and also strengthen academic standards at Australia's universities, the number of new foreign student visas granted for tertiary study in Australia should be wound back by at least 10 per cent per year for the next five years (commencing from 2021). These reductions should also be accompanied by: cancellation of student visas for any violation of work restrictions (regardless of stage of completion of studies); and phased tightening of the Working Holiday Maker (WHM) visa stream, to reduce its role as a source of labour for low-skilled jobs.

Proposal (Complementary Changes to Newstart): Reductions in WHM numbers should be accompanied by changes to New-start for young Australians (under 30) in designated areas where unemployment is high, but substantial employment of WHM visa holders is occurring (e.g. fruit growing areas during picking season). In these areas, for the period of designation, Newstart should be converted to a HELP-style loan, to be recovered in due course from individuals through the tax system.

Proposal (Further Reform of Skills Lists): The skills lists for both permanent and temporary skilled worker visas should be further tightened. There is no good reason for the list for the new short-term temporary work visa, for example, to still include occupations such as hairdresser, signwriter and youth worker – or for there still to be over 200 categories on the new Medium and Long-term Strategic Skills List.

Proposal (Parent Visas): The government should: immediately double all fees, charges and bonds associated with Contributory Parent Visas for new applicants (with existing applicants grandfathered); lower the annual number of such visas to be issued by 10 per cent a year for five years from 2020-21; and also, from 2020-21, reduce by 50 per cent the annual number of Non-contributory Parent Visas issued. These changes would complement the recent introduction of a temporary Sponsored Parent Visa category and, within 10 years, could be saving taxpayers around $1.0 billion p.a. (and still growing).

Epilogue

Compared with the proposals above for substantial but orderly reductions to net immigration, the impact of the Wuhan virus pandemic has been much more dramatic – a sudden, almost complete cessation of both permanent and temporary migration until further notice.

What difference, if any, should this unexpected development make to the policy changes the Commonwealth should pursue to our immigration settings? The main changes concern implementation and ambition, rather than direction.

In particular, it should be much easier, politically, to change the permanent migration cap to 110,000 now that the annual rate is running around zero, rather than 160,000. This is especially so when the number of unemployed and idle workers has skyrocketed – so that the government can note the imperative to help Australians get jobs again, before such jobs are provided to foreigners.

Rather than wait for the 2020-21 Budget, the government should therefore announce an immediate cut in its annual permanent migration cap to 110,000, to be maintained indefinitely.

It should also announce that this cap is further reduced to (say) 80,000 until such time as the unemployment rate is back below 6 per cent; and that the annual issuance of all temporary work visas (and Working Holiday Maker visas) will be likewise reduced by at least 50 per cent (compared with the average level over the five years to 2018-19) until the labour market has recovered.

These announcements would have the additional benefit of formalising the idea that the scale of our permanent and work-related temporary migration programs should be sensitive to the state of the labour market, being reduced when unemployment rises or wage growth is persistently weak.

Finally, one specific issue which the pandemic has starkly and suddenly highlighted, and which directly concerns immigration, is the appalling over reliance on foreign students which our universities have built up over the past decade – including many of our most prestigious campuses.

In defiance of every tenet of basic risk management, and with complete disregard for the damage being caused to the quality of education provided to Australian students, many universities – including Sydney, Melbourne, the Australian National University (ANU) and UNSW – lifted their (higher fee paying) foreign student numbers to over 40 per cent of total students, by the time the pandemic struck. With the virus having brought this to a juddering halt – thereby wreaking havoc on university budgets – this appalling state of affairs should never be allowed to recur.

In place of the phased scale back of student visas proposed above, the government should exploit the fact that such visas have already been slashed much more severely to introduce a cap of 10 per cent or less on the share of foreign students which any university may have. This would be enforced by simply declining to issue visas for numbers beyond this – ideally with strong preference given to non China source countries (given China's behaviour throughout the pandemic, and the resulting urgent need for Australia to begin decoupling itself from that totalitarian nation).

The government should also unhesitatingly use the threat of refusing to issue foreign student visas to encourage institutions to co-operate, individually and collectively, with the excellent reform package for universities announced by Education Minister Dan Tehan on 19 June 2020.

3

ON KEEPING RIGHT
THE CASE FOR LIBERAL
PARTY REFORM

JOHN RUDDICK

The purpose of the Liberal Party is to provide the gutsy parliamentary leadership Australia needs to keep advancing. Since 2007 Australia has had seven prime ministers. The only era of greater prime ministerial turnover was the dozen or so years after federation when we were finding our footing in the new constitutional arrangements.

Recently I spoke to a friend who is about to retire from the job he's had since school – the NSW public service. He's a politically interested, big-time leftie. Over the decades we've had countless rows but this time he surprised me. He said he was happy Scott Morrison was prime minister: 'He's made politics boring. We need a rest from chaos.'

Perhaps he's right but we can't let a rest become a national slumber. At some point the federal parliamentary Liberal Party is going to have to roll up its sleeves and get on with fighting for tough reforms.

The Liberal Party and its ancestors have won 32 of Australia's 46 federal elections. For as long as Australia's centre-left party is under the hegemony of the trade union movement, its more than conceivable the lopsided political scoreboard continues for another 75 years. So if we want good Australian government the most critical ingredient is an optimally structured Liberal Party.

In the past six years we have had three hues of Liberal Party prime minister – conservative, moderate and now centre-right. All have governed with either no agenda, no mandate or both. The country is stalled because the Liberal Party is bound by archaic, byzantine rules that deprive the nation of the best possible parliamentary Liberal Party.

The future of the Liberal Party is as simple as it is monumental: wholesale democratic reform will transform it from a 19th century relic into a 21st century best-practice political organisation. Reform is inevitable – the variable in the equation is timing. It could take half a decade or half a century but the sooner the better.

The most consequential reform will be a triennial 'national leadership convention' open to all party members to elect our federal parliamentary leader. This is the reform that will deliver the good and gutsy leadership Australia needs this century. We'd have parliamentary leaders who will first have convinced the party's true believers that they have the right combination of policy, popularity and persuasiveness. Such a leader would then go into a federal election campaign with a policy agenda to fight for … and in government would have a bold mandate.

Some dismiss 'national leadership conventions' with two arguments: John Howard and Jeremy Corbyn. They argue "Howard is against the reform and Corbyn is a product of the reform, therefore the reform is wrong". Let's drill down on both.

In the long battle for some democratic reform of the factionally charged NSW Division of the Liberal Party (2011-2017), Howard was an early and at key moments, a valuable supporter of that partially successful movement. Howard is on the record as supporting all members voting for both our lower and upper house candidates. He is however opposed to the party membership electing our parliamentary leaders. It's curious as to why. Howard identifies with other national leaders on the right like Margaret Thatcher, Ronald Reagan and Stephen Harper … all top advocates of their parties' democratising the election of leaders.

Robert Menzies contested nine federal elections as leader. He won eight and retired on top. Obviously Menzies is the Liberal Party's gold medal champion. Howard contested six federal elections and won four … which easily awards him the party's silver medal. The bronze goes to Malcolm Fraser who won three from four since no other Liberal has won more than one.

As the silver medalist, Howard is rightly regarded by the party membership today as near-infallible … but near-infallible is not infallible and therefore we need more than his pronouncement that national leadership conventions are unwise.

Perhaps Howard is defending the 'party room ballot for leader' because it was a system that was good to him … but was it? Despite empirically being the second greatest Liberal, the party room repeatedly denied the leadership to the 'legend-in-the-making.' Let's review the seven times Howard put his hand up for the leadership before becoming Australia's second longest serving prime minister.

Malcolm Fraser won his third federal election in 1980. A year later his ambitious foreign affairs minister, Andrew Peacock, dramatically resigned from Fraser's cabinet. In a blistering 5,000-word parliamentary speech Peacock declared:

> Over recent months I have regretfully concluded that the Prime Minister is fracturing Cabinet government and the parliamentary

system as we know it. What I in fact have shown reveals the Prime
Minister's determination to centralise power and satisfy a mania for
getting his own way.

Peacock's strike against Fraser was dressed up as concern about
principle but it was just a routine attempt to destabilise Fraser
in the hope he (Peacock) would become leader. After Peacock's
purposefully damaging resignation he spent a year on the backbench
undermining Fraser ... so in April 1982 Fraser called a party room
meeting and threw open the leadership. Fraser won 54-27 ... but
his government was mortally wounded. Another by-product of
the turmoil was that Fraser's treasurer, John Howard, was elevated
to the deputy leadership.

When Fraser lost to Bob Hawke in 1983 he resigned the party
leadership. There were two contenders with a decent claim to
be 'next in line' – the recent challenger (Peacock) and the deputy
(Howard). That 1983 contest was remarkably amicable but the
seeds of chaos were sown when the two agreed before the ballot
that whoever lost would be deputy. They should have learned from
the Billy McMahon and John Gorton party room war a decade
earlier that whoever comes second in a leadership ballot should
never be deputy.

Peacock thumped Howard - 36 votes to 20. Peacock then lost the
1984 federal election but did enjoy an encouraging swing so his
leadership appeared secure. But Peacock was annoyed Howard
(his deputy) was publicly refusing to rule out ever being leader.
It went on for months. It quickly escalated into acrimony. As
it reached its crescendo Peacock was publicly calling on Howard
to rule out a challenge while Howard refused to budge from his
formula: "someone who has given the Liberal Party the lifelong
service I have is not required to answer that question."

In a rage, Peacock blundered. He should have plainly said (with his
Hollywood smile) that he 'encourages ambition in my colleagues'

and moved on. Instead Peacock called a party room ballot to boot Howard out as deputy. The press said Howard was gone but he narrowly defeated John Moore (38-31). Peacock was stunned. He paused the meeting and took the three other members of his leadership team to his office (weirdly including Howard) where he said he was thinking of resigning the leadership. The other two advised him not to. Howard stayed silent. Peacock walked back into the party room, announced his position untenable and quit.

The Sydney Morning Herald (SMH) the next day reported, 'Mr Peacock, who struck against Mr Howard this week to try to forestall a leadership challenge, became the victim of his own strategy.' Howard was now leader but by default. A decade later Howard reminisced on how he got the leadership in 1985 and concluded it was a mistake: "what should have happened was Andrew should not have resigned and we both should have said to the party we accept what the party wants is Andrew remaining leader and you John remain deputy leader."

Four years later at 8.30pm on 8 May 1989 Peacock knocked on the door of the Leader of the Opposition. He informed Howard he wanted his old job back. Within 12 hours the party room met and Peacock again thumped Howard 44 to 27.

Peacock's coup was perfectly executed. Neither Howard nor the media had an inkling. It was over quickly and decisively. The party replaced its legend-in-waiting with Peacock ... who would lose again to Hawke in less than a year giving Peacock a score of two losses from two attempts.

After Peacock's second loss in 1990, he considered nominating to retain the leadership but then decided against. A new leader therefore was needed. On the Tuesday after the 1990 election the SMH reported:

> The shadow Treasurer, Dr John Hewson, is coming under a lot of

pressure from within the party to stand for the leadership ... Dr Hewson appeared to leave open the possibility of a challenge when he arrived at the meeting of the Coalition leadership yesterday. He would certainly not stand if the former leader, Mr Howard, decides to contest the position. Mr Howard still retains a substantial body of support within the Liberal Party." Senator Michael Baume went on ABC and said Howard was the best person for the job.

Howard's sole public statement at the time was, 'I will continue to watch events and do whatever is in the best interests of the Liberal Party.''

The outgoing leader Peacock was decisive – he publicly swung in behind Hewson. At first the deal was that Peacock would be Hewson's deputy but that was howled down within hours by the press and public. Howard wanted the leadership in 1990 and he signaled his interest but the party room didn't want him so he didn't formally nominate. Hewson defeated Peter Reith 62-13.

After Hewson lost the 1993 federal election he ungraciously fought to retain the leadership (it would be akin to Bill Shorten re-contesting after losing the equably unlosable 2019 federal election). On the night of that crushing defeat Howard all but announced he would be a candidate for the leadership. Five days later the SMH reported:

> Mr Howard, who has been aggressively lobbying for party room support over the past few days, visited Dr Hewson in his Sydney office and told him of his intention to nominate for the leadership. He will announce that decision today. In announcing the special party-room meeting, Dr Hewson reaffirmed his intention to stand again as leader. This was a clear setback to Mr Howard who has been 'working the phones' over the past few days in the hope of getting his leader to pull out of the ballot. Dr Hewson also rejected the assertion of Mr Howard's supporters that a majority of the party-room of about 80 had already swung Mr

Howard's way.

A week after the 1993 federal election the Sun Herald's front page had a huge headline: Civil War Hits Liberals. It read:

> Still reeling from election defeat, the Liberal Party's leadership tussle broke out into civil war yesterday ... Despairing Liberal MPs preparing for Tuesday's leadership showdown between John Hewson and John Howard are describing it as 'Hobson's choice' – no choice at all. Liberal insiders acknowledge the Liberals are facing their greatest crisis since the Party's founding by Sir Robert Menzies in 1944. While the Hewson and Howard camps claim they are ahead in the leadership race, some Liberals reject both frontrunners. 'The candidates are seriously flawed and, whatever decision we make, we can't be sure it is going to stick anyway,' a Liberal front bencher complained yesterday."

Howard was now just three years away from starting his golden 12 years as prime minister ... but the 'all-wise' party room in March 1993 returned the now shattered Hewson (47 to 30).

Hewson's post-election leadership was across-the-board terrible. Prime Minister Paul Keating wasn't popular but Hewson couldn't land a glove. Hewson had been the most right-wing parliamentary leader that party had ever had but he then attempted (and failed) to reinvent himself as a 'moderate.' Worried about his leadership, on 6 March 1994 Hewson tried to damage his most likely challenger when he said of Howard's immigration policy in the 1980s: "It was very, very bad politics and morally and intellectually wrong in my view." Howard was rightly furious.

Peter Reith (a Howard ally) was in Hewson's shadow cabinet but routinely speaking out on contentious issues. He was openly contemptuous of his failing leader. On 17 May 1994 Hewson publicly berated Reith: "there is a perception that he's been disloyal and he needs to deal with that perception." Hewson's ultimatum was the spark that lit the bushfire. That night Hewson was ambushed on ABC TV with leaked polling from Liberal HQ that was atrocious.

The next day the SMH reported:

> Support for the embattled Opposition Leader, Dr Hewson, is beginning to waver as backers question his long-term future amid sliding poll ratings and obvious party-room disquiet over his performance. Although they are publicly remaining loyal to Dr Hewson, sources within the Hewson camp say they are aware of discussions about the alternatives. These include trying to build support for either of the so-called 'young Turks' – Mr Alexander Downer or Mr Peter Costello, or a combination ticket involving the former leader, Mr Howard, and one of the 'young turks.' Mr Howard has indicated in the past few days that he is still a leadership contender.

Two days later in the SMH the lead story was: 'Howard starts his run.' It read:

> Dr Hewson's position has deteriorated, with the former Opposition leader Mr John Howard now actively promoting his own candidacy while Dr Hewson's key support wavers. Mr Howard unsuccessfully approached Mr Costello to his deputy on a 'blended ticket.' The anger within the Victorian Liberals is helping Mr Howard in his bid to regain the leadership, although there is a widespread concern that replacing Dr Hewson with Mr Howard may leave lasting internal divisions.

Hewson tried to take control by announcing a leadership spill in the hope of clearing the air and rebooting his leadership. The 'Dream Team' of Downer and Costello announced their ticket within a few hours of Hewson calling the ballot and the press gave the young guns a big thumbs up.

On the day before the ballot (23 May 1994) Howard reluctantly ruled himself out of the race but refused to endorse either Downer or Hewson. Howard had a bloc of around 15 votes and some defected to Hewson. Michael Millett in the SMH explained why:

> One loyal Howard man said the maneuvering of the past 10 days had left the party room with only two choices. He described a Hewson win as a 'holding pattern' enabling fresh alternatives to emerge - a clear reference to Howard.

That would turn out to be the best plan ... but the party room didn't agree and Downer defeated Hewson 43-36.

For a short time Downer was riding high which coincided with the party celebrating its 50th anniversary. The ABC made a documentary on the party and interviewed Costello who said of Howard wanting to contest in 1994:

> I started ringing senior people in the party and I rang John Howard and informed him of this. And I told him my assessment which was that he couldn't run. And he couldn't win. I think there was a certain sadness yes because I think John Howard always wanted to be the leader and the prime minister. He's always had a claim on it. Circumstances conspired against his one opportunity and I think it was a ruling off of a long-time ambition."

Costello was simply reflecting the consensus view of the party room ... and the near future would demonstrate how faulty that view was.

Downer soon entered a bad patch which quickly turned diabolical. I recall listening to the John Laws radio show around this time when his Canberra reporter phoned in with some breaking news: John Howard was now determined to throw everything at one last all-out effort to grab the leadership. Howard was lobbying for support but then Downer (in a rare act of self-awareness in a leadership tussle) invited Howard to a private meeting. The most convenient location for both was a motel room on the outskirts of Melbourne. The meeting only went for 20 minutes but an unscripted photo showed big smiles all around. The next day Downer resigned and endorsed Howard to become leader without a ballot. Peacock had lifted his veto. Finally, Howard's path was clear.

That night Howard continued with his scheduled diary and by chance his next event was guest speaker at the humble Bankstown Young Liberals. He had accepted the invitation months earlier and to his credit turned up along with what seemed like the entire press gallery. Howard was radiant. He had the aura of an incoming prime minster (I know, I was one of 15 or so Young Liberals there weaving my way through all the TV cameras).

Finally, after all other options had been exhausted, the broken party room relented and gave Howard a go. Overnight the polls said Howard would smash Prime Minister Keating in the election. For the first time since the 1970's the federal coalition enjoyed a sustained polling ascendancy over Labor. The rest is history – Robert Menzies II would go on to win four federal elections on the trot and could only be defeated when a Labor opposition leader pleaded on TV, 'I'm just like John Howard.'

The party and the nation are indebted to Howard for his tenacity in seeking the leadership. But what if someone was, say 90% as good as Howard? We'd happily still want someone who was 90% John Howard as leader and PM … but it required the 100% effort of Howard to overcome his biggest stumbling block to the prime ministership – the silly party room.

On seven occasions between 1983 and 1995 Howard had contested (or wanted to contest) the leadership. Thrice Howard stood against an opponent and didn't come close to a majority (1983, 1989 and 1993). Twice he backed out of running due to a dearth of support (1990 and 1994). He won by awkwardly in 1985 when Peacock resigned and he won in 1995 as the sole nominee. The party room had the party's second biggest legend in its midst ... and conspired for over a decade to deny him the leadership.

Had the entire membership been invited to a national convention to elect our federal parliamentary leader Howard would have won in 1983, 1985, 1989, 1990, 1993, 1994 and 1995. How do I know? Because I know the rank and file party membership and they are overwhelmingly Howardites – now and in the 1980's. So while Howard himself may be against the membership electing leaders at a national convention, his life story is a towering testament as to its obvious need. Can the Liberal Party afford to have a leadership election process so prone to making such a big error?

The party room gets the leadership so wrong, so often because too many MPs are blinded by self-interest. Immediately post a party room ballot for leader, one third of those voting will be promoted to the front bench and two thirds will not. A sizable number of MPs will cast their vote according to a calculation about who is their best bet to get themselves into the top one third. Its scandalous – they're meant to be acting in the national interest.

The second uniformed argument against 'membership elections of leader' is today's British Labour leader Jeremy Corbyn. Clearly Corbyn is a dangerous left-wing radical. He was first elected leader in 2015 via an ultra-democratic ballot involving all the members of the Labour Party plus anyone who was willing to pay £3 and become a registered party 'supporter.' Corbyn won a massive 59% of the vote – no other candidate got above 20%. The party hierarchy was in uproar so the next year the party room deposed him (172 to 40). They thought they were rid of him but Corbyn was grudgingly permitted to recontest as the party HQ feared a party split. Corbyn won again with an increased margin (62%).

Is this evidence that too much democracy is a bad thing? No quite to the contrary. Tony Blair won three big general election wins by campaigning as a centrist ... but we now know that was spin. The organisation which was delivering all the Labour MPs in the Blair government was is, in fact, a radically left-wing morass who believes Corbyn should be PM. Blair's 'centrist' government engineered the public service decisively left but without the public registering what was going in.

Isn't it better the British public knows the naked truth about Labour? Of course it is – and now they do. Won't it result in the demise of British Labour as the main party on the British left? Hopefully and quite possibly yes – the UK's leftie-centrist party, the Liberal Democrats, are vying with Labour in recent polls. Either way, Corbyn will never win a general election and so the danger he poses is a mirage.

Labour can't be forgiven for electing Corbyn twice with the claim he only won because of the £3 memberships. It's true those 'members' voted over 80% for Corbyn ... but if their votes were not included Corbyn would still have won comfortably. Corbyn is a truthful representation of what British Labour is ... and they'll rightly wear the consequences. We should celebrate Jeremy Corbyn and be grateful the true Labour Party has come out from behind the curtain.

While on British politics, there is no better example of the benefit of 'membership elections for leader' than the leaderships of Teresa May and Boris Johnson. Immediately after the successful Leave vote in the 2016 Brexit referendum Prime Minister David Cameron (who campaigned for Remain) honourably resigned as PM and party leader.

In an act of utter stupidity the party room conspired to deny the Tory membership a vote and chose Teresa May as leader and PM. But May too was a Remainer! Its recently been revealed she sobbed on the night of the referendum ... but the all-wise party room thought May was the one to lead the nation through Brexit. Britain has suffered the consequences since.

Had the membership voted for Cameron's replacement they would have elected Boris Johnson – we know that because when May did resign and the membership were invited to elect the leader, Johnson (a Leave champion) won 66.4% of the votes to the Remain candidate's 33.6%. May had a painful period as PM. The Conservatives were reduced to a hung parliament in the 2017 general election and then the polling just kept getting worse. When Johnson became leader and PM in mid-2019 he immediately transformed a broken party into a party that is set to win big at the next general election.

The most significant political force in mid to late 19th century Australia were the radical democrats known as Chartists. After failing to achieve democratic reforms in Britain, Chartists flooded into Australia around the time of the gold rushes. Very quickly the Australian colonies had the most democratic parliaments in the world. When the newly independent United States were drafting a constitution in the 1780's the people were excluded from the process and the deliberations were strictly among the political elite. It was similar in Canada in the 1860's – the people were shut out of the process.

When the federation movement began in Australia our political elite assumed they would manage the entire process but the democracy loving Aussies would have none of it. They insisted the people elect delegates to a constitutional convention who would draft the constitution and then their work could only be approved by a referendum of the people.

When the Commonwealth came into force on 1 January 1901 it was a triumph of people power the like of which the world had never seen before. Australians were rightly proud of their democracy but we've since rested on our laurels. We now have the least democratic political parties in the Westminster world and our politics are the poorer as a result.

Australia faces great challenges. The chances of a Pacific War in the 21st century is not zero. We need the best possible political leadership possible and that won't happen until the men and women of the Liberal Party membership elect our federal parliamentary leader.

4

ECONOMIC POLICY

Robert Carling

Preamble

The SARS-CoV-2 coronavirus and its spread to the rest of the world rapidly became a major issue for economic policy in early 2020. Such was the expected economic impact that by March the Australian government had announced a series of emergency economic measures that would have been unthinkable in their scale and nature just a few weeks earlier.

These measures have been characterised by the government and the Reserve Bank of Australia as providing a bridge across the expected sharp economic downturn to the recovery on the other side. This essay is best described as a vision for economic policy on the other side of the bridge, rather than a commentary on the bridge itself.

It is to be hoped that both the measures and the economic scars — although inevitably long-lasting — prove ultimately to be temporary. However, it is already clear that one lasting legacy of the crisis will be a level of public debt -- both Commonwealth and state — much higher than previously projected, which will be an ongoing challenge for economic policy.

The federal budget for 2020-21 has been postponed from May to October. That will be the time for the government to spell out a macroeconomic management and reform program consistent with the principles spelt out in this essay.

Introduction

The ideas and principles of classical liberalism provide the best framework for economic policy. Those who agree with that proposition will hope it guides the policies of the re-elected Morrison government, but the government's record to date gives cause for doubt.

A classical liberal framework includes adherence to the rule of law, policy predictability and consistency, emphasis on markets and incentives, and limitations on government size and regulatory activities.

It is an understatement to say that the Morrison government up to the 2019 election — and its Coalition predecessors under both Turnbull and Abbott — were not guided primarily by classical liberal and free market ideas but by the pragmatism of electoral survival. There were some policies consistent with classical liberalism, such as tax cuts, but they had to share the stage with distinctly illiberal policies such as the 'big stick' approach to energy markets, threats to control gas exports, the deeply interventionist bank executive accountability regime (BEAR) and increasing dominance of the central government in the federal system.

The government sometimes spoke the language of free markets and incentive, but mixed it with the language of intervention and redistribution, leaving the impression it did not follow a set of consistent principles.

Advocates of classical liberalism must hope for better from the current term of the Morrison government. The government could hardly be said to have been re-elected on a platform of classical liberal policies, but governments are defined as much by how they deal with the inevitable stream of unanticipated external and domestic events as by how they implement their election promises. If it were to move further in the direction of classical liberal policies, it would not be the first government to make a course correction in office.

Australia's economic performance

While Australia has maintained its world-beating record of economic expansion in terms of longevity, in other respects our performance of recent years is wanting. This is partly a result of external events beyond our control — such as fluctuations in commodity prices and the sub-par performance of the world economy — but it can also be traced to policy deficiencies at home and in particular to the drift away from policies of free and open markets.

Economic performance and living standards are suffering from the combination of weak productivity growth, low levels of business investment and flat real household disposable incomes. The problem is often described in terms of weak consumer spending, but this is a consequence of the more fundamental and related weaknesses in business investment, productivity and household incomes.

Business investment is historically low as a proportion of GDP, and this is even more the case for non-mining investment than it is for total business investment. Non-mining investment in recent years (up to 2017-18) has been at the lowest proportions of GDP since the series started in 1959-60. Total business investment, similarly defined, is the lowest in 25 years. The Productivity Commission speaks of a stalling in innovative activity, with both research and development (R&D) activity and the R & D capital stock in absolute decline.[5] Business has faced an inhospitable climate for so long that it could be argued there is an investment strike under way.

The decline in innovative activity augurs badly for productivity growth, which is already weak. In the market sector labour productivity growth and multi-factor productivity growth averaged 1.7% and 0.8% respectively in the six years to 2017-18. These were both low by the standards of earlier periods of strong economic performance. More concerning still, both measures of productivity actually declined in absolute terms in 2018-19.[6]

Real living standards have either stagnated or slowed to a crawl — depending on the measure used — since reaching a peak in 2011-12 after the long, steep climb associated with the resources boom. For example, although real net national disposable income per capita rose in the last two years as the terms of trade recovered, this increase merely reversed the decline from 2011-12 to 2015-16. Other measures less sensitive to terms of trade fluctuations have been less volatile, but show a similar picture of flat real household disposable income since 2011-12. For example, the Melbourne Institute's 2019 HILDA survey reveals real household disposable incomes flat (for the mean) or slightly down (for the median) from 2012 to 2017.[7]

Thus, while Australia's economic expansion has continued, there are signs that not all is well and we could be doing much better, particularly in the vital indicators of investment, productivity and

5   Productivity Commission, *Productivity Bulletin*, May 2019 (Commonwealth of Australia, Canberra, 2019)

6   Australian Bureau of Statistics, *Australian System of National Accounts, 2018-19*, Cat No 5204.0.

7   Melbourne Institute, *Household, Income and Labour Dynamics in Australia (HILDA) Survey* (melbourneinstitute.unimelb.edu.au/hilda)

real income growth. Weakness in these areas has taken a toll on the real GDP growth rate in recent times. The problem is often diagnosed as a lack of structural economic reform, but this sidesteps the question as to what kind of reform. The classical liberal prescription is that we need reform consistent with greater economic freedom.

Australia's performance in international surveys of economic freedom has levelled out or deteriorated. For example, the Fraser Institute's index of economic freedom shows a long, slow advance in Australia's ranking from 12th in 1985 to 5th in 2010, followed by a retreat to 10th in 2016.[8]

Macroeconomic policy framework

A stable macroeconomic policy framework with consistently applied rules of fiscal and monetary responsibility is something any government should strive for — whether or not they adhere to classical liberal principles. Such a framework is a necessary but not sufficient condition for a thriving private sector. It does not mean the business cycle can be abolished, but its amplitude can be reduced through judicious economic management. A more stable framework also fosters greater confidence for long-term business investment decisions.

The inevitability of the business cycle means that the budget cannot always be in balance but will swing between deficits at times of weakness in the cycle and surplus at times of unusual strength. Australia has long had a balanced budget rule that recognises these cyclical swings, as it calls for the budget to be balanced on average over the business cycle. (In fact, both Labor and Coalition governments took this further and aimed for surpluses on average

---

8   Fraser Institute, *Economic Freedom of the World: 2018 Annual Report* (fraserinstitute.org/studies/economic-freedom)

over the cycle.) The problem is that the rule has not been met. If it had, the budget would have climbed out of deficit several years ago.

The budget actually reached balance in 2018-19, which was a much better result than seemed likely even a short time ago — a deficit of $21 billion having been projected for that year in the 2017 budget, for example. The Morrison government aimed for surpluses in 2019-20 and beyond, but no surplus was achieved and the Covid-19 pandemic and fiscal policy responses to it have overwhelmed any prospect of surpluses for years to come. The risk now is that the inevitably very large deficits of 2019-20 and the following two years will become entrenched structural deficits. One key task for fiscal policy is to ensure this does not happen. In fact, even before the Covid-19 shock, Treasury's central estimate of the structural budget (which abstracts from cyclical effects) continued to show a small structural deficit in 2020-21 even if the government's budgeted surplus was achieved (meaning that the surplus would have been entirely cyclical) and did not reach balance until 2021-22.[9]

Although there are many uncertainties, in all probability more work was needed on fiscal discipline to secure balanced (let alone surplus) budgets, on average, over the medium term. The problem is that the government long ago gave up talking about the expenditure savings measures needed to secure such discipline, with the exception of continually ratcheting up the nebulous efficiency dividend.

It has relied on tighter control of government running costs and enforcement of social security benefit eligibility rules to keep total expenditure growth under reasonable control (average real growth of 1.6% in the five years to 2018-19) in the face of rapid growth in some large programs such as the NDIS and child care subsidies. But it has also relied heavily on tax revenue growth – and

---

9   Mid-year Economic and Fiscal Outlook, 2019-20, Treasury, Canberra, 2019.

particularly bracket creep – to bring the budget close to balance.

The budget's return to deficit as a result of economic weakness reflects the working of automatic fiscal stabilisers, such as the decline in tax receipts as unemployment goes up and business profits go down. Such responses should not be resisted by fiscal policy. The bigger question is whether fiscal policy should become active in trying to dampen an economic downturn through stimulus measures, as it did in large measure in response to the 2008-09 global financial crisis.

The Charter of Budget Honesty does not rule out a role for active counter-cyclical fiscal policy, but the amount is a matter for careful judgement. The 2008-09 stimulus was very large by both historical and international standards and arguably was destabilising in the medium term, whatever short-term benefits to economic activity it delivered. The government would be wise to avoid going down the same path, keep any discretionary stimulus to modest proportions and be as quick to withdraw it – when it is no longer needed – as to apply it.

Government spending

How the budget is balanced is as important as whether it is balanced. Limiting government size is a classical liberal prescription, and the Centre for Independent Studies was on this track when it advocated in 2013 that total general government spending should be no more than 30% of GDP.[10] The figure at the time was 35% and it remained at that level when last measured in 2017-18.

What a reduction to 30% would mean for the federal government depends on the distribution of expenditures across the three levels of government, but it is clear that the current ratio of

---

10 Simon Cowan et al, *TARGET30 — Towards Smaller Government and Future Prosperity* (The Centre for Independent Studies, Sydney, 2013).

Commonwealth budget payments to GDP of around 25% would be inconsistent with 30% for total general government expenditure. It also remains above the average for the years 2000-01 to 2007-08 (a period that included the structural effects of the GST on the federal budget and excluded the effects of the GFC and associated stimulus spending).

The government's medium-term fiscal projections to 2029-30 show payments falling to 23.6% of GDP. This would be a good step in the direction of smaller government but has been criticised by some observers as unrealistic. However, the projections are based on the usual technical assumption of no new spending policy initiatives, and on that basis it is likely that payments would drift lower relative to GDP, particularly once the NDIS completes its ramp-up phase and no longer boosts the growth rate of total payments.

The key issues, rather, are whether there will be new spending policy initiatives, and how significant they will be. If they are as large as they have been over the past ten years, then spending is likely to remain at its current elevated proportion of GDP. However, this is a policy choice of government. As the former Treasurer Peter Costello has often said, the easiest expenditure saving is the new spending initiative *not* adopted. The current government would be well advised to follow that advice and avoid new initiatives such as the increase in the Newstart allowance being urged upon it from numerous quarters.

Beyond avoiding new initiatives, the Morrison government should resurrect the search for savings in existing programs that was embraced by the Abbott government in 2014 but subsequently largely abandoned by it and the Turnbull government under intense political pressure. At the very least, the government should operate under a fiscal rule that every dollar of new spending must be matched by a dollar of savings from existing spending. Then, it has a chance of lowering the spending to GDP ratio.

Taxation

The Coalition governments of 2013-2019 put more effort into increasing taxes than reducing them — remember the budget repair levy on the top bracket of personal income; reinstating indexation of fuel excise; continuing with the Labor government's massive increases in tobacco excise; springing a complete surprise with the levy on major banks' liabilities; and increasing superannuation taxes in the name of 'fairness'. Admittedly they also tried to cut company tax, but ran into the Senate brick wall and were only able to cut the rate for small companies.

Since 2018 the government has changed its tune and put emphasis on cutting personal income tax. This was a key plank in its 2019 election victory and the tax cuts were swiftly passed into legislation by the new parliament. Praise for these tax cuts must be tempered by the observation that they do little more than hand back the proceeds of bracket creep and won't be fully implemented until 2024.

The government is now on the right track of limiting rather than adding to the tax burden, but it should aim for a lower tax-to-GDP ratio than the 23.9% cap it has set for itself, which is based on the historically high pre-GFC tax take. As for specific measures, there is much more to be done beyond what it has promised and enshrined in legislation. In personal income tax, the top marginal rate needs to be cut from 47% and the top threshold raised beyond the $200,000 level now set for 2024. Once the new thresholds are in place in 2024, they need to be automatically indexed to annual growth in average wages to stop the charade of bracket creep and periodic tax cuts financed from its proceeds.

In company tax, the two-tier system based on business size needs to be abolished and the single rate restored at a lower level than 30%. That argument was lost in the last parliament but needs to be re-prosecuted. If there is no cut in the rate, then the government needs to consider something like a permanent investment allowance.

Beyond income taxes, the government could show a commitment to neutral, efficient taxation with a small revenue loss by abolishing the luxury car tax. And the whole area of taxation of savings income (such as interest, dividends, rent and capital gains) needs attention — not that the overall taxation of such income is too low, as some argue, but that the important principle that savings income be taxed at a low rate is being inconsistently applied.

Needless to say all of the above will require a much more disciplined approach to government expenditure than we have seen in the past.

The GST is the other major tax, but is inextricably linked to fiscal federalism and is taken up in the next section.

Federalism

Federalism is a constitutional and governance topic but it is also an economic policy topic because it has an important bearing on the allocation and use of resources in the public sector. A federal system is the best for Australia but our system has lost sight of the basic principles of federalism and is operating way below potential. In some respects we are operating more like a unitary system because of the growing dominance of the central government.

There is scant regard for the principle of subsidiarity. The federal government uses its financial muscle to influence policies in the states' constitutional domain. Accountability is confused. The states are too dependent on money raised by the Commonwealth and are left with a bundle of mainly inefficient taxes.

None of this will change until there is a Commonwealth government that wants it to change, and there are no signs yet that the Morrison government fits that bill. It could start to get federalism back on the rails by withdrawing completely from funding state responsibilities such as education. It should also desist from vote-buying through Commonwealth grants for local purposes such as sports ovals and leave those matters to local government, where they belong.

If it follows this prescription it would be left with spare money, which it should use either to grant the states a share of personal income tax revenue for their general and untied use, or cut its own taxes to make room for a state income tax surcharge on Commonwealth rates.

Increasing the GST would be the easiest way to give the states more general purpose funds in place of tied grants, but it would also be the easiest way to increase the overall national tax burden and for this reason should be resisted. However, some broadening of the GST base should be considered in exchange for the abolition of inefficient state taxes.

Trade and investment policies

Openness to trade and foreign investment are hallmarks of the competitive market economy. There is a hierarchy of ways to achieve this, with global trade and investment liberalisation at the top, regional liberalisation as second, and bilateral trade deals a distant third.

The last attempt at global liberalisation (the Doha round) was a failure and the prospects for another attempt have worsened considerably since then. While global liberalisation should always be Australia's first choice, it is obvious that no Australian government can do much to bring it about, other than advocate it and join or attempt to form coalitions of like-minded countries.

In the meantime the world of trade policy has degenerated into a tangled web of overlapping regional and bilateral deals that probably do as much to divert trade than to create it, and create a lot of complexity for business.

In this setting, the best realistic option for an Australian government is to promote and participate in multilateral regional initiatives drawn as broadly as possible, such as the Trans Pacific Partnership (TPP) and the Regional Comprehensive Economic Partnership (RCEP).

The government should also be open to unilateral trade liberalisation, resist domestic pressures for unilateral increases in protection and maintain an open door to foreign investment and the technology it brings. The reduction in protection in the 1980s and 90s was largely unilateral, and the government should lower the remaining protective barriers to trade whether or not as part of agreements with other countries. It should keep the nationalistic blinkers off when it considers foreign takeover proposals.

Structural reform to foster productivity growth

There is more to economic management than balanced budgets and low unemployment and inflation. The term has a broader meaning in which microeconomic policies are at least as important as the macroeconomic. The efficient and innovative allocation and use of the nation's resources (in the broadest sense of economic resources, not just what is in the ground) are vitally important to productivity and potential growth.

Governments can contribute to productivity growth through the allocation and efficiency of their own spending on goods and services and how they run their own business enterprises, but there is little they can do to *directly* affect productivity growth in the market sector. However, public policies have an important *indirect* effect by shaping some of the determinants of market sector productivity.

Public policies can be thought of as drivers (the incentive framework) and enablers of productivity growth.[11] These include the policies discussed above such as taxation policies with an emphasis on incentive and trade and investment policies that emphasise openness. However, domestic economic policy can go further through what is often called structural reform. These include the following, in no particular order of importance:

- Competition policy, such as avoiding concentration of market power and avoiding interference with the forces of creative destruction of failed businesses large and small.

- Development of skills in the labour force, and ensuring TAFE are not squeezed out by universities in the allocation of funding.

- Infrastructure projects that are selected according to rigorous cost/benefit analysis, and overall programs that do not strain the public finances.

- Ensuring low cost and reliability of energy and that these goals are not compromised by carbon emission reduction objectives. Among other things, unwarranted state restrictions on onshore gas field development need to be removed.

- An industrial relations system that gives primacy to enterprise bargaining and ensures the award system serves only as a safety net.

- Reducing red tape and regulation, particularly in major project approval processes. This includes not strangling

---

11   For example, Gary Banks, *Productivity Policies: the 'to do' list*, address to the Economic and Social Outlook Conference, Melbourne, 1 November 2012.

the banking system with post-royal commission regulatory overkill.

The role of state governments in this agenda is at least as important as the Commonwealth's. The latter has direct responsibility in some areas, such as industrial relations, and in other areas can work as leader of the National Cabinet (formerly the Council of Australian Governments (COAG)) to facilitate state actions in the national interest.

Inequality and redistribution

The ALP sought to make inequality and the need for more redistribution a major issue in the 2019 federal election. The election result suggests this agenda does not resonate with the Australian people to the extent many thought. However, the issue is unlikely to go away, and the government will need a sensible position on it.

Under classical liberalism there is no place for attempting to engineer greater economic equality for the sake of it through coercive measures such as redistributive taxation. As free and competitive markets are the best way to organise economic activity and maximise living standards, a degree of inequality must be expected. It is an essential feature of a market-based economic system in which differences in talent, effort and luck result in wide disparities in income and wealth.

This does not mean the government can or should disregard economic inequality or attempt to dismantle all forms of social security and welfare. Most advocates of classical liberalism accept the case for a social safety net and that its level should have regard to average real incomes broadly. Call that redistribution if you like, but it is a very different proposition from that of imposing greater economic equality for its own sake and regardless of adverse economic consequences.

As well as explaining that economic inequality is an essential and positive feature of a successful market economy, the government should respond to pressures for greater forced equality by emphasising that inequality in Australia has not changed greatly over the long run and is not exceptional by international standards. If there were to be a sudden increase in measures of inequality, it would be important to understand and treat the underlying causes rather than just the symptoms.

Classical liberals will always feel more at home with equality of opportunity than with equality of outcomes. The principle of equality of opportunity provides some guideposts for policy, particularly in education policy and the distribution of public funding. However, in the real world absolute equality of opportunity is pie in the sky and policy makers should never be deluded into thinking they can achieve it.

Policy development process

Policy predictability and consistency is an asset but is unlikely to be achieved without proper policy development processes being followed. The government must resist being stampeded into rash policy announcements by social media campaigns and pressures from shock-jocks. It should not spring policy surprises 'out of the blue'. All significant policy proposals should be thoroughly aired through green papers, white papers, Productivity Commission reviews where appropriate, parliamentary inquiries and public consultation.

Concluding remarks

Low levels of business investment and productivity growth are a recipe for continuing disappointment with real household income performance. Australia's economic performance will always be conditioned by the global economy, but there is much to be done to lift our performance relative to whatever the global economy is doing at any point in time.

This requires policies consistent with free and open markets with limited government spending and regulation in a framework of responsible macroeconomic policies. Such policies, as outlined above, are unlikely to be deliverable in full in one term, but the government should at least move in this direction and be consistently guide by classical liberal principles in all areas of public policy.

5

LABOUR RELATIONS

JOHN SLATER

Keeping Australia's economy 'strong' has been a long-standing fixture of the Coalition's daily talking points. The problem for the Morrison Government is that since the Coalition came to power in 2013, Australia's economy hasn't performed as strongly as its boosters would have you believe. Productivity has grown at a miserly average of 1.1 per cent per year. Wage growth in the private sector has also been anemic, barely nudging 1.5 per cent. Meanwhile, business investment – a key measure of our economic dynamism - has shrunk by one fifth. The 1.3 million jobs created under the Coalition's watch have overwhelmingly been in the public sector. In 2018, only one in five new jobs were generated by private enterprise.

What should the Morrison Government do about industrial relations? It's a question which many in the Government's ranks are reluctant to answer. Since the repeal of *WorkChoices* following the defeat of the Howard Government in 2007, the Coalition's industrial relations policy has largely been a case of "don't ask, don't tell". But as Australia enters the third decade of the 21st century, there is mounting evidence that IR reform is not something which the Coalition can ignore much longer.

The World Economic Forum ranks Australia 53rd in the world for labour-employer relations and 95th for flexibility in wage determination. One in four business leaders say industrial relations is the biggest barrier to doing business in Australia. An overregulated, outdated industrial relations system isn't the only reason why Australia's economy is failing to emulate the strength of Trump's America or the steady prosperity of the Howard years. But it does explain some things.

The bottom line is that Australia's labour market is significantly more regulated than those of the vast majority of its peers. In a world where capital is mobile and competition for goods and increasingly services is global, this is not a desirable state of affairs.

Liberalising industrial relations was once a core part of the Liberal Party's political identity. Today, the topic is treated by many MPs as a liability - if not an embarrassment. Apart from crackdowns on trade unions, the Coalition has spent more time downplaying its differences on IR with the Australian Labor Party since the Rudd Government's *Fair Work Act 2009* was passed than highlighting them.

The Liberal Party has become Australia's natural party of government at the federal level principally on its record of sound economic management. If the Morrison Government intends to seek re-election on this basis, it can't treat its *bona fides* on the economy as a self-fulfilling prophecy. It needs to make good on its pledge.

So what should an IR agenda equal to the task of re-invigorating Australia's economy look like? Could inspiration be drawn from the Dries who mounted the case that the market for labour should be liberated from the shackles of compulsory wage arbitration?

The 2019 Liberal Party room could certainly use the ballast of Peter

Reith, Nick Minchin and Peter Costello. But the political climate today is vastly different.

Recall that in the 1980s, Big Government was on the nose. A decade of high unemployment and crippling inflation in the 1970s had undermined the Keynesianism Consensus of pump-priming economic growth through high taxes and big spending. Amid this malaise, free-marketeers successfully made the case that lower taxes, deregulation and freer trade would end the stagnation that had beset much of the western world.

The Dries' push for a less rigid industrial framework was still vigorously opposed. As Prime Minister, Bob Hawke denounced as 'economic lunatics' the HR Nicholls Society, an activist group set up to champion the cause of workplace deregulation. But eventually, their arguments cut through. In 1992, the Keating Government moved to dismantle compulsory arbitration in favour of moving to a decentralised system of bargaining at the workplace level.

Today, the *Zeitgeist* is very different. In the years since the Global Financial Crisis, public confidence in the free market has been badly shaken. As the wealth of the richest in the world has climbed to dizzying new heights, many workers haven't received a real pay rise since downloading Uber to their smartphone. Large-scale job losses in manufacturing have prompted fresh doubts over whether the 'rising tide of freer trade' really does lift all boats. And trust in corporations has been debased by a long list of misdemeanours perpetrated by big banks and social media barons.

It's no coincidence that successful Right-leaning politicians in recent times have channelled these anxieties, not resisted them. Donald Trump and Boris Johnson for instance, sought to reclaim the nation state as the bedrock of public life and to address legitimate concerns spurred by globalisation. Scott Morrison recast the Coalition's message away from ideology and around practical goods: letting people keep more of what they earn while providing a fair-go all round.

Notably, all three leaders owe their success to the support outside their traditional support base: non-professional wage earners no longer represented by the increasingly identitarian, and post-material politics of the left.

When it comes to industrial relations, the political upheaval of recent times underscores the dangers of re-heating the arguments made in the 1980s. A case for reform built on the supposedly self-evident virtues of deregulation risks being received as a euphemism for slashing workers' pay and conditions. Instead, the Coalition must frame its pitch for reform around practical outcomes and common sense. To that end, here are two ways Morrison could get started.

Ending closed shops

One of the more interesting upshots of the 2019 election was the total failure of the Australian Council of Trade Union's 'Change the Rules' campaign to have virtually any discernible impact on how people voted. Despite a $25 million campaign spend ($3 million more than the resources industry spent campaigning against the Rudd Government's mining tax) Labor's vote among low and middle-income earners went down, not up.

You might think such a humiliating result would prompt some introspection about what went wrong. At a minimum, the result would suggest a rethink of the campaign's overwrought claim that the Coalition and Big Business were conspiring to turn Australia into a country of working poor. Not so. By the end of the year, the union movement had launched yet another hyper-partisan campaign – *Stop Morrison's Attack on Working People and Our Unions*.

The union movement's refusal to acknowledge its disconnect with the workers it used to represent isn't a new development. It's one of the core reasons why its membership has fallen so rapidly over the past four decades. The truth is that the union movement's class war-obsessed, anti-business screed bears little relevance to the worldview held by the mainstream of the Australian workforce. Most workers are reasonably well-paid, enjoy a comfortable standard of living, and have no desire to join 'The Resistance' – much less partake in a workers' revolution. Indeed, eight in ten Australians trust their employer – double the amount who put their faith in media and Government.

Unions have wilfully ignored that most workers no longer share their appetite for industrial conflict. Instead, they've spent recent decades trying to change the outcome of federal elections and doubling-down on Left-wing hobby-horses like refugee rights, boycotting Israel and climate change to name a few. The results speak for themselves: union density has fallen from 51 per cent of the workforce in 1976 to 14 per cent today.

Despite this precipitous decline, unions remain a dominant force in Australia's industrial landscape. Under the Fair Work Act, unions are the *de-facto* representatives for workers in collective bargaining – even if the vast majority of workers covered by a proposed agreement aren't members. More than two thirds of collective agreements are negotiated by trade unions. For major projects which are yet to recruit a workforce, negotiating an agreement with a union is compulsory.

In the construction industry, these institutionalised privileges have enabled unions to secure eye-watering salaries that have made Australia's building costs among the highest in the world. Labourers on CFMEU agreements for major projects can earn as much as $200,000 per year – more than double the salary of an experienced teacher. Registered trade unions also have de-facto standing to make submissions and be heard by the Fair Work Commission in relation to a range of its regulatory functions, including reviewing modern awards and setting the minimum wage.

These rules have preserved the union movement's power while its membership has fallen. This is true not just of union influence, but of the unions' financial clout. As research by this author for the Menzies Research Centre revealed, unions have used their privileges under the Fair Work system to generate new sources of revenue to offset declining membership dues. Between 2003 and 2017, the 15 largest trade unions increased their yearly revenue by 89% while trebling their asset holdings to nearly $1.6 billion.

Since coming to office in 2013, the Coalition has taken a range of sensible measures to curb the worst abuses of union power. Reinstating the ABCC has brought greater scrutiny to the standover tactics and anti-competitive collusion that besets the construction industry. Likewise, the Registered Organisations Commission has helped bring union governance standards into line with the private sector. The Ensuring Integrity Bill which remains in the Senate at the time of writing, will deservedly strip law-breaking officials and unions of their right to represent workers.

The problem is that the Coalition's lack of industrial relations agenda beyond these policies has given credence to the claim it is 'anti-union'. Indeed, with the exception of plans to introduce penalties for deliberate wage underpayments, every major piece of industrial relations legislation proposed by the Government has been characterised as a crackdown on trade unions. The narrowness of this agenda, coupled with mis-steps, like the botched leaking of the AFP's raids on the AWU, have reinforced the perception by unions that the Coalitions is a tribal enemy. This has given the union movement a powerful call to arms, fortifying its narrative that the Coalition is intent on crushing unions at all costs.

When it comes to reducing the union movement's outsized and entrenched influence on industrial relations, the Coalition has better options than passing more laws, creating new agencies and hiring more regulators. Instead, it should turn its focus to the privileges that protect unions from paying a price for their underperformance.

It's a little known fact that in Australia, trade unionism is a closed shop. Under the 'conveniently belong rule', a trade union cannot be registered under the Fair Work Act if there is already an organisation that caters to workers in that occupation or industry. In effect, this is a ban on choice in workplace representation that gives the existing class of mostly ALP-aligned trade unions a monopoly over their chosen industry.

It's well established that monopolies promote inefficiency and undesirable behaviour. Without the check of competition, monopolists become bloated and indifferent to the needs of their consumers. The result is higher rents and poorer services – enriching the monopolist at everyone else's expense.

It's a familiar story neatly borne out by unionism in Australia. Despite amassing $65 million in penalties and more than 2200 convictions in the last fifteen years, the CFMEU remains the only choice for workers in construction, mining, forestry and maritime jobs seeking workplace representation. Likewise, after the AWU negotiated enterprise agreements that resulted in cleaners being paid $400 million less than the award, the workers dudded would have had no other alternatives but to resign their membership or stay with the wayward AWU.

In recent years, this cosy protection racket has begun to show cracks. In much the same way that Uber bypassed the taxi industry's wall of self-serving regulation, traditional unions are now being disrupted by a new generation of employee associations.

The Nurses Professional Association of Queensland Inc. (NPAQ) was formed in 2014 with the object of providing nurses with no-frills workplace representation without politics. Instructively, NPAQ had its beginnings in a discussion between nurses frustrated by the Queensland Nurses and Midwives Union's (QNMU) campaigning against the Newman Government. The nurses wanted the support services and insurance offered by a union, but resented funding hyper-partisan campaigning.

Unlike the QNMU, NPAQ stays at arm's length distance from the dog fight of partisan politics. Political donations are banned under the association's Constitution, allowing it to provide expert industrial advice and support, professional indemnity insurance and representation in enterprise bargaining at roughly half the membership rates charged by the QNU. This extraordinary price difference highlights the premium charged by traditional unions, much of which is used to finance campaigns and political donations.

NPAQ has 5,000 members and growing, placing it among Queensland's ten largest employee associations. Yet because of the "conveniently belong" rule, it faces an uphill battle representing its members on a level playing field with the QNMU. The Department of Health has banned NPAQ from being a party to an award or enterprise agreement, and refuses to allow it to represent its members in workplace disputes or consultations.

NPAQ's success, in spite of these roadblocks, highlights three ways the existing union monopolies are giving workers a rotten deal.

First, a lack of competition has seen existing unions become wasteful and greedy. Too many union leaders behave like the top end of town they claim to disdain. Disclosures to the Registered Organisations Commission have revealed that 59 union officials are paid more than $200,000 per year, with some earning as much as $400,000.

Second, the conveniently belong rule has encouraged unions to behave like the rulers of a fiefdom; not service providers. According to senior NPAQ officers, their employees are frequently subject to hissing and foul-mouthed abuse by QNMU officials. The Queensland Labor Government has point blank refused to recognise NPAQ, with one Queensland Minister even refusing to be in a photograph with NPAQ's staff at an office opening. It's difficult to see how such tribalism can be reconciled with maintaining an undivided focus on the interests of workers.

Third, despite how our workforce has changed, there continues to be a real market for workplace representation. Particularly in occupations such as nursing which involve dealing with high-risk situations, many workers understandably want the assurance of a third party to advise them on their rights and represent them if something goes wrong. The same can be said about teachers, bus drivers, police officers as well as construction and mine workers where occupational risk is a fact of daily life.

Repealing the "conveniently belong" rule will make unions that put political empire-building before workplace representation accountable to consumer choice. From a political standpoint, repealing the conveniently belong rule would shift the debate away from union-busting to the far friendly terrain of freedom of association. Morrison wouldn't be arguing that unions should be brought to heel, but simply that workers should choose the union that best suits their needs. And Labor would be left to defend why the largest power bloc in its own party should continue to receive its own set of privileges.

Cutting through complexity

When the Coalition took office in 2013, the underpayment of workers was thought to be a marginal problem, confined mostly to small and unsophisticated businesses. By the time of Scott Morrison's unlikely election win, that assumption had been spectacularly debunked. Dozens of businesses, many reputable, household names, have been caught out paying their staff less than the lawful minimum.

The number of employers and scale of underpayments – some as high as $300 million – has stoked an escalating sense of crisis. The list of victims has grown from vulnerable groups like backpackers and international students to include managers and even salaried professionals. Payroll company Ascender estimates at least one in five workers are left out of pocket and that bosses are unlawfully withholding as much as $1.8 billion in wages each year.

The notion that wage theft has reached epidemic proportions has been eagerly fomented by the union movement. ACTU Secretary Sally McManus, says wage theft is "systemic… often [involving] deliberate manipulation of the system" and "cannot be blamed on ignorance of the rules."

What was once a compliance issue has quickly morphed into a far-reaching conspiracy by large corporations to steal from the mouths of their benighted workers. The unfolding scandal has given the union movement a more potent rallying cry than any policy, real or imagined, proposed by the Morrison Government.

The problem for the union movement in posing as the saviour of underpaid workers is that its record on wage theft is also actually fairly poor. Before underpayments became a national issue around 2018, traditional unions had little interest in ensuring workers' payslips matched their lawful entitlements. This work was largely left to law firms, community legal centres and the Fair Work Ombudsman.

Even more embarrassing, however, is that several of Australia's largest trade unions have been complicit in a different type of wage theft. The SDA – the Australian Council of Trade Unions largest affiliate – has negotiated scores of enterprise agreements with the biggest names in Australian retail and fast food that stripped workers of penalty rates and overtime loadings, resulting in lower wages than if they'd been paid under the relevant award. A conservative estimate has these agreements saving major corporations hundreds of millions of dollars by reducing the take-home pay of low-skilled workers, many young, working unsociable hours.

Is it still wage theft when the co-conspirators are unions and the industrial umpire responsible for enforcing minimum conditions?

The other problem with denouncing all underpayments as 'theft' is the list of culprits. The claim that big chains like Woolworths, Grilld and Michael Hill operate a business model of exploiting staff is conceivable, albeit hyperbolic. But in the cases of Victorian State Government Departments and the ABC, it verges on the absurd. Even Maurice Blackburn, a nationwide plaintiff law-firm that has led several underpayment class actions, has been exposed for underpaying 400 staff $1 million. The error was caused by an ambiguous overtime provision, with the firm agreeing to back-pay workers in June 2018 after months of negotiations. Can Maurice Blackburn, a firm with the pedigree of having represented unions in a host of epoch-making court battles, be accused of running a business model based on worker exploitation? Or is there more to the wage theft saga than the ubiquity of corporate greed and malfeasance?

In truth, the phrase wage theft has been loosely applied to what are two very different classes of conduct. There are employers who conspire to deprive workers of their lawful entitlements. And there are employers, who for reasons ranging from inadvertence to genuine oversight, do not make good on every one of their employees' lawful entitlements.

Since a host of 7-Eleven franchises were exposed for systematically underpaying their migrant workers – paying some as little as 47 cents an hour – it's become apparent that Australia has more of a problem with the first class of wage theft than was previously thought. According to the Migrant Workers' Taskforce formed in response to the 7-Eleven scandal, the exploitation of foreign workers, especially temporary visa holders and international students, has become widespread and entrenched. Apart from receiving meagre wages, the Taskforce found workers on temporary work visas often had their passports seized, were housed in rooms with up to eight people and made to work punishingly long hours under the threat of being reported to immigration authorities for breaching their visas.

The culpability of employers in the second class is not nearly as black and white. On the one hand, it's hard to sympathise with employers who are seemingly indifferent to whether basics, such as minimum wages and casual loadings, are being properly paid. For what else, other than sheer indifference, could explain salubrious restaurateur George Calombaris failing to pay hundreds of casual staff the minimum award rate for years on end?

However, the question of blame becomes murkier where underpayments are caused by errors in payroll administration. Wesfarmer's $15 million underpayment of 6,000 former and current staff following its migration onto a new payroll system is a case in point. The underpayments were not for ordinary wage rates, but for superannuation that wasn't added to sporadically paid allowances for cars and clothing. Similar mistakes have plagued the payroll systems of Bunnings, Beaurepairs, and the Get-Up backing, Adani-bashing cosmetics outlet Lush.

Relying on software or outsourcing shouldn't absolve employers of their obligations at law. But it says something about the complexity of modern awards that specially trained managers and purpose-built systems are being repeatedly caught out. Payroll managers typically earn a six figure salary, and yet, the Australian Payroll Association estimates a staggering nine in ten find awards contradictory and confusing. Even in large organisations with inhouse teams dedicated to achieving compliance those responsible are regularly stumped, with seven in ten seeking advice from lawyers and external consultants. If award compliance is vexing for major companies, it's hard to imagine the bureaucratic nightmare it presents to Australia's more than two million small businesses.

The costs this adds to the bottom line is significant. According to a survey conducted by PwC, payroll costs large businesses $1,400 annually per employee and mid-sized businesses $2,000.Employers beset by payroll errors may be guilty of being suboptimal administrators. But if trained professionals and bespoke software is getting it wrong, the system itself is ripe for a rethink.

The term 'thieves' is more specious still in the case of allegedly underpaid managerial or professional employees. These cases involve full-time employees paid lump sum salaries which, on their face, seemed more generous than the equivalent hourly rate under the award. Yet because of the often long hours of work such roles demand, it's come to light that many of these employees would have earned more receiving the full suite of award loadings and penalty rates for their actual hours of work.

Woolworths is a case in point where 5700 store-level department managers are being back-paid the shortfall between their salary and the overtime, penalty rates and allowances mandated by the award. However, professional white-collar workplaces are also at risk. In 2019, defence manufacturer Thales began backpaying more than 400 engineers and middle managers earning an average salary of $120,000 per year – roughly 40 per cent more than the average full-time salary and over three times the minimum wage.

Professionals Australia Chief Executive Chris Walton, a union representing engineers, pharmacists and scientists, insists it is a 'myth' that professionals aren't underpaid and that 'all workers are being affected by this widespread epidemic of wage theft.

But the demands of professional life bear little resemblance to workers earning under $10 an hour. Lofty rhetoric about work life balance notwithstanding, long and unpredictable hours of work is an unavoidable part of professional life. The responsibilities of management and meeting client demands in a competitive market don't always neatly fit into a 9-5 working week.

It may be easy for some to believe that supermarket department managers deserve to earn more than a salary in the low $60,000s. Yet these salaries were agreed to by Woolworths' employees, presumably on the basis that they offered managerial experience, secure income and the prospect of advancement. The lack of penalty rates was not a sleight of hand. It was an explicit part of the deal.

For those who do sacrifice for the sake of professional advancement, the rewards of future opportunities, higher income and personal gratification are obvious. Indeed, if the gruelling competition to enter professions such as law, medicine and consulting is any indication, it's a trade-off that many are willing to make.

If you're still in doubt about how simply paying staff correctly could cause so many headaches, it's worthwhile opening an award and reading it for yourself. The Contractors Call Centres Award, for instance, is 76 pages long and consists of 31 individual clauses and eight schedules. The document looks and reads like a statute and has been varied at least ten times over the past five years.

To determine what minimum wage rate an employee must be paid, employers must select between twelve individual job classifications, each with their own comprehensive set of definitions, qualifications and indicative tasks. Applying these classifications to what employees actually do in the workplace can require drawing fine legalistic distinctions, and even guesswork.

Whereas a Clerical and Administration Officer Level 1 will 'work under direct supervision with regular checking of progress and apply knowledge and skills to a limited range of tasks' a Clerical and Administration Officer Level 2 will 'work under routine supervision with intermittent checking and apply knowledge and skills to a range of tasks.'

Such ambiguities notwithstanding, the cost of getting it wrong can be punishingly high. There are ample instances of businesses relying on guidance provided by the Fair Work Ombudsman, only to later be issued with a notice to back-pay employees on the grounds of an award misclassification.

That awards have become unworkably complex is not a partisan view. Fair Work Commission President and former ACTU Assistant Secretary Iain Ross has said small businesses 'overwhelmingly… want to meet their legal obligations' but that "super-complex" awards were the biggest obstacle to them doing so. Likewise, former Fair Work Ombudsman Natalie James has admitted that the regulator has struggled to enforce the law when awards are ambiguous on basic questions such as which pay rates should apply at different times of the day.

The *Fair Work Act* lists as one of its objects 'the need to ensure a simple, easy to understand, stable and sustainable modern award system for Australia'. By that test, it has dismally failed.

At the time of writing, the Government has committed to introducing criminal penalties for systematic and organised wage theft. This is a reasonable proposal. But without addressing the root issue of complexity, the problem is sure to continue.

Rather than incremental reform, the Government needs to join the rest of the world in recognising that awards are no longer fit for the purpose of regulating the minimum pay and conditions of the modern Australian workforce. Yet in pursuing that goal, the Coalition must learn the lessons of the Fair Work era. The Fair Work Commission's award modernisation process, in which unions, lawyers and employer associations joust with each other over the most marginal of changes, is a lesson in what the Government must strenuously avoid. An 'inquiry' or 'taskforce' manned by lawyers and regulators is guaranteed to be a hiding to nothing.

Ideally, the award system should be abolished altogether, leaving minimum wage entitlements, types of leave, and notices of termination to be provided by the ten National Employment Standards. But given the difficulties inherent in achieving a change of this scale in Australia's fractious polity, a two-stage simplification process could be more prudent.

Initially, the key entitlements in the existing awards could be consolidated in a set of no more than twelve industry awards. In the short-run, there may be a case for retaining certain entitlements, for instance additional loadings for shift-workers required to exceed their standard rostered hours. But the overarching goal should be the creation of a simple, straightforward safety net with as few prescriptions as possible on how individual employers manage their workforce. Arbitrary job classifications based on task, pay rates based on seniority and outdated allowances for items such as laundry or clothing should all be abolished.

Easing the compliance burden when it comes to minimum pay and conditions is sensible regulatory policy. But it's also in the interests of fairness. Employers who take reasonable steps to pay their staff correctly would be at far less risk of being dubbed a wage thief based on mere technicalities. And those who set out to underpay their staff shouldn't have the fallback of complexity to sheet home the blame.

6

HEALTH

Terry Barnes

Since Medicare was established in 1984, the Australian healthcare system has stayed largely unchanged, preserved in political aspic while everything around it has been transformed beyond recognition.

The reason is not its perfection. Rather, it is that in a political world, Australians have been conditioned to believe it is totally free and totally fair. Just as Britain's National Health Service has become the most sacred of political sacred cows, with the 2016 Leave campaign and Boris Johnson's 2019 leadership and general election campaigns dumping billions of pounds, no questions asked, into a slush bucket marked "Our NHS", in Australia the Whitlam-Hawke healthcare settlement, with Medicare at its heart, is all but sacrosanct.

Anyone who even dares whisper the words "healthcare reform" is deemed by self-interested defenders of the status quo and social media keyboard warriors to be a Harvey Weinstein or Jeffrey Epstein of public policy. To even suggest the slightest changes to

Medicare is akin to killing Bambi.

As Tony Abbott, his treasurer Joe Hockey and then health minister Peter Dutton found out the hard way in 2014, challenging the healthcare establishment is treacherous indeed. Reformers and innovators swim in a shark-infested ocean of powerful egos and cashed-up vested interests, all of whom believe ministers come and go, but they go on and on.

The panjandrums' power is underpinned by the political potency of health. Healthcare consistently rates as one of the very top issues in voter issues surveys. It is an issue the Australian Labor Party – in no small part due to Gough Whitlam's founding Medicare, and Bob Hawke's making it a stick with which to beat the Coalition – largely has made its own.

When the Coalition has been able to make inroads into Labor on health, it has not been because of policy innovation and imagination. It is by being more Labor than Labor. Tony Abbott could successfully boast "the Howard government is the best friend that Medicare ever had" because the Coalition out-Labored Labor in spending lavishly on Medicare, the Pharmaceutical Benefits Scheme, public hospitals and, especially, by pushing up bulk-billing rates with a range of bribes for general practitioners to bulk-bill as many patients as possible.

Good policy, no. Great electoral politics, yes.

But to achieve this in a traditionally Labor preserve, the Morrison government cannot afford to waste its energy, voter goodwill and political capital on attempting wholesale, across-the-board reform, however much many on the Right see a crying need for that. Instead, it should focus itself on targeted but substantial changes to health infrastructure and financing, and on changing complacent community attitudes to the real cost burden of having one of the best healthcare arrangements in the world.

In doing so, the Morrison government should play to the Coalition's strengths and values of smaller government, self-help, and personal responsibility, and reject a pale pink imitation of Labor in its use of taxpayer funds. But given healthcare is an imperfect market, that also means being unafraid to use its massive purchasing power as payer and subsidiser to leverage change that benefits patients and users well ahead of vested interests.

It certainly should not pretend that for Medicare, the Pharmaceutical Benefits Scheme (PBS) and public hospitals, there is a bottomless public money pit, tempting as it may be for health ministers to assert that the Coalition's prudent economic management gives government the means to spend lavishly on Medicare items and costly PBS listings for rare conditions benefiting a very few.

Good health policy should never be a pissing contest between adolescent boys to see who can go furthest. It is about quality, reliability, and affordability, the latter a virtue to be pursued unashamedly.

Framing health policy for a post-coronavirus Australia

When this chapter was first written nobody had heard of coronavirus, COVID-19 – Wuhan flu – or even Wuhan, where it all began.

While Australia and New Zealand have weathered the coronavirus storm better than most Western countries – not least due to our being, geographically, at what Paul Keating called "the arse end of the world" – enforced social isolation and economic shutdown measures taken by federal, state and territory governments have created public debt on a hitherto unimaginable scale, put hundreds of thousands out of their jobs while even more were stood down for the duration, and the healthcare system braced for demand shocks not experienced since the Spanish flu pandemic of 1919.

Others will argue whether what was done was appropriate or an overreaction, but we all must live with the economic and financial consequences of those profound early 2020 decisions. The reality is that, having jolted into recession, much of what we took for granted in 2019 no longer applies. Not least, the relationship between the state and the individual has changed, perhaps irrevocably, in favour of the supposedly benign, but authoritarian, state. The rush to safeguard as many jobs as possible has led to whole sectors of the private sector being bailed out or quasi-nationalised, including private hospitals which suddenly found themselves free of income dependency on private health insurance and elective surgery. The way many Australians look at their healthcare system, and the private healthcare choice, has been upended, and the public-private healthcare divide is now very blurred indeed.

But even if the economy and politics "snap back" to something like the *status quo ante*, the scale of the coronavirus response means the public money tap will at best slow to a trickle if not stop altogether. The rest of the Morrison government's term will not be one of grand scale healthcare investment: there simply won't be the money or political energy for it.

Therefore the plan outlined in this chapter, adjusted to reflect the impacts and lessons of the coronavirus pandemic, is necessarily fiscally modest but intended to make the most of our straitened circumstances, scarce resources, and changes in the political mindset that Bismarck would have called "the art of the possible".

A six-point plan to make Australian healthcare more Right

Our healthcare system has long been captured by the political, activist, and bureaucratic Left. They prattle on endlessly about the social determinants of health and more recently on how man-made climate change is a capitalist conspiracy against the poor.

A truly conservative government therefore should at least try and turn the health ship back towards the centre, something made much tougher by the Morrison government's "we're all socialists now" response to Wuhan flu. Post-pandemic, the Morrison government should start reverting to ideological normality, avoiding cash splashes, and then pursuing at least some systemic reform consistent with conservative principles of fiscal prudence, personal responsibility, and social duty.

But to help the coronavirused-out folks on Capital Hill, here is a mix of hard policy and cultural change, that could help make our healthcare services, policies, and programmes more responsible, more conservative-principled, and more genuinely fair:

- Change the mindset of the Australian public that too easily assumes medical services, pharmaceuticals and public hospital beds are free goods.

- Stop treating Medicare as middle-class welfare.

- Use the Commonwealth's powerful healthcare monopsonies to protect taxpayers against blatant rent-seeking vested interests, including by the States.

- Make the private health sector and private health insurance fitter for purpose; and

- Start a difficult public debate with Australians about the costs and benefits of providing healthcare, including when it does not improve the quality of a person's existence.

Changing the mindset

Both the 2014 GP co-payment debacle and the 2016 election's Mediscare showed how diabolical it is to pursue structural and efficiency reform in Australian healthcare.

Australians have all too readily bought the free universal healthcare myth, thanks to bulk-billed Medicare, prescription medicines costing them next to nothing and free public hospital admission and treatment as a patient. We as a nation now spend nearly $200 billion annually on medical, hospital and other health services, but who pays for it is somehow always someone else's problem.

The 2020 pandemic response was free care on steroids. The introduction and massive take-up of, particularly, telehealth consultations solely bulk-billed to Medicare was intended as an emergency measure but, long coveted by doctors and medical centre operators and popular with patients, that costly genie will be very hard to put back in the bottle. A similar critique applies to the broadening of Medicare-subsidised mental health services, on which mandatory bulk-billing also has been imposed.

But even in normal times, moral hazard rules the politics of health.

This is not helped by politicians of all colours talking incessantly about money. For governments, they are always claiming, "the healthcare system is wonderful because we're spending billions more here, billions more there".

Or, "When we came to office the health/hospitals/whatever budget was x billion, and now it's x billion plus 50 per cent".

And when critiquing the system's performance, the Opposition of the day (let alone power-without-responsibility Greens, One Nation and crossbenchers) promises "however much the government is spending, we'll spend that and a heck of a lot more".

Then come the vested interests – the doctors, hospital operators, pharmaceutical manufacturers and pharmacists and, indeed, State governments – that are complacent or do very well financially out of the status quo. In healthcare more than any other area of government activity, partly due to image and partly information asymmetry, the public attaches a ponderous weight to whatever these interests say, regardless of its intrinsic merit. It is why doctors and pharmacists are so frequently wheeled out in lab coats or scrubs before a camera: their White Coat of Truth means their every utterance is widely taken as gospel.

Moreover, the politics of healthcare reform are made more fraught by voters conditioned to the "Medicare settlement". Bob Hawke, Paul Keating and health ministers Neal Blewett and Brian Howe entrenched Medicare and the free and universal myth, and John Howard conceded in 1996 that the battle was lost and accepted that challenging Medicare was electoral poison.

Given the political obsession with the *quantity* of health spending, the Australian Institute of Health and Welfare expenditure data for the start and end of the decade 2007-08 to 2017-18 therefore gives a ready snapshot of the scale of what Australia as a community is willing to spend on its healthcare.

In 2007-08, Australia's health expenditure was $104 billion, representing 9.1 per cent of Gross Domestic Product (GDP)[12]. This included all federal, state, PHI, and other private health-related outlays. Of it, the Commonwealth's share of the healthcare cake was $45 billion, or four per cent of GDP.

A decade later, in 2017-18, total health expenditure had skyrocketed to $185 billion, representing 10 per cent of GDP[13]. Of it, the Commonwealth's share was $77.1 billion. Real growth of health-related spending through the decade was 22 per cent, so the real annual health spend was $46 billion more than it was a decade earlier.[14]

Whichever way one looks at it, healthcare in Australia is hugely expensive, not free.

---

12 Australian Institute of Health and Welfare, *Health Expenditure Australia 2007-08* (2009) Chapters 2 and 3.

13 Australian Institute of Health and Welfare, *Health Expenditure Australia 2017-18* (2019), Chapters 2 and 3.

14 Reserve Bank of Australia, Inflation Calculator website, https://www.rba.gov.au/calculator/financialYearDecimal.html

Until voters can be convinced reform does not mean the world will end tomorrow, the healthcare "system" will continue to bump along under increasing strain, as vested interests defend their lucrative patches. A Right-thinking government can at least set out the true facts about what all this costs us, and especially demolish the myth that our basic healthcare is free. That mindset change is a precondition of any substantial reform. Otherwise, as in 2014, political and vested interest opponents will sink any reform attempt at its moorings.

The well-off should not be bulk-billed

The bulk-billed better-off are bludging on those who are less affluent.

Medicare ensures Australians affordable access to world-class healthcare, regardless of means. Those on very low incomes and pensions, the elderly and those with costly chronic conditions, do need protection. They are the ones for whom bulk-billed "free" medical services were intended.

But for millions of us in good health and on equally healthy incomes who visit a GP a handful of times a year if that, Medicare should be about fair, not free, access. If a key underlying principle of Medicare is that everyone pays according to their means, surely those with adequate means can pay at least something at the point of use.

The bipartisan political obsession with bulk-billing rates has turned Medicare into a gigantic and electorally untouchable middle-class welfare scheme. It is misguided to say, smugly, "I pay my Medicare levy so bulk-bill me". That levy covers just two-fifths of the cost of Medicare and pharmaceutical benefits. Other taxes and government borrowings do the real heavy lifting.

There is no such thing as a free lunch, and there should be no such thing as a "free" visit to the doctor if you can afford to chip in. If you earn a good income, can afford a nice car, dine out, and take regular holidays in Bali, Europe or Port Douglas, then for a few times a year you can easily afford up to $45 a pop for a handful of standard GP consultations (the Australian Medical Association's recommended $83 fee less the Medicare rebate) – let alone the paltry $7 co-payment that so damaged the Abbott government in 2014.

In 2018-19 there were 158 million Medicare-billed GP services, a whopping 86 per cent of which were bulk-billed.[15] A 2015 report by the former National Health Performance Authority found one-third of us visit the GP just 1-3 times a year, and one half no more than five times.[16] The standard GP consultation Medicare rebate is $38.30.[17] If just 15 per cent of all GP services were not claimed by the reasonably well-off, low-use patients, then taxpayers would save almost $1 billion a year from these alone.

To protect the more vulnerable, why can't the trendy affluent who claim to care about those less well-off put their money where their mouths are, and willingly stump up to pay to see the doctor? If they will not, a Right-thinking government should make them do it.

Bulk-billed GP and specialist services should be only for pensioners and Health Care Card holders. For the rest of us, the first five GP visits in a calendar year should be charged at full price to the patient, with no Medicare rebate at all. For generally healthy people on even moderate incomes, surely an unrebated $90 or so will not bankrupt anyone. For additional services, a co-payment of at least

---

15 Department of Health, *Annual Medicare Statistics.*
16 And a further 15 per cent don't visit the GP at all in any given year: National Health Performance Authority, *Healthy Communities: Frequent GP attenders and their use of health services in 2012-13*, page 8-9.
17 As of December 2019.

$10 should be standard and a maximum co-payment could be capped by regulation as a condition for a GP billing Medicare.

To avoid gaming, public hospital emergency departments also should charge patients for GP-type services.[18]

As for specialists, relatively few bulk-bill now. The issue with them is ensuring their charging co-payments that are reasonable and affordable for the patient, and that they do not gouge. That is the only aspect in which government should take a regulatory interest in specialist billing.

Current emergency measures aside, both Labor and the Coalition waste billions of dollars bribing doctors to boost bulk-billing rates, treating their own polling numbers rather than improving the country's standard of primary healthcare. As John Howard's health minister, Tony Abbott himself introduced lavish loadings on Medicare rebates to encourage GPs to bulk-bill pensioners and families with young children. His successor Greg Hunt boasts of an 86 per cent GP bulk-billing rate as a good thing.

Politically it may be. Economically it isn't.

Using the Commonwealth's healthcare monopsonies to taxpayers' advantage

As Theodore Roosevelt supposedly said, "If you have them by the balls, their hearts and minds will follow".

When it comes to government health spending, the Commonwealth government potentially has a firm grip on Australia's health cojones, particularly in relation to:

- Medicare ($26 billion in 2020-21).
- The Pharmaceutical Benefits Scheme (PBS) ($10 billion in 2020-21); and the big one:

---

18 Triage categories 4 and 5.

- Public hospital funding ($130 billion for the 2020-25 National Health Agreement)[19]; and

- Private health insurance rebates ($6.5 billion projected in 2020-21).

One would think that with this sort of leverage at its disposal the Commonwealth would be challenging any vested interest standing in the way of good policy.

In fact, it is the other way around. The Commonwealth's chain is yanked shamelessly by an array of interests, each of which treats taxpayer-supported healthcare funding pools as "their" money. While in economic terms monopsonies, like monopolies, are perversions of free markets, in political terms they confer real power on their holders – if they choose to use them and not let powerful rent-seekers treat them as a doormat.

For each of the following three areas, the Morrison government could flex its monopsony muscles and stand up for the taxpayers instead of for the price-takers and rent-seekers.

Medicare

The national president of the Australian Medical Association is *de facto* federal health minister. Both sides of politics defer to the AMA far too much: as a result, the AMA determines the pace of change in the healthcare system, and always in a way that protects its members' interests.

The Medicare provider number is the goose that lays the golden egg for Australia's GPs and specialists. Whether or not they bulk-bill, Medicare income is the vital base of their practice income, and on top of Medicare benefits doctors are subsidised in wider ways, not least by highly-costly specialty training.

---

19 Figures taken from Department of Health, *Portfolio Budget Statements 2019-20.*

Government should use its provider number and training place leverage to keep patient costs down and generally to give back more to the community, such as return-of-service obligations in return for training subsidies and a provider number. The "civil conscription" constriction of the Constitution[20] should be the only impediment to decisive action, but it is high time the constitutional boundaries around civil conscription were tested again.

Government should also crack down on business models that exploit public subsidy and are inimical to good public policy. These include corporatised, high-throughput medical centres and unlimited access to Medicare-subsidised In-Vitro Fertilisation (IVF) regardless of a patient's age and likelihood of success. Controversial "woke" treatments, such as gender reassignment surgery or IVF for same-sex couples, also should not be automatic under Medicare: a flexing of the government's monopsony would send a message to both socially conservative quiet Australians as well as to noisy activists.

The PBS

PBS dispensing and distribution fees are governed by five-year Australian Community Pharmacy Agreements between the Commonwealth government and the Pharmacy Guild of Australia, the trade organisation of pharmacy owners. These are closed negotiations excluding all other affected parties.[21] Besides fixing generous pharmacist remuneration, the Agreements preserve blatantly anti-competitive practices, especially pharmacist-only

---

20 Australian Constitution, section 51(xxiiiA): The Parliament shall have power... to make laws for the provision of maternity allowances, widows' pensions, child endowment, unemployment, pharmaceutical, sickness and hospital benefits, medical and dental services (but not so as to authorize any form of civil conscription).

21 Although the Pharmaceutical Society of Australia, the pharmacists' professional body, has been included for the 2020-25 Community Pharmacy Agreement negotiations. The relationship between the Guild and the Society could be, however, likened to that between a great white shark and a remora fish.

ownership of pharmacies and pharmacy location rules that protect the inefficient and incompetent pharmacy businesses from direct competition.

If it wants to leave a powerful policy legacy, the Morrison government should repudiate this pharmacy cartel, tear up the Community Pharmacy Agreements and deregulate dispensing fees altogether. It should also throw its market power behind opening up retail pharmacy to genuine price and service competition by joining with the states to abolish pharmacist-only ownership of pharmacies: as long as professional services are under professional supervision, it doesn't matter a tinker's cuss who actually owns a pharmacy business.

Or, rather, it shouldn't.

Public hospital funding

Heads of Agreement for the 2020-25 National Hospital Agreement was signed by the Commonwealth, State and Territories unnecessarily early in 2018[22]. But given that federal money comprises almost half of public hospital recurrent funding, and the 2019 election is won, why can't the Morrison government reopen negotiations to drive a better bargain, and demand States make their hospitals more operationally efficient?

In the coronavirus emergency, the Morrison government increased its share of public hospital recurrent funding to 50:50 to help states cope. Good luck with winding that back, Prime Minister, but why not try?

For starters, the agreed National Funding Cap "limits" Commonwealth funding growth to 6.5 per cent per year. The

---

22 https://www.publichospitalfunding.gov.au/public-hospital-funding/about-agreement

States say that is not enough to cover health cost inflation; the man in the street would say that's blatant featherbedding.

Why could not the growth factor be tied to the Consumer Price Index, or the average annual increase permitted for private health insurance premiums? Why should the States not be expected to find efficiencies just like their private sector counterparts? And why should the States pocket revenue from private patients in public hospitals funded by Commonwealth-subsidised private health insurance, or cost-shift their responsibilities to Medicare? And if the States want still more to fund their money-hungry hospital services, why can't they raise their own taxes and be politically accountable for it?

In an ideal federation, states would run public hospitals and raise their own money to do it, or contest services entirely paid for by a single national funder. In post-coronavirus Australia, however, that is beyond the art of the politically possible. In dealing with lazy mendicant States, however, surely in these straitened times the Commonwealth at least using its health monopsony to contain public hospital cost growth would be a step in the Right direction?

Concentrating on real private health reform

The private health sector – not just private health insurance but private hospitals, doctors and the wider array of other health professionals whose services PHI pays for – is an indispensable feature of the Australian healthcare landscape. In health politics, it is the Coalition's home turf.

Numbers speak for themselves:

- Australians with hospital cover have bounced around the 45 per cent mark since 2000.

- Around two of every three elective surgical procedures are done in a private hospital.

- PHI premium subsidies (the PHI rebates) contribute $7 billion a year to meeting the costs of privately-insured healthcare services.

- 37 health insurers in a thriving, profitable PHI market.

But there are darker numbers too:

- PHI premiums consistently rise significantly ahead of CPI in a low-inflation economic climate, and currently health cost inflation (the cost of healthcare goods and services) is more than double CPI.

- The PHI-insured population is ageing as "younger and healthier" people aged between 20 and 34 drop out – 48,000 in the December 2019 quarter alone.[23]

- Consumer complaints about their cover, their premiums, and especially their unexpected out-of-pocket costs continue to increase.

Then there are the still-emerging side effects of the 2020 pandemic. Health insurers may have gained a huge temporary windfall in the mass cancellation of non-urgent elective procedures, allowing them to defer or cancel scheduled 2020 premium increases. But beyond this crisis, the resumption of normal business will cause a hugely expensive spike of demand in 2020-21, limited only by the availability of doctors and hospitals to process it.

The biggest consequence of 2020's upheaval, however, is attitudinal. Suddenly millions of Australian households have lost income permanently or temporarily. Equally suddenly, PHI looks like something best foregone in favour of mortgages, school fees, and utility and food bills – especially if they are paying to cover services that have become unavailable or greatly reduced for the indefinite future.

---

23   Australian Prudential Regulation Authority regular reporting data.

To keep PHI both relevant and affordable post-Wuhan virus, more substantial reform is needed. Insurers and providers hoping to ride the crisis out with suddenly boosted reserves, and kick the reform can further down the road, are foolish.

The PHI industry doesn't set its own agenda

An industry letting others define it will not survive. For too long, private health insurance has been just such an industry, far more reactive and defensive than on the front foot, and it risks paying the price existentially.

Debate on PHI reform currently is being led by one with no great love for it, the Grattan Institute's Stephen Duckett. He claims a PHI membership "death spiral", with the younger and healthier voting with their feet.[24] Duckett has been joined by the industry regulator, the Australian Prudential Regulation Authority (APRA), which says industry should stop blaming others and get its own house in order.

In truth, the decline in membership is real but greatly exaggerated. Hospital cover participation rates have hovered in the mid-40s since then health minister Michael Wooldridge legislated "the trinity": the 30 per cent PHI rebate; Lifetime Health Cover with premium penalties for late joiners aged over 30; and the Medicare Levy Surcharge on people on reasonable incomes who don't take PHI.

But the post-coronavirus world will not be PHI-friendly. Many younger and healthier likely will drop PHI cover. Meanwhile,

---

24 Duckett et al: *The history and purposes of private health insurance* (July 2019); Saving private health insurance 1: reining in hospital costs and specialist bills (November 2019); Saving private health insurance 2: making private health insurance viable (December 2019), all published by the Grattan Institute. In conversation with the author, Duckett said his papers were planned and written anticipating an incoming government determined to "do something" about private health insurance consistent with Labor ideology.

the "older and sicker" will stick to their PHI like glue: the likely problem is that, with community rated PHI[25], there will be fewer lower-risk members to cross-subsidise the higher-risk, meaning premiums will spiral just to cover the costs of treatment for those higher risks. This was the vicious circle that existed in the 1990s prior to the Wooldridge trinity; good risks drop out – premiums rise – more good risks drop out, and so on down and down.

Furthermore, in carrying a massive post-coronavirus deficit Morrison and future federal governments will not have deep subsidy pockets. Any future reform therefore must be cost neutral, and ideally offering savings as far as taxpayers are concerned. It is up to the PHI industry to propose policy solutions to the government as regulator, not simply complain.

In 2018 health minister Greg Hunt implemented useful but modest PHI cover reforms, particularly around tiered policies; updating the pricing regime for medical devices (protheses) paid for by PHI; extending cover of Hospital in the Home and mental health services; and making token efforts to confront the medical out-of-pocket problem. These measures improve the PHI value proposition *vis a vis* the public alternative but were band-aids to get the Coalition honourably through a supposedly unwinnable election: they are nowhere near as extensive as what the whole private health sector needs.

Recently I reopened an archive box from my time as senior adviser to then health minister Tony Abbott. It included briefing papers on PHI reform, cabinet submissions and policy proposals from the industry association now known as Private Healthcare Australia.

Some of these proposals were adopted, but many were set aside by

---

25 Community rating: the underlying concept of Australian PHI that says everyone pays the same premium for a given policy regardless of age and degree of health risk. Effectively, the young and healthy cross-subside the older and sicker in the insurance risk pool.

the Howard government as too difficult, expensive, or politically contentious. These included boosting PHI rebates, giving substantial Fringe Benefit Tax (FBT) concessions to employers paying health insurance premiums, cracking down on prostheses costs and making the PHI product more consumer-friendly by tackling medical bill shocks.

What has the main industry association been urging the Morrison government to consider since its re-election? Boosting PHI rebates, giving substantial FBT concessions to employers paying health insurance premiums, cracking down on prostheses costs and making the PHI product more consumer-friendly by tackling bill shocks. It is as if Private Healthcare Australia's research department is a rusty filing cabinet containing a broken record.

To be fair, this intellectual bankruptcy is endemic right across much – but not all – of the private health sector. The prevailing mentality is "Just fork out another couple of billion, Minister, and we'll continue to bump along". It will be no surprise if that remains the industry's mantra post-coronavirus.

But that is not enough. A realistic and affordable further reform plan is required. Any realistic Right-thinking post-coronavirus PHI reform agenda must target five things:

- Wind back universal community rating of health insurance risks and premiums.
- Deregulate the PHI coverage and make managed care lawful.
- Remove contracting obstacles that overly protect providers.
- Spike the guns of medical and other providers who fleece patients in need by egregious fee-gouging; and
- Build a reform coalition across the private health sector, where payers and providers work with each other in common cause, not set them at each other's throats.

Community rating

Duckett and others may overegg the PHI "death spiral" claim, but their point that PHI is no longer as attractive to the healthy, low-claiming under-40 cohort is valid.

The sacred cow of community rating, whereby all policyholders pay the same premium, can only work effectively if the pool of no- and low-claimers is deep enough to cross-subsidise the older and sicker. If too many younger and healthier walk, the claims of the older and sicker drive community-rated premiums up still higher for those remaining.

Universal community rating itself is a relic of a bygone demographic age when few lived many years after their working lives ended. It cannot remain so: at least partially risk-rating PHI should be on the agenda. Duckett proposes much lower but risk-rated and unrebated premiums for under 55s to keep them, while redirecting resultant rebate savings to the older and sicker.

The Duckett dividing line is flawed – not all frail and chronically ill people are over 55, and cancers and other intensive-treatment illnesses can strike at any age – but his premise is correct: community rating is too rigid and absolute, a relic of a time when life expectancy was much shorter. It, coupled with sclerotic risk equalisation rules forcing insurers with good risk profiles to cross-subsidise those with bad ones, kills PHI competition based on price and the quality of offering to consumers.

This could start small, by offering significantly lower premiums for people who do not smoke, drink moderately and actively keep themselves fit. This would not be constrained by excessive regulation from underwriting services supporting positive behaviour. Treating injuries from high-risk activities and from self-inflicted stupidity, such as fractures after a drinking binge, could also be denied PHI cover, just as there are uninsurable acts in general insurance.

Alternatively, instead of Lifetime Health Cover driving good risks into community rating, premiums could be actuarially aged-stepped over a lifetime, rather than Duckett's arbitrary age 55 cut-off. A 20-30-year-old could pay, say, 30 per cent of full premium for a hospital policy; 30-45 50 per cent; 50-65 75 per cent; and over 65 100 per cent. This might drive down insurers' returns from any given PHI product, but if it retains current low claimers and brings in many more, it could do the job without sending full premiums through the roof.

But if community rating must continue untouched its perverse subsidies, bonus premium rebates for over 65s, costing taxpayers$1 billion or more[26], should be removed and the savings redistributed to incentivising the under 30 to take up PHIs. These counterintuitive (in terms of subsidising high-risk older and sicker users) bonus rebates were designed as Coalition election carrot for older voters in the 2004 election, despite their being bad policy.[27] If those additionally subsidised youngsters take up PHI, and stick to it with the right premium incentives, the whole private health sector ultimately benefits.

Deregulate what PHI covers

Private health insurance is regulated to within an inch of its life, not least in dictating what it can and cannot cover.

Hospital cover still essentially means just that. A specialist can be covered for seeing a patient in hospital, but not for consultations in his rooms. Despite cover reforms at the end of the Howard government, health management programmes and interventions

---

26 The precise cost of the elderly rebate bonuses is buried in the aggregate expenditure on PHI rebates.

27 First modelled, as it happens, literally on the back of the envelope by the author.

are still a grey area. GPs and PHI still largely have a mutually exclusive relationship. And extras cover, often the main attraction to the young and healthy, is constrained by regulation as to what it can offer: gym membership assistance yes; gym shoes no.

What insurers offer in the coverage essentially should be left to insurers. Provided the purpose of the coverage is to maintain and improve the health and well-being of the member, what an insurer covers is best left as a matter between insurer and consumer. With hospital and medical cover especially, the patient's whole clinical journey should be insurable, from the first referral to a treating specialist to post-acute stepdown, rehabilitation and recovery.

And if a patient is bewildered by the "system", and uncertain about their treatment options and who is best to look after them, insurers should have the legal freedom to guide or even be delegated those choices by the patient, effectively becoming their agent and care manager in dealing with providers.

Critics would call this "US-style managed care"; realists would call it long overdue common sense that would improve the patient's buying power, overcoming the information asymmetry between doctor and patient, and serving as a brake on provider overpricing and over-servicing, not least for costly and debilitating treatments, like spinal fusions, that clinical evidence indicates has little or no greater efficacy than alternative non-invasive treatments.

Remove contracting obstacles to beat down provider costs

Because of the politics of private health, governments shy away from muscling up to providers. Ever since the mid-1990s, when the Keating government first legislated for purchaser-provider contracts, provider interests have ensured heavy checks and (im) balances tip negotiations in their favour, ensuring PHI-derived revenue remains their source of viability and profitability while giving as little as possible in return.

It is high time that these checks on market efficiency were removed, giving payers a freer hand to negotiate with private hospital and other providers. Above all, insurers should be free to *not* contract with a greedy or uncooperative provider: that means abolishing the "second tier default benefit" insurers must pay to non-contracted hospitals which is 85 per cent of the average benefit for a given service in comparable hospitals in a State[28]. Besides guaranteeing revenue for hospital operators, and allowing them to resist insurer pressure to concede better prices or commit to greater efficiency in contract negotiations, second-tier defaults incentivise any Tom, Dick or Harry entrepreneur to promote marginal hospital and day-procedure centre ventures with a promise revenue will flow to them regardless of any other factor. This is a rort whose abolition is well overdue.

Something similar applies as regards prostheses and medical devices. The Turnbull government took some steps to reform the rigidly regulated prostheses market, but more can be done to eliminate profiteering by suppliers and wholesalers. Insurers being able to take a managed care advocacy role on behalf of their members, including questioning whether doctors' choices of prostheses are the most clinically or cost-efficient, would go a long way in this respect.

If it is a question of market power, there is no reason insurers and providers should be treated differently than any other sector. If there are abuses of market power in contracting and purchasing, the Competition and Consumer Act, the Australian Consumer and Competition Commission and APRA as industry regulator can deal with them.

---

28 Department of Health, *Second-tier default benefits*, fact sheet, March 2020: https://www1.health.gov.au/internet/main/publishing.nsf/Content/private-second-tier

Lasso greedy provider cowboys

Another much-needed area of decisive private health reform is tackling callous and greedy price-taking by medical specialists and other providers who refuse to accept generous PHI benefits and who charge whatever they like.

Patient out-of-pockets, or co-payments, of a few or even of a few hundred dollars for surgical procedures, are acceptable if they are reasonable and known in advance. But excesses of thousands and even tens of thousands are beyond the pale. Relatively few specialists indulge in such outrageous behaviour, but the Lamborghini-driving avarice of the few that do besmirches their profession and trashes the private health choice. By contrast, free public patient care may involve inferior standards of care, foregone personal choice, and long waits for elective treatment, but at least you are not sued for big bills no-one warned you about.

A Coalition government should use its powerful healthcare monopsonies to protect patients and taxpayers from medical buccaneers, sharks and scoundrels infesting the waters of private health. Government gives these cowboys the right to print money, as it – we, the taxpayers – finances not only Medicare and PHI subsidies, but their specialist training, their professional privileges and even their medical indemnity insurance.

If these gouging shysters will not exercise some personal responsibility of their own, then possible remedies include:

- Suspending or cancelling the offending specialist's Medicare provider number, if his Medicare billing record consistently shows he or she charges patient out-of-pockets outside a reasonable range – say, more than 1.5 times the Medicare rebate plus available PHI benefit for a given item;

- Allowing a surgeon, obstetrician or lead doctor to quote an all-up cost for a procedure binding all their team (who usually are recommended by them): assistants, anaesthetists and so on, effectively making them the patient's project manager responsible for the total delivery of service.

- Suspending any taxpayer subsidy of medical indemnity insurance for serial offenders.

- Making the public funding of a doctor's specialist training conditional on his signing an enforceable covenant to charge reasonably when qualified, and repaying some or all their training subsidy if his billing practices breach that covenant; and

- Legislating to ensure patient debts for bills more than the range suggested above are legally unenforceable.

Tough. But Right.

Build a reform coalition of the willing

Lastly, government should get the private health sector off its well-dined posterior and demand it gets its innovation act together.

Instead of rent-seeking, industry leaders should be innovative, not reactionary and self-serving. Instead of whingeing to government and blaming providers for their problems, Private Healthcare Australia especially can live up to its whole-of-sector name and build a whole-of-sector coalition of reform consensus in which the wider health insurance industry, doctors, other health professionals, hospitals and prostheses manufacturers advocate a common reform agenda to government and the Australian public.

Surely government would welcome this. Politicians like the Prime Minister and Greg Hunt know collective goodwill and cooperation, not confrontation, is needed to adopt workable and politically sellable solutions to the most acute problems private health faces. The one criterion government should impose is that sector-driven innovation involves not *one* more cent of public subsidy. Besides this being consistent with Coalition principles, the post-coronavirus national budget cannot afford more subsidy billions, especially when subsidy rewards inefficiency and price-taking.

Since the 2019 election, Labor says it wants wholesale PHI reform. Instead of dismissing this as political posturing, Health minister Hunt should treat it as a mandate to go much further than he already has. But an industry regulation and mendicant mindset apparently stuck in 2005 indicates that the necessary coalition-building might be too big a ask for the whole private health sector.

Confronting tough social questions

The full social and economic scale of the coronavirus crisis, the economic shutdown, mandatory lockdowns, and social distancing, was motivated by society's collective obligation to protect the most vulnerable from infection and death – especially the elderly with multiple co-morbidities. We effectively put an exceedingly high price on already long-lived lives of which, as a share of total Australian population, there are a great many more than even half a century ago.

- In 1962, the year I was born, Australia had 10.7 million people. Male life expectancy at birth was 68 years and female 74 years.

- In 1984, the year Medicare commenced, the Australian population was 15.5 million. Male life expectancy at birth was 72 years and female 79 years.

- In 2000, at the turn of the century, the Australian

population was 19.2 million. Male life expectancy at birth was 77 years and female 82 years.

- In 2017, the Australian population was 24.6 million. Male life expectancy at birth was 80 years and female 85 years.[29]

While our healthcare infrastructure and funding arrangements largely have stayed static for decades, these data highlight that demographics, in terms of population size and life expectancy , have been transformed. Back in the 1960s, a centenarian was as rare as hens' teeth. Even twenty years ago, the Queen didn't have many 100th birthday telegrams to send. But now centenarians are commonplace, and in a decade's time they will be ho-hum.

The population is ageing at an even greater rate than it is growing. In 2013, the Productivity Commission (PC) projected:

> The population aged 75 or more years is expected to rise by 4 million from 2012 to 2060, increasing from about 6.4 to 14.4 per cent of the population. In 2012, there was roughly one person aged 100 years old or more to every 100 babies. By 2060, it is projected there will be around 25 such centenarians.[30]

In that same report, the PC projected that Australia's death rates would continue to fall strongly into this century. Its data showed that from the 1920s to the 2010s, the chance of an 80-year-old dying in the next year fell from nearly 15 per cent to just five per cent.[31]

Thanks to the wonders of medical science and research, enviable

---

29 Population figures: Australian Bureau of Statistics. Life expectancy figures: World Bank tables https://data.worldbank.org/indicator/SP.DYN.LE00.FE.IN?locations=AU

30 Productivity Commission, *An Ageing Australia: Preparing for the Future*, November 2013, page 2.

31 *Ibid*, page 5.

healthcare services and facilities, and *mostly* sensible public health practices, Australia excels at keeping older people alive for longer. For younger people with what previously were early fatality diseases, like cystic fibrosis, medical and pharmaceutical breakthroughs are prolonging life, but at great financial cost. Similarly, cancer survival rates have increased steadily even as cancer prevalence has done likewise.

One might presume from data such as these that Australians not only are living longer and dying less, but are universally "enjoying" (as the statisticians like to describe it) those added years, a happy, healthy long twilight to lives already well-lived.

Wrong.

Certainly, despite the 2020 pandemic, many "old old" and chronically ill Australians keep in tolerably good health, retaining their physical movement and their mental faculties, and thereby are able to enjoy a good quality of life for their age or condition.

But a great many more are being kept alive merely because we can. And when it comes to Alzheimer's Disease and dementia, too often the body survives as an empty husk while the person's mind checked out ages ago. Yet we keep these people going.

Those people merely exist, miserably. They have little or no quality of life now. Yet they are counted as success stories simply because they somehow drag themselves through another miserable day, racked by pain, too often abandoned or neglected by family, their friends already gone, and nothing to look forward to barring Death itself.

Doctors, committed by the Hippocratic oath to save and preserve life, feel driven to do whatever they can for those patients. The more egotistical of them chalk up their patient's survival as a testament to their own skill and genius, regardless of the patient's quality of life. Families, reluctant to lose a loved one, too often insist on continuing treatment when all it does is prolong existence, not meaningful life. They know taxpayer-funded health, aged care and other services are there to carry most of the cost, and moral hazard therefore applies to their choices.

Public policy in a range of healthcare areas, including electronic health records and organ donation, now favours people opting out rather than in. As part of the social contract between the individual and the state as payer, perhaps that should apply to complex primary and acute care for the very old. Could, for instance, an Advanced Care or Do Not Resuscitate directive be presumed to apply to people above, say the age of 85, unless they or their authorised representative expressly declare otherwise?

For many such an approach is unpalatable, but the 2020 pandemic – especially in Europe and the United States, but certainly anticipated by Australian governments too –highlighted that tough utilitarian choices must sometimes be made in prioritising people for intensive care and other life-saving treatment where available resources are insufficient for all. Nevertheless, this searing recent experience highlights there are many difficult moral and social questions here that need a sensible public airing.

Should medical science save or prolong some people's lives at the cost of their ability to have a meaningful life? Is it right to spend billions on hugely expensive treatments and drugs benefiting handfuls of patients with rare conditions? Is there a widespread public benefit in such spending or does it simply allow governments the satisfaction of boasting about the cost to prove they care? Should we put more effort into research that might find a cure for a blight like dementia? Is it ethical to declare that when a person reaches a certain age, we can lawfully scale down the publicly-funded medical services because they have already had a good innings?

Similarly, for costly medicines for conditions suffered by only a handful of people, should they expect taxpayers to pay the full costs of those medicines through the PBS? Should there be a minimum number of people who can benefit before a drug is listed in the PBS?

In short, is 21st century man tampering too much with the course of nature?

As a society, Australians need to discuss the downside of our ageing population and our ability to treat the previously untreatable. A compassionate but rational Right-thinking government whose ethical DNA values human life should lead it. As this century continues, there will be yet more medical breakthroughs, and yet more costly ways to keep more people alive but just ticking over. Certainly, a great many people will not only survive but thrive, but many more will be left in living limbo, miserably waiting for God.

Knowing this challenge is going to become even more pressing in coming decades, as people live to great ages in great numbers and medical science marches on, now is the time to get a national consensus on what's right and how best to fund it. Socially and economically, we cannot afford – and the people directly affected cannot afford – to sweep this challenge under an ethical carpet.

Conclusion

With the Coalition gifted an unexpected third term by Bill Shorten, the Morrison government cannot take a fourth for granted. While it strives for re-election in 2021-22, it should also be thinking of the policy legacy it will leave whenever its number is up.

As of now, however, the government has a post-coronavirus golden opportunity to be more reformist in its health policy, drawing on truly Right-leaning values of prudence, personal responsibility, and social duty. If it is sensible but bold it can entrench a legacy difficult for a future left-wing government to undo.

Doing this nevertheless will take political courage and capital, and a willingness to eschew the lazy big-money announcements that even Coalition Health ministers love- to make as a vote-winning substitute for hard reform, regardless of the fiscal havoc wreaked by COVID-19. The Coalition therefore must stop out-Laboring Labor, make our fragile healthcare system much more fit for purpose, and end the prodigality of incumbency that wastes taxpayer's money.

It's time to take a truly Right-leaning approach to health policy, financing, and administration.

7

CONSTITUTIONAL RECOGNITION

Morgan Begg

Among the litany of major public policy issues to enter public debate over the last 12 years, few have united the corporate, legal, political and media elite quite like the question of "constitutional recognition".

Constitutional recognition refers to the process of enshrining some form of substantive change in our legal and constitutional institutions to "recognise" the history of indigenous Australian's occupation on the Australian continent prior to the arrival of European colonists in the 18th century. It is an agenda that is based on the corrosive ideology of identity politics which is in contrast both to Australia's legal traditions and to its history of constitutional change.

A key legal development in Australia in the twentieth century, in common with other western nations such as the United States and the United Kingdom, was an acceptance of the principle that the historical use of the law to divide people on the basis of their race was inconsistent with more established legal traditions such as the principle of equality before the law. By this point, it was no longer tenable that the legal status of an Australian should be determined by their skin colour or racial background. Accordingly, many of the legal barriers between indigenous and non-indigenous Australians began to be repealed, leading to the momentous referendum held on 27 May 1967. The question put to Australians voters at that referendum proposed to omit specific references to indigenous Australians in the Australian Constitution and was overwhelmingly approved by voters on the basis that this was an advancement of racial equality. While the reality of this is more complex – the expansion of the commonwealth's objectionable race power and centralisation of power to Canberra have caused problems in their own right – the removal of words purporting to treat Australians differently in the Constitution on the basis of their race meant the document treated Australians of all backgrounds more equally than before.

However, this clear principle is being undermined by a concerted campaign to divide Australians further in our nation's founding document through the constitutional 'recognition' of Aboriginal and Torres Strait Islanders.

Recognition has not always meant the same thing. Back in 2007, both Liberal party and Labor party leaders, Prime Minister John Howard and Opposition Leader Kevin Rudd respectively, made identical commitments ahead of that year's federal election to achieve constitutional recognition by holding a referendum to insert a declarative preamble into the Australian Constitution. While even a symbolic preamble would have led to expectations for other political change and exposed the Constitution to the predations of activist decisions at the High Court, this has nonetheless been viewed as a minimalist proposal. Perhaps reflecting the belief that this did not go far enough, the demands for constitutional recognition have radically transformed in a relatively brief period of time.

Currently, advocates for "recognition" are calling for the Commonwealth government to hold a referendum to implement the recommendations of the constitutional convention held in Uluru in May 2017, also known as the Uluru Statement from the Heart. The Uluru Statement recommended the establishment of a "First Nations Voice" (the Voice) enshrined in the Australian Constitution to be a special advisory body to parliament on issues relevant to indigenous Australians. It also recommended the establishment of a "Makaratta Commission" to supervise a process of "agreement-making" and "truth-telling" between Australian governments and indigenous Australians.

There is considerable uncertainty about how a Voice may work. For instance, just the issue of the Voice's composition raised the question of whether its office holders will be elected, or experts and elders appointed by the government, or a composition of both. Although the finer details of what the Voice would look like and how it would operate have not yet been determined, it has already generated significant support from the nation's political, economic and media elite. During the time of National Reconciliation Week in May to June 2019, a major push for the Voice took place, with no fewer than 21 law firms, 21 investment banks, superannuation funds and accounting firms, and a group of 14 major organisations from the Elevate Reconciliation Action Plan, and Australia's premier business group, the Business Council of Australia, each issuing a statement in support of the Voice. Each statement promised unwavering support for constitutional change to enshrine the Voice, saying "thank you" for the invitation to "walk with" or "work with" recognition advocates, and asserting that the Uluru Statement was a significant or important historical development.

At the same time, the *Sydney Morning Herald* launched a campaign to lobby the parliament to implement the Uluru Statement and to promise to hold a referendum accordingly. The 27 May 2019 edition of the newspaper included unambiguously favorable news, editorial, and opinion coverage of the Voice. Likewise, the national broadcaster has adopted a pro-Voice editorial position, almost without question and to the exclusion of alternative views. For example, the ABC's flagship current affairs program, *Q&A*, on August 18 2019 held an episode solely about proposals for indigenous recognition. Of the six panelists on the program (including host Tony Jones) only Jacinta Nampijinpa Price, the Director of the Indigenous Program at the Centre for Independent Studies, was opposed to the Voice.

Australian governments at a state and federal level have also demonstrated a commitment to some form of referendum on indigenous recognition. It is estimated that federal government funding for the recognition campaign has amounted to $25.73 million since the campaign to raise awareness officially began in 2012 to the period ending in October 2017.[32] This money was provided to Reconciliation Australia to make the case for Constitutional recognition. In the 2016/17 financial year alone, over $11 million dollars were granted to Reconciliation Australia and equivalent state bodies that focus on campaigning for constitutional change. [33] Several government bodies and government-funded bodies also signed on as Reconciliation Australia supporters, including the ABC, the Australian Council of Social Services, the Federation of Ethnic Communities Council of Australia, and the National Aboriginal Community Controlled Health Program.

Despite the absence of details about how the Voice would operate, the public has been given sufficient information to make some determinations about the practical problems of the

32 Stephen Fitzpatrick, 'Indigenous recognition campaign risked guideline breach', *The Australian*, 10 October 2017.
33 Figures for the 2016/17 financial year are from a forthcoming publication of the Institute of Public Affairs authored by Morgan Begg and Daniel Wild.

Voice. Constitutional law professor Anne Twomey prepared a draft constitutional amendment in 2015 to provide guidance on how a constitutionally-enshrined Voice might work. The first part of Professor Twomey's proposed amendment states that an Aboriginal and Torres Strait Islander body 'shall have the function of providing advice to the Parliament and the Executive Government on matters relating to Aboriginal and Torres Strait Islander peoples.'[34] Similarly, former Chief Justice of Australia Murray Gleeson argued in a speech delivered in Sydney in July 2019 that 'it is difficult to see any objection in principle to the creation of a body to advise Parliament about proposed laws relating to indigenous affairs.'[35]

An obvious problem that Twomey or Gleeson have failed to envisage is the issue of mission creep. The assertion that the Voice would be confined to matters which solely affect indigenous Australians could not be upheld in practice. Since all major policy issues apply to and affect all Australians, indigenous and non-indigenous alike, there are in practice likely to be very few policy areas where the Voice is solely confined to matters affecting indigenous Australians and indigenous Australians only. Inevitably, the Voice would give "advice" on all policy areas.

This is particularly a problem if the Voice is to have a forceful influence on public debate. While the Voice would not be granted a formal veto power, the power of the body would be to shame Australian parliaments into agreeing with its advice, or risk "going against" the official Voice of indigenous Australians. It would be almost impossible for a majority non-indigenous parliament to defy the advice of an indigenous-only body. While an attempt

---

34 Anne Twomey, 'An indigenous advisory body: Addressing the concerns about justiciability and parliamentary sovereignty' (2105) 8(19) *Indigenous Law Bulletin* 6, 6-7.

35 Murray Gleeson, 'Recognition in keeping with the Constitution: A worthwhile project' (Speech to Uphold and Recognise, 18 July 2019) 12.

to maintain parliamentary supremacy could be written in, the allegation of "racism" would in many, if not most, conceivable situations nullify any such protection.

Concern about the consequences of this model has led to it being labelled a "third chamber" of parliament. It is true that the Voice is unlikely to become a third chamber *de jure*—although even this is not clear until a detailed proposal for how the Voice would work in practice is provided. Australia's peak representative body for the legal profession, the Law Council of Australia, said in October that the Voice would share some characteristics of a parliamentary chamber:

> The whole point of the Voice to parliament is to ensure that our First Nations peoples have an opportunity to propose bills, be consulted on bills, and to express their views on bills before they are enacted as laws of the Commonwealth which may impact upon First Nations peoples. This includes bills about fundamental issues which matter on the ground to First Nations peoples, such as health, welfare and education.[36]

Even Gleeson was only able to say it was "unlikely" that parliament would "propose a change in the Constitution in aid of indigenous recognition if the effect of the change will be to curtail its own legislative power."[37] Professor Twomey has argued that the Voice is not a radical concept as it would join numerous other bodies "whose job it is to ensure that the parliament is better informed about particular subject matters", similar to the Productivity Commission, the Australian Law Reform Commission, and Australian Human Rights Commission, and the Auditor-General.[38]

---

36 Law Council of Australia, 'Uluru Statement should be respected' (Media release, 1 November 2019).

37 Murray Gleeson, 'Recognition in keeping with the Constitution: A worthwhile project' (Speech to Uphold and recognise, 18 July 2019) 13.

38 Anne Twomey, 'Why an Indigenous Voice would not be 'third chamber' of parliament', *The Sydney Morning Herald*, 28 May 2019.

There is already a myriad of specialised government bodies intended to inform parliament on a range of matters that do not attract the criticism of being a third chamber of parliament. Yet the entire premise of the Voice is that it must not be just another Canberra-based body, but one which is more influential and with a more privileged place within the policy development and implementation process. That is why proponents insist on it being constitutionally enshrined—to elevate it above the other bodies and to prohibit its abolition by parliament. The distinct nature of the Voice explains why regarding the proposal as a third chamber *de facto* is unreasonable.

The practical flaws of the unprecedented Voice proposal should not suggest that so-called moderate alternatives could or should be safely adopted in its place. The current federal government has resolved to forego constitutional change and is proceeding with a co-design process to develop a model to establish a Voice in legislation, as opposed to being written into the Constitution. In reality, a Voice would bear many of the same practical flaws whether it was created by legislation or was constitutionally enshrined.. Further, even a legislated Voice will not necessarily halt momentum for its enshrinement in the Australian Constitution at a future date. Tom Calma, who along with Professor Marcia Langton, was selected to lead the federal government's co-design process for the Voice, urged indigenous Australians to support the legislated Voice on the basis that it could be the basis for future constitutional change:

> I would like to get the opportunity to establish the bodies and the process and look at all the models and how they might work, and then at a future time look at – and this is the government's role – to look at constitutional enshrinement or whatever.[39]

---

39 Katherine Murphy, 'Tom Calma urges Indigenous support for design of voice to parliament', *The Guardian* 29 October 2019.

Other proposed forms of recognition include the idea of a treaty, or the insertion of a declarative provision explicitly recognising indigenous Australians, as proposed by the major political parties ahead of the 2007 federal election.

Under a treaty, Australian governments would sign an agreement of some kind with indigenous Australians in some way; and this is a process in which a proposed Makaratta Commission might also play a role. Conceptually, the idea of a treaty is confusing. The legality of what a treaty actually is and who can enter into a treaty, has long been an obstacle to using this as a form of recognition.

From a strictly legal perspective, a nation cannot sign a treaty with itself. Article 2 of the Vienna Convention on the Law of Treaties provides that a treaty "means an agreement concluded *between states*", whereas a state is usually "defined as a community which consists of a territory and population subject to an organized political authority; that such a state is characterised by sovereignty."[40] In other words, a treaty requires two sovereign parties. To sign a treaty with indigenous Australian would mean a concession of sovereignty of some kind.

In 1998, Prime Minister John Howard delivered a succinct statement explaining what this would mean:

> I don't like the idea of a treaty because it implies that we are two nations. We are not, we are one nation. We are all Australians before anything else, one indivisible nation.[41]

If a treaty is signed between Australian governments and representative indigenous groups, it is certain to go beyond symbolism and will create legal obligations and policy outcomes. In their book *Treaty*, published in 2005, Sean Brennan, Larissa

---

40 Thomas D. Mulgrave, *Self-determination and national minorities* (Oxford Monographs in International Law, Oxford University Press, 2000) 235.

41 John Howard, Election debate, 13 September 1998 <https://australianpolitics. com/1998/09/13/howard-beazley-1998-election-debate.html>.

Beehrendt, Lisa Streilin and George Williams defined a "treaty as a document comprising three key elements: a starting point of acknowledgement; a process for negotiation; and outcomes in the form of rights, obligations, and opportunities. In discussing the third element, they explained that

> For government it might mean accepting, as a legal obligation, its responsibility to provide long term funding and administrative support for programs in health and education, or to follow a particular negotiation protocol before embarking on changes that affect a particular community. For indigenous peoples it might be taking on primary responsibility for an important and difficult area of public policy, such as child protection, community justice or substance abuse.[42]

Indeed, a pact or agreement with indigenous groups to "address" historical disadvantage through positive action could give rise to a potentially limitless range of obligations, including separate indigenous representative bodies, additional land rights, expansion of government-provided social programmes, or new hate-speech laws.

The least disruptive model of constitutional recognition is the declarative preamble or statement inserted into the Australian Constitution, as proposed by the major parties ahead of the 2007 federal election. Still, this is not without legal risk. Preambles are legal instruments, and legal instruments are intended to have an effect in law. As Quick and Garran noted in their authoritative annotated commentary on the Australian Constitution:

> The proper function of a preamble is to explain and recite certain facts which are necessary to be explained and recited before the enactments contained in an act of parliament are to be understood. A preamble may be used for other purposes; to limit the scope of certain expressions or to explain facts or introduce definitions.[43]

---

42 Sean Brennan et al., *Treaty* (The Federation Press, 2005) 10.
43 Sir John Quick & Sir Robert Garran, *The Annotated Constitution of the Australian Commonwealth* (The Australian Book Company, London, 1901) 284.

Even when a provision is explicitly intended not to have a legal effect, this can not necessarily be guaranteed. In a paper to the Samuel Griffith Society in 1999, former Chief Justice of Australia, Sir Harry Gibbs, noted that it would be "illusory" to imagine that a referendum proposal to insert a new preamble could not be guaranteed to be of no legal force in the future. :

> The Courts have held that a preamble may have wider effects than as an aid to interpretation. A reference in a preamble to a matter will make evidence of that matter admissible. Recitals in a preamble are prima facie evidence of the facts recited. It would be arguable that these rules were not excluded by a provision that the Preamble has no legal force.[44]

Moreover, declarations of "fact" in a constitution may also lead to political claims or demands from some groups on the basis that parliament has a moral obligation to honour the words or the spirit of the preamble.

Beyond the practical problems posed by the proposals, they each share one key feature: the permanent division of Australians along racial lines. In this respect, constitutional recognition is the policy manifestation of the ideology of identity politics, which in turn is an affront to the concept of human dignity. Human dignity recognises that humans possess unique and intrinsic value by virtue of being human. Rather than uniting Australians under the one parliament, constitution, and set of laws, the demand for legal and constitutional change based on group identity is an exercise in identity politics that would permanently divide Australians by race.[45]

Identity politics holds that an individuals' immutable characteristics,

---

44 Sir Harry Gibbs, 'A Preamble: The issues' (Paper presented to the 11th Conference of the Samuel Griffith Society, 9-11 July 1999).

45 This discussion on identity politics is adapted from a forthcoming publication of the Institute of Public Affairs, authored by Daniel Wild and Morgan Begg. See also Andrew Bushnell and Daniel Wild, 'How identity politics divides us' (2017) 69(3) *IPA Review* 15.

such as sex, race, ethnicity, nationality, or their chosen characteristics such as religion, are determinative of the views they ought to hold. This leads to the assumption that there are uniquely group-specific views of the world which exclude other groups. This view therefore holds that there is an indigenous interpretation of events that is only relevant and available to indigenous Australians.

The concept of a group-specific interpretation of events is at the heart of the Voice. Implicit in arguments for the Voice is the assumption that, at least on some issues, a non-indigenous Australian could not accurately speak on behalf of, or represent the interests of, an indigenous Australian. This assumption undermines the notion of individual autonomy and ignores the commonality of challenges that Australians across the country face. Joblessness, suicide, family breakdown, violence, and drug and alcohol abuse, for example, are not problems unique to certain indigenous communities, and they are not necessarily the product of a unique indigenous culture. Rather, these challenges are tragically present for Australians of different backgrounds.

Inversely, just as many social, cultural, and economic challenges do not emanate from one's biological background, so too are the fundamental building blocks of a successful life independent of race. Access to the dignity of work, communities free of crime, stable families, economic opportunity, and adequate provision of education, health, and infrastructure resources are foundational to human flourishing. Access to such resources does not guarantee a successful life will always follow; nor does the deprivation of such resources guarantee failure. But the existence and availability of these resources is obviously preferable, and an indigenous-only voice to parliament is not required to communicate this basic truth.

Not only do the tenets of identity politics segment those who may speak for which group, the members of a group are assumed to have a collective voice, further denying individual autonomy.

Sublimating the voices of individual indigenous Australians to the one collective "Voice" also denies the differences between different indigenous groups across Australia and within those groups themselves. There are over 500 different indigenous "tribes" or "clans" across Australia, many with distinct languages, cultures, and beliefs, comprising some 460,000 people – around 2.5 per cent of Australia's total population.

Indigenous Australians bring a range of views to different policy issues and ought not to be assumed to all provide one, equivalent "voice". There is no more a single indigenous view on policy than there is a single non-indigenous view. A number of prominent indigenous Australians have made this point. Nyunggai Warren Mundine argued in the *Australian Financial Review* on 10 September 2019 that the proposal for a national Indigenous voice "doesn't reflect the way indigenous Australians are." According to Mundine, "We aren't one people and we don't think of ourselves as one people. We think of ourselves in terms of the countries or nations we're born into or descended from."

Most importantly, Mundine observed that a national Voice would not carry legitimacy amongst the various indigenous nations or tribes: "only traditional owners can speak for their country. Bundjalung speak for Bundjalung country. Yuin speak for Yuin country. Yolngu speak for Yolngu country. But a national voice can't speak for any country."[46] Similar views were expressed by Price who argued in July 2019 that attempts to lump all indigenous groups together and treat them the same is a "grotesque denial of their rights to see themselves as different and distinct linguistic and cultural groups, with their own distinct histories of contact with Europeans and experience of colonisation."[47]

---

46 Nyunggai Warren Mundine, 'Why a national voice to Parliament is doomed to fail',
    The Australian Financial Review, 10 September 2019.
47 Jacinta Nampijinpa Price, 'Power, inclusion and exclusion; my concerns about a
    'Voice', *NITV SBS Online*, 20 July 2019.

Further, according to the analysis of identity politics, the received institutions of a nation-state are compromised by their historical origins. The claim here is that social, political, and economic interactions reflect a zero-sum power struggle between different classes in society. The demographic composition of the hierarchy of the major institutions of society reflects the interests of that hierarchy and exists only to protect those interests. In this view, the institutions which are derived from Australia's British colonial history are not capable of representing indigenous Australians, and need to be deconstructed.

It does not follow that the deconstruction of Australia's governing institutions will resolve hardship in indigenous communities. It would likely have the opposite effect. To understand hardship within some indigenous communities as an issue to be solely addressed by indigenous-only institutions is then to relieve all other Australians of their duty to their fellow citizens. To attribute all disadvantage to institutionalised structural oppression is to remove any sense of individual or local responsibility for the improvement of one's condition. This message denies individual agency, autonomy, and free will. It is fundamentally disempowering and destructive.

The Voice to parliament will create permanent division of Australia along racial lines. Australians have been asked to ignore this element of the proposal. Recognition advocates, such as Noel Pearson, have argued that there is a meaningful distinction to be made between race and "indigeneity", where the basis for the claim is to recognise a pre-existing culture and society connected to a homeland.[48] But this is a distinction without a substantive difference. In the case of the Voice, rights of representation in the Australian Constitution are being offered to some Australians and not others, and the basis for this is a person's membership of a group based on immutable

---

48   See for instance Noel Pearson, 'All we seek is our rightful place' (Speech to the Key Forum of the Garma Festival of Traditional Cultures, 5 August 2019).

biological identity or descent. Fundamentally, it is in opposition to the principle of racial equality to treat people differently based on biological traits such as indigenous membership.

Many indigenous Australians and indigenous communities face real and significant challenges. . But despite the relatively high levels of welfare spending directed towards indigenous Australians,[49] the lives of many do not appear to be improving.[50] Indeed research suggests that 35 per cent of indigenous Australians are dependent on welfare in one form or another.[51]

We are all Australians and we all share a responsibility to care for one another and create a better future. Instead of pursuing a divisive agenda based on identity politics, policy-makers should look to practical solutions to the numerous challenges confronting remote indigenous communities. This would mean:

- Investigating how native title over traditional lands can be altered to more closely reflect the rights and opportunities of freehold title that other Australians can enjoy. This ought to allow, for example, indigenous Australians to buy and sell their own property, borrow against that property, and decide what types of economic development will be allowed to take place;

---

49 Research by the Centre for Independent Studies in August 2016 calculated state and federal government expenditure explicitly targeted towards indigenous services and programmes to be at least $5.9 billion per year: Sara Hudson, 'Mapping the Indigenous program and funding maze' (Research report 18, Centre for Independent Studies, August 2017).

50 See the health and welfare statistics collected in Andrew Bushnell, 'Indigenous Australians and the Criminal Justice System' (Research report, Institute of Public Affairs, 2019) 16-24.

51 Sara Hudson, 'Mapping the Indigenous program and funding maze' (Research report 18, Centre for Independent Studies, August 2017) 1, citing estimates based on Helen Hughes and Mark Hughes, *Indigenous Employment, Unemployment and Labour Force Participation: Facts for Evidence Based Policies* (Policy Monograph 107, Centre for Independent Studies, Sydney, 2010) Other studies into indigenous welfare dependency are summarised by Francisco Perales et al., 'Intergenerational Welfare Dependency in Australia: A Review of the Literature' (Paper, ARC Centre of Excellence for Children and Families over the Life Course, 2018).

- Lifting barriers to economic opportunity and job creation in regional areas. This should include reducing regulatory barriers to business investment, laws which restrict the development of private farmland, such as native vegetation regulations, and those which provide urban activists with special legal privileges to thwart projects in regional areas; and

- Embracing localism in policy design and implementation. This would involve the Commonwealth devolving more functions to state governments and state governments devolving functions to regional bodies who are closer to the lived experiences of remove indigenous communities.

Indeed, one of the main deficiencies of policy-making in Australia, for both indigenous and non-indigenous, is that too much centralisation removes it from the concerns and lived experiences of local communities. Ken Wyatt, Minister for Indigenous Australians in the Morrison government, acknowledged this challenge in an address to the National Press Club in July 2019 when he argued that, "Even the most well-intentioned modern policies and programs have still tended to take a top-down command-and-control approach".[52] The Voice would suffer from the same flaw.

All Australians have a shared destiny, but any attempt to undermine the universality of the Australian Constitution will erect a wall between indigenous and non-indigenous Australians. Even just putting the proposed referendum to the Australian public for a vote would be divisive: Australians would be asked whether or not they want to divide themselves and their nation along racial lines. This is a lose-lose proposition. If the referendum succeeds, the nation will be formally and permanently divided in our governing institutions. If the referendum fails, advocates will inevitably and disingenuously use the result as evidence of continuing ill-

---

52 Ken Wyatt, 'Walking in partnership to effect change' (Address to the National Press Club, 10 July 2019).

will against indigenous Australians, fuelling further resentment between members of the Australian population.

The question itself defies our history. In the landmark 1967 referendum, Australians took a significant step in removing references to race in the Australian Constitution, with almost 91 per cent of electors approving of the proposal. This should be seen as the first step in a larger process of making the Australian Constitution blind to such concepts as "race".

Two references to race remain in the Australian Constitution. The first is the defunct section 25, which penalises states that ban an entire race from voting in state elections by reducing their portion of seats in the federal house of representatives. The second is section 51(xxvi)—also known as the "race power"—which gives the Commonwealth the power to make laws for the 'people of any race for whom it is deemed necessary to make special laws.' Gleeson acknowledged the moral problem with section 51(xxvi), arguing that, "The race power, by its very nature, calls into question the assumption of equality." Hence why it ought to be removed.

Any proposal for constitutional change must be measured against fundamental principles underlying Australia's liberal democracy. This is a test that the Voice will always fail. Parliaments, being open for participation of all Australians, remain the best body to represent all Australians. Only by rejecting the proposals to insert references to race will we secure the Australians Constitution as a race blind rule book and properly honour the spirit of the Australian people as expressed at the 1967 referendum. The alternative – to accept toxic identity politics as a feature of our governing institutions will divide Australians along racial grounds forever.

8

GENDER DYSPHORIA IN CHILDHOOD AND ADOLESCENCE

Hugh Puttenham

While the history of Western medicine has been largely a story of incremental progress, it has also born witness to harmful fads. Although usually brief and self-limiting, they are often only identified as being dangerous in retrospect. Even in today's age of evidence-based treatments, spurious diagnoses and unethical treatments can still achieve mainstream acceptance.

The medical sub-specialty of psychiatry has also promoted discredited diagnoses and therapies. The once widespread practices of lobotomy and insulin coma therapy are embarrassing examples of deviations from the scientific method. In the 1990's, the epidemic of recovered memories led to innocent teachers spending many years in jail following false accusations of sexual abuse. In relation to disorders of childhood and adolescence, previous psychiatric classification manuals are awash with questionable diagnoses such as intermittent explosive disorder, oppositional defiant disorder, and childhood bipolar disorder.

Childhood transgenderism is an example of a dangerous,

contemporary medical fad. The inherent intangibility and subjectivity of psychiatric disorders render them especially susceptible to ideological, environmental and political influence. The manufacturing of novel psychiatric diagnoses progressively fattens each new edition of the APA's Diagnostic and Statistical Manual of Mental Disorders (DSM).

Normal human experiences are increasingly pathologised; a phenomenon described by the eminent US psychiatrist Allen Frances.[53] These 'artificial' diagnoses frequently fail to reach thresholds of validity, utility and reliability. The construct validity of 'gender dysphoria' (GD) in childhood as it is currently conceptualised is highly questionable. Gender identity is itself unverifiable and has no physical manifestations. The high desistance rates of children with gender confusion after puberty suggest that GD is an unstable diagnosis. We are playing fast and loose with our approach to diagnosis and treatment.

Take for example Melbourne's Royal Children's Hospital transgender service that offers a service to children as young as age 3. Very young children function at a *preoperational* level and hence lack the capacity for abstract reasoning. Indeed, infants even have very weak understanding of *natal sex*. They are prone to conflating external appearances (clothes, hair) with corresponding biological essences.

For example, a 3-year-old might understand a 'boy' to mean a person with short hair who wears blue. The term 'gender' is itself a sociological construct that enjoys a whimsical and inconsistent relationship with biological sex. Apparent deviations from stereotypical sex norms may just be a normal developmental phase in a proportion of children. Each of us occupies a position on the normal distribution curve for femininity and masculinity. This does

---

53 Frances, Allen. "Saving normal: An insider's revolt against out-of-control psychiatric diagnosis, DSM-5, big pharma and the medicalization of ordinary life." *Psychotherapy in Australia* 19.3 (2013): 14.

not mean that we each exist on a spectrum of 'genders'.

Ironically, those who most vociferously object to the binary nature of gender are the first to fall back on crude and sex outdated stereotypes. The process of social transition alone involves the creation of an ersatz version of the opposite sex. Activists avoid the use of the term *transsexualism* but it is a more honest appraisal of what is attempted.

The child who transitions is in the strict sense *transsexual*, not transgender. 'Affirmation' therapy (affirming the child's perceived gender) is another misnomer because it prioritises the fleeting, abstract and unstable over the fixed, and objective and measurable. Doctors are ordinarily very careful about their use of medical terminology. Nevertheless, confusing, imprecise and contradictory terminology abounds in transgender medicine. For example, the term 'gender assigned at birth' is patently false; hospitals record *sex* at birth.

Gender clinics across the country are in receipt of healthy governmental funding; Victoria's two services have received $12.4 million since 2015. Clinics at Australian hospitals are facing unprecedented demand for the assessment and treatment GD. Freedom Of Information (FOI) requests made to gender clinics across the country were recently analysed by Professor Dianna Kenny[54] showing the ballooning numbers of children referred for assessment and treatment. Despite some clinics either providing incomplete data, or refusing to comply with the FOI requests, the numbers are still startling.

According to Professor Kenny, the Royal Children's Hospitals Gender Service in Melbourne reported a 250-fold increase in new referrals to their service between 2003 and 2017. Similar increases

---

54 https://www.diannakenny.com.au/k-blog/item/12-children-and-young-people-seeking-and-obtaining-treatment-for-gender-dysphoria-in-australia-trends-by-state-over-time-2014-2018.html

have been recorded overseas, for example in referral rates to the Tavistock Gender Identity Development Service (GIDS) in the UK. Looking at Australian data, over a five-year period from 2014 to 2018, 2,415 children and young people were enrolled in one of four gender clinics in Australia. Over the same period, 492 children and young people were receiving puberty blocking agents (stage 1 treatment) from three gender clinics in New South Wales, Western Australia, and Queensland. Victoria did not supply figures. A total of 286 children and young people were commenced on cross sex hormone treatment (stage 2) in gender clinics that provided data.

Professor Kenny believes that these data significantly under represent the actual numbers of children receiving some form of treatment for gender dysphoria, given that only four of seven states have gender clinics and could supply data. Her research also suggests significant differences between the states in treatment patterns. Explanations for discrepancies include the rigor of initial assessments of the child in determination of gender identity status, and differences in cut-off criteria to commence or delay intervention.

Shockingly in Victoria, there has been a 70-fold increase over the study period of young people receiving cross sex hormones. Some young people bypass the local system due to the growing waiting lists at gender clinics and source cross-sex hormones through the internet or travel for them. Clearly, there is a growing demand for services. It should not be so difficult for the public to know what is taking place in our hospitals; we urgently need greater transparency and reporting. The public has a right to know.

In June 2018 The Department of Health and Human Services in Victoria released their report 'Development of Trans and Gender Diverse Services in Victoria'.[55] In the 115-page service blueprint, the DHS proposed major changes to referral pathways including

---

55 https://www2.health.vic.gov.au/about/publications/researchandreports/development-trans-gender-diverse-services-victoria-final-report

expanding the role of general practitioners in facilitating services for trans-children. The report stated that there could be at least 73,800 trans and gender diverse people in Victoria! Nevertheless, it accurately identified the high rates of mental illness in young people seeking transition. It cited a 2017 study[56] on trans and gender diverse people aged between 14 and 25 years, which found that 75% had been diagnosed with depression, 80% reported self-harming, 82% reported suicidal thoughts, and 48% had attempted suicide.

It is a common fear of parents that their child's dysphoria could progress to suicide. It is easy to empathise with these concerns. This narrative is emotionally compelling and is effective in shaping public policy – but only tells half the story.[57] Much of the truth about suicidality has been buried under the weight of activist disinformation, some of it emanating from academic institutions, professional organisations, and gender clinics. We know that suicide rates post-transition remain very high suggesting the persistence of underlying distress after 'best practice' treatment.[58]

Yet despite this, the Victorian DHS is quick to call for limits to the role of a psychiatrist in referral pathways where they deem it unnecessary. They cite a perceived double standard in the health system where "cis-gender people do not require a mental health assessment to access surgery such as breast augmentation, whereas trans and gender diverse people require rigorous mental health

56 Strauss, P, Cook, A, Winter, S, Watson, V, Wright Toussaint, D, & Lin, A 2017, Trans Pathways: The Mental Health Experiences and Care Pathways of Trans Young People - Summary of Results., Perth, Australia.

57 https://www.diannakenny.com.au/k-blog/item/11-key-issues-in-decision-mak-ing-for-gender-transition-treatment-questions-and-answers.html

58 Dhejne, C., Lichtenstein, P., Boman, M., Johansson, A. L., Långström, N., & Lan-dén, M. (2011). Long-term follow-up of transsexual persons undergoing sex reas-signment surgery: cohort study in Sweden. PloS one, 6(2), e16885. doi:10.1371/journal.pone.0016885

assessments and approval letters".[59] They state that in Victoria, mental health practitioners mainly diagnose gender dysphoria, and acknowledge the role of psychiatrists in playing a gatekeeping role in facilitating access to hormonal and surgical services. However, the report's authors imply that psychiatric referrals contribute to long waiting lists and potentially reduce access to affirming interventions. The ambivalence about the functions of the psychiatrist in the assessment process evinced by DHS activists reflects a fundamental misrepresentation of the nature of the problem. The role of psychiatrist as gatekeeper needs to be strengthened, not weakened.

Psychiatrists must accept some of the blame for this confusion. Their professional college, the Royal Australian and New Zealand College of Psychiatrists (RANZCP), finds itself in the odd position of being pro-affirmation, but seems reluctant to hitch its wagon to the latest progressive guidelines from the RCH –presumably to avoid guilt by association. The RANZCP in its relevant position statement[60] does support international consensus guidelines recommending that adolescents who fulfil minimum criteria undergo reversible treatment to suppress puberty, generally with the use of gonadotrophin-releasing hormone analogues. The evidence they offer in support of this approach is a small, low-quality study of only 77 young people with a high drop-out rate.[61] A number of psychiatrists I speak to in private have expressed their concerns about the reversibility of hormone blockade and feel that the RANZCP has afforded this issue insufficient deliberation.

The internal machinations behind the public position statements that emanate from our medical organisations are largely opaque.

---

59 https://www2.health.vic.gov.au/about/publications/researchandreports/develop-ment-trans-gender-diverse-services-victoria-final-report

60 https://www.ranzcp.org/news-policy/policy-and-advocacy/position-statements/recognising-and-addressing-the-mental-health-needs

61 Wallien, M. S., & Cohen-Kettenis, P. T. (2008). Psychosexual outcome of gen-der-dysphoric children. *Journal of the American Academy of Child & Adolescent Psychiatry, 47*(12), 1413-1423.

Highly controversial diagnoses such as GD should be open to debate within the wider professional membership. Many doctors are worried about this development in our culture and practice; firstly, because this is a high stakes game of human experimentation that irrevocably changes the biology of an individual, and secondly because important safeguards enshrined in evidence-based medical practice and ethics have been abandoned to expedite diagnoses, potentially bringing the profession into disrepute.

Despite the continued presence of GD within psychiatric taxonomy, there has been a paradoxical divorcing of this diagnosis from its association with mental illness. Readers will no doubt be familiar with the shift in the Diagnostic and Statistical Manual of Mental Disorders (DSM) terminology over time to achieve this end. Transgenderism was initially considered a paraphilia, then an identity disorder, then a dysphoria, it will soon be an 'incongruence' before it disappears altogether.

At the start of the 21st century, the numbers of children and adolescents seeking sex change were virtually negligible. Indeed, psychiatrists would have considered the adoption of traits traditionally associated with the opposite sex as either a normal phase of psychic development ('tomboyism' for example), or if severe and persistent, to be an externalizing manifestation of disordered family dynamics and/or childhood trauma.

Notwithstanding the previous rarity of such cases, there is a psychoanalytic literature dating from mid to late last century exploring the contribution of developmental traumas and parental attachments to childhood transvestitism and transsexualism. For example, the presence of a pathological 'symbiosis' between some mothers and their sons was seen as a possible causal factor in the development of sex confusion in boys. Typically, psychiatrists deployed a range of exploratory psychotherapeutic techniques, often grounded in family dynamics and attachment styles.

Medications were rarely, if ever, prescribed.

Critics state that these approaches were ineffective. There are limited data to support or refute this claim – partly due to a low disorder prevalence and because systematic research into therapy was not widely undertaken. Today, individual and family psychotherapy remain the best forms of treatment for other causes of disordered self-identity such as in anorexia nervosa, body dysmorphia and dissociative identity disorder. For reasons both political and ideological, GD has been uncoupled from this analytic tradition, and finds itself orphaned in the murky limbo of invisible physical disorders. What potential insights have we lost by turning our backs on unconscious reactions to trauma?

The contemporary understanding of GD makes the a-priori assumptions that there can never be an abnormal psychological process underpinning gender confusion (meaning no 'false positives') and that the person's intuition that their body and gender identity do not align is unassailable. To highlight the extent to which this fallacy is widely accepted, a panel of trans clinicians from the prestigious Mayo Clinic recently declared at an international psychiatric conference that ''nature had screwed up'' by causing some children to be "born into the wrong bodies". One of the presenters asked the assembled audience if they were ''all on board'' with this premise. Nobody demurred; or at least had the courage to do so.

The concept of "follow the child" stems from this shaky premise. According to the orthodox view of gender dysphoria endorsed by the Royal Children's Hospital and based on international protocols (e.g., the WPATH guidelines and the 'Dutch' Protocol), if the child believes that they are in the wrong body, then this subjective conviction is immediately placed beyond reasonable doubt. Furthermore, this disordered self-concept is reinforced through praise and validation by the clinicians who were involved in 'supporting' transition in the first place.

Paradoxically, the self-perception that the person is a victim (in the face of prejudice, bigotry and discrimination) also serves to reinforce the sense of being uniquely different further justifying the decision to transition *post-hoc*. The transitioning child occupies a world of confirmation bias enforced by books, those such as the infamous "Gender Fairy", which expose children to these ideas in infancy.

The assessment process for GD in children outlined by The Royal Children's Hospital (RCH) generally proceeds from the premise that the person already has the disorder rather than from assuming the null hypothesis – a strange starting point for any medical assessment. In listing the roles of mental health professionals in the assessment of children desiring to transition, the RCH guidelines state that the psychiatrist or psychologist is there to assess capacity, assist the young person manage their dysphoria, assess co-morbidities, and support adjustment to their "new" body. There is no stated imperative for clinicians *to* question the underlying diagnostic premise. While most gender dysphoric children cannot be considered delusional in the classical sense, they do adopt, with growing conviction, a false but culture-bound syndrome sustained and reinforced by a number of sociocultural factors.

According to the requirements of current practice, competing accounts of the causes of dysphoria are not to be entertained. To that end, symptoms of depression, anxiety, anorexia, self-harm, autism, OCD and personality disorder are viewed as co-morbidities and consequences of the mismatch, rather than *confounding* symptoms caused by the same trauma that led to the development of GD. Supporters of the affirmation model attribute these symptoms and behaviours to the distress of stigma and discrimination. Is this a valid assumption? Do all people who are the victims of other kinds of stress and trauma harm themselves or attempt suicide? Why are rates of self-harm and suicide in individuals post transition high in trans- tolerant jurisdictions like the Netherlands and Sweden where self-reported episodes of discrimination are low[62]? Perhaps there are personality and temperamental factors at play here that pre-date the desire to transition.

The greater the sunken emotional and physical cost of transition for the child, the harder it is to change course. Early social transition (an ostensibly 'soft' stage of transition) is the first stage of the affirmation model. In this phase, the child adopts the stereotypically external manifestations of the other sex- for example, hairstyles, clothes and vocal tonality and binding of the chest. This seems at first glance harmless enough, but is it? These measures normalise and reinforce the 'living of a lie'. Social transition is the fall of the first domino; once the child has made this step, they have made an early foreclosure on competing explanations for their distress, ruining their chances of an open future and committing them to more radical interventions. Activists claim that transition should commence with great urgency. Puberty is considered an impending psychological "Armageddon" rather than a sometimes painful but necessary and healthy developmental hurdle. In some instances, children remain on puberty blockers for more than 5 years and face the real possibility of infertility.

Indeed, we know very little about the long-term safety of hormonal interventions. The use of puberty blocking drugs is highly contentious. In a recent letter to *Archives of Disease in Childhood*,[63] Christopher Richards and colleagues noted that use of these hormones is likely to threaten the maturation of the adolescent mind. They referenced evidence from animal models that pubertal hormones promote cognitive maturity, and are

---

62 https://research.vu.nl/ws/portalfiles/portal/42198051/complete+dissertation.pdf
63 Richards, Christopher, Julie Maxwell, and Noel McCune. "Use of puberty blockers for gender dysphoria: a momentous step in the dark." *Archives of disease in childhood* 104, no. 6 (2019): 611-612.

necessary for structural brain development and characterise the use of puberty blockers for GD as "a momentous step into the dark". The RCH standards of care do list the medical complications of cross sex hormones and of reassignment surgery. It even candidly concedes that delaying the onset of puberty with hormones may have psychological ramifications for the child who now lags behind their peers in terms of physical development. Yet none of these facts seems to alter the general direction of travel.

The RCH has just published a study protocol in the British Medical Journal[64] called Trans20, which aims to examine the health outcomes of 600 children who attended the Gender Service at the Royal Children's Hospital between 2017 and 2020. The authors note that the study is limited by the absence of an untreated control group. They admit that this will limit the potential of their research to offer conclusions about the effectiveness of their affirmation based interventions. They also claim, as one of their goals, to study the "natural history of gender dysphoria". It is difficult to see how this could be possible when all 600 subjects are in the treatment group. We need more studies examining the "wait and see" approach combined with targeted psychotherapy where appropriate. We also need to better understand the long-term psychological effects of artificially delaying puberty. What becomes of those who desire to revert to their natal sex and what interventions are made available to these unfortunate young people? Supporters of the affirmation model like to disavow the very existence of so-called 'de-transitioners', but we know from anecdotal reports that they exist.

Another area that deserves greater consideration is that of rapid-onset gender dysphoria;[65] a concept that has also received rapid-

---

64 Tollit, M. A., Pace, C. C., Telfer, M., Hoq, M., Bryson, J., Fulkoski, N., & Pang, K. C. (2019). What are the health outcomes of trans and gender diverse young people in Australia? Study protocol for the Trans20 longitudinal cohort study. *BMJ open*, *9*(11).

65 Littman, L. (2018). Rapid-onset gender dysphoria in adolescents and young adults: A study of parental reports. *PloS one*, *13*(8), e0202330.

onset condemnation by the orthodoxy. Brown University's Lisa Littman surveyed a group of parents whose children experienced a rapid onset of GD. She found that in post pubertal females, GD often arose around the same time in clusters of friends, with parents noting their daughter's heavy social media/internet use preceding disclosure of a transgender identity.

This phenomenon highlights two issues: first, the possible impact of social contagion on the "spread" of the disorder; and second, the possibility that GD is multifactorial in its aetiology which makes it all the more important to conduct research rigorously for individual-specific causes. Heterogeneous disorder subtypes warrant an array of different treatments. The problem with the affirmation approach is that it is essentially 'one size fits all'. Further epidemiological studies are required to better un-pack some of the sociocultural determinants of GD. How prevalent is rapid-onset GD in Australia? What role do social media and governmental programs such as Safe Schools have in increasing disorder prevalence? Is this a case of diagnosis *following* treatment as the number of GD services grow?

The issue of capacity to consent is also crucial. "Gillick-competent" adolescents (those who have purportedly attained decision-making capacity in relation to treatment) wishing to undergo transition may now do so without requiring the blessing of the Family Court. Parents can also consent on behalf of their children to both stage 1 and stage 2 of treatment providing they have medical approval.

Questions remain about whether or not adolescents have the capacity to make decisions about sex reassignment. The teenage brain tends towards impulsivity and risk taking. Long-term consequences of biological interventions (of which the teen has no personal experience) are often obscured by proximate feeling states, the influence of peers and social media. I am skeptical about whether even the most insightful and rational teens are able to give informed consent to complicated, largely untested, hazardous and life-altering interventions which will permanently change the way the world sees them, and which will invariably produce sterility. We desperately need some external oversight of the process by which informed consent is obtained at our clinics, ensuring that families are sufficiently aware of the risks of intervention. A parliamentary enquiry into transgender services would help shine a light on shortfalls in current practice.

Australian doctors should be taking note of developments in the UK where a number of dissenting voices have expressed concern at the alarming surge in young people and their families seeking treatments. The pre-eminent clinic in the UK, The Tavistock and Portman NHS Trust's Gender Identity Development Service, has recently become subject to embarrassing scrutiny after a number of whistle blowers expressed concerns about some of the practices they witnessed including 'fast-tracking' diagnoses.[66] The Royal College of General Practitioners in the UK has also expressed reservations about current approaches to GD. According to the college:

> There is a significant lack of robust, comprehensive evidence around the outcomes, side effects and unintended consequences of such treatments for people with gender dysphoria, particularly children and young people, which prevents GPs from helping patients and their families in making an informed decision.[67]

The crushing of calm, rational dissent extends to the issue of compelled speech (use of the 'correct' pronouns) which functions chiefly as a political test. It is the discursive equivalent of an oath of allegiance. Failure to adopt the pronouns for whatever reason exposes the speaker to criticism as an unbeliever. Demands that a trans person's interlocutor adopt a novel, arbitrary neo-Orwellian

---

66 https://www.dailymail.co.uk/news/article-6897269/Workers-transgender-clin-ic-quit-concerns-unregulated-live-experiments-children.html

67 https://www.rcgp.org.uk/policy/rcgp-policy-areas/transgender-care.aspx

lexicon is grossly narcissistic and attempts to enslave that other someone into this distorted worldview. I have at any given time a cohort of patients who claim to be Jesus; but I refuse steadfastly to address them with the moniker "Lord". The pronouns trap is designed to snare the unwitting for the purpose of confecting outrage and humiliating the transgressor. The lexicon of novel pronouns, presented as a *fait accompli* in governmental and educational missives, is intentionally capricious, changeable and confusing.

Activist squawking is drowning out dissenting physician voices. Professor John Whitehall, who has put his neck on the line many times in print, on radio and TV, has had Medical Board complaints made against him for speaking out. His 'crime' was to have questioned the chronic physical and psychological effects of hormone blockade in the young. He also warned us that governments (state and federal) are moving to criminalise 'conversion therapy', a practice that traditionally relates to the attempted changing of sexual orientation in homosexuals. Under such legislation being proposed in Queensland (and vigorously supported by the Andrews Government in Victoria), any clinician advocating a 'watchful waiting' approach to GD, using psychotherapy preferentially, or delaying referral to a gender service could face criminal or civil prosecution.

We need to oppose laws that compel clinicians to refer cases of GD to clinics where the child will receive affirmation-based treatments. The government needs to offer safeguards to those who conscientiously object to the affirmation model. Doctors should be freely allowed to express dissenting views without fear of harassment or vexatious reporting to medical boards. This is indeed a most troubling business, and Australia has the dubious distinction of leading the world in promoting this madness.

9

WOMEN IN POLITICS

KARINA OKOTEL

From the philosophy of its founder right through to the present day leadership, Liberals do not hesitate to have women fill the parliamentary benches. As Sir Robert Menzies said: 'Of course women are at least the equals of men. Of course there is no reason why a qualified woman should not sit in the parliament ...'[68]

But who is this "qualified woman" to whom Menzies refers? Does it matter if she subscribes to the values of the party? Does she have to demonstrate aptitude to advocate for her community? Must she be able to contribute new ideas to address the problems facing our nation?

---

68 Robert Menzies, 'Women for Canberra' (Radio Broadcast, 29 January 1943), cited in Margaret Fitzherbert, *Liberal Women: Federation to 1949* (Federation Press, 2004) 250.

The Australian people deserve the very best candidates put forward by political parties who will fight with integrity for the betterment of their electorates and country. Menzies used very deliberate language in specifying the "qualified woman". Both male and female candidates must be qualified to meet the expectations of the community. This is what we term "merit".

The opposite of merit-related policies involves the imposition of some sort of quota, direct or indirect, in the context of increasing the number of female parliamentarians. Gender quotas were first introduced by the Labor Party in 1994 mandating pre-selection of women in a third of all winnable seats. In 2015, the Labor Party resolved that 50 per cent of Labor parliamentarians would be women by 2015. In the current 46th parliament, 45 per cent of Labor parliamentarians are women. No one argues against the fact that gender quotas do increase the number of female parliamentarians. But do they address the systemic issues that prevent women from running for parliament or are they a mere Band-Aid, an easy solution to a constructed problem?

The view that we need to do whatever we can to get more women into parliament in the belief that this will somehow address inequality distracts us from dealing with the underlying issues as to why it is many women – women of merit – do not join political parties or stand for pre-selection in the first place.

There are two parts to this chapter. The first part explores the prevailing assumption that we must have more women in parliament as an end in and of itself. This is the narrative of the left which the media have lapped up unquestioningly.

To some extent, the left have already succeeded in convincing many Australians that getting more women into parliament is the solution to discrimination against women. The reality is that modern-day discrimination against women is an issue that quotas can never solve. The second part of this chapter explores the real issues of systemic discrimination against women which government must finally address. These are the issues that need a light shone on them. Sadly, the focus on parliamentary gender quotas does nothing but continue to divert government's attention.

PART ONE

A. (Re)defining the problem

In the age of information technology and the 24-hour media cycle, a good headline, such as a party having a "woman problem" and "needing more women in parliament", resonates. But we are rapidly losing the capacity to interrogate whether or not this really is a problem and, if so, why.

Politics is about the contest of ideas not the contest of chromosomes. The notion that having more females in parliament could alone generate better ideas is overly simplistic. Ideas are generated through one's life experience, environment, sharing and observation. Diversity in these areas provides the best foundation for developing the innovative ideas that can take our country forward. But a headline suggesting this would be complicated, nuanced and would not retain the attention of a modern audience that is constantly bombarded with more information than ever before to have cut through.

In the current 46th Parliament of Australia, of the 227 members, 44 per cent are former political staffers. Moreover, 63 per cent were either former staffers, union officials, industry association officers, internal party employees or bureaucrats.

Women account for 37 per cent of members of parliament. Amongst this cohort, 45 per cent are former political staffers and

65 per cent were either former staffers, union officials, industry association officers, internal party employees or bureaucrats.

What do these figures tell us? Whether a parliamentarian is male or female, the same proportions, almost two-thirds, have either worked for, in, or very close to government. This inevitably has the effect of perpetuating the existing culture and ideas; it mimics the echo chamber. Fresh ideas and perspectives that come from outside the Canberra "bubble" are simply out-muscled.

If we want fresh eyes and new ways of doing things, we need more parliamentarians with varied experiences who do not come from within the bubble and who are able to put forward new ideas. This defect is not cured simply by having more women in parliament.

When people talk about diversity in politics, they often base their remarks on the flawed premise of tokenism. This is the idea that someone possessing two X chromosomes instead of one will be better able to generate more diverse ideas. Rather, the critical problem is the uniformity that comes from being part of the bubble and having spent a lifetime soaking in the existing views and prejudices that permeate that bubble.

Why, then, are so many preselected and elected candidates cut from identical cloth? Consider that if someone works as a political staffer, they build relationships and are loyal to their Member of Parliament and their employer's faction. Such loyalty is valuable because that Member of Parliament will regard the staffer as another number in a party room to support their rise up the ladder to Cabinet and the top job. It is this self-interest that drives sitting parliamentarians to promote a former staffer over other candidates in a pre-selection. Similarly, those who work closely with government, such as union officials, industry association officers, internal party employees or bureaucrats, develop relationships of trust and are also more likely to be considered loyal and worthy of promotion by parliamentarians in a pre-selection.

Can this problem be solved? Only if parties are prepared to remove the oversize influence of parliamentarians in pre-selections. This applies to both men and women as existing and wannabe MPs.

It is not just lack of connection to the Canberra bubble that often prevents someone from attaining pre-selection. Regardless of whether you are male or female, limited means or connections can lead to you being excluded from being a candidate.

This is because it does take money to attend functions or to be a donor to the party in order to build relationships and garner support for pre-selection. If you are a breadwinner who has a full time job, you often cannot attend daytime meetings or catch-ups with influential party members. And without savings or a financial backer, it is difficult to run as a candidate for election, which is itself a full time voluntary job.

Again, if we want diversity of life experience and ideas, we must make it easier for people to stand for pre-selection, regardless of gender, who do not necessarily come from families with means and political connections. This will necessitate parties being willing to provide financial support to candidates in the lead up to an election who do not have a parliamentary wage or the same fundraising capacity as sitting Members of Parliament.

It is time the conversation shifted from the superficial issue of gender balance to the real issue of diversity of ideas which challenges the genuine tyranny of "cookie cutter" uniformity produced by the Canberra bubble and the personality-based power structures of political parties that often prevent candidates with diverse life experience and ideas from succeeding at preselection.

B. The number of women in parliament is reflective of the number of women in political parties

An initial assumption might be that the only women who run

for pre-selection are those who do not have children or who are older and have completed their child-rearing years. The statistics, however, disprove this hypothesis.

Of the current parliamentarians, the average age calculated for women entering parliament is 44.46 years, and the average age for men is only slightly younger being 42.26 years.[69] So what is it that actually prevents women from standing for parliament?

The reality is that we have fewer women joining political parties than men. This means that the talent pool from which to pre-select women is smaller and is comparable to the number of women presently serving in parliament. If more women were active in politics, more qualified female candidates would emerge.

There are no barriers to women signing a membership form to join a political party. Research from 2015 in the United Kingdom, a similar jurisdiction to Australia from which parallels can be drawn, showed that:

> Members are notably more male, middle class and educated than supporters… members are more socially liberal than supporters in both left- and right-wing parties. Members also have a decidedly greater sense of personal political efficacy than do supporters.[70]

It also found that:

> Party supporters believe that party members must derive intrinsic pleasure from involvement in party life, and career or material benefits, and that they must be embedded in a social network that draws them into the party. Actual members are far less likely to believe that this is the case – especially with respect to selective

---

69 Averages are calculated based on the ages of all current parliamentarians besides three females and three males whose ages are not published.

70 Tim Bale, Monica Poletti and Paul Webb, 'Why do only some people who support parties actually join them? Evidence from Britain' (2019) 42(1) *West European Politics* 156 [20].

outcomes or social norms [71]

It is important to note the recommendation the authors make to political parties seeking to increase their membership:

> By respectfully and sensitively challenging supporters' narratives about members – perhaps by encouraging activists to talk more about the realities of membership wherever possible – political parties may be able to convert more supporters into members.'[72]

This conclusion is one which should be heeded and applies to both recruitment of new male and female party members.

Encouraging members to authentically reach out to supporters to challenge the common belief that political parties are only for the elite who are seeking material benefit through political connection, and to talk to supporters about the reality of being a party member is also likely to increase membership. Making members aware of the need to focus their efforts, in particular, on reaching out to female supporters is therefore likely to bring in more female party members which, in turn, will help to increase the talent pool of qualified women available for pre-selection.

C. The Q word

The Band-Aid solution for increasing the number of female parliamentarians is typically to suggest quotas for women. This ignores the real reasons why women do not join political parties and why they may not seek pre-selection in the first place.

Introducing quotas when there is a significantly smaller pool of women to choose from makes it less likely that the best candidates on merit are being presented by political parties to the public

---

71 Ibid [29].
72 Ibid [33].

for election. The first step to increasing the pool of qualified women able to stand for pre-selection is to increase female party membership as outlined above.

Good potential candidates are often overlooked at pre-selections if they are unable to demonstrate loyalty to a faction generally through time served in the Canberra bubble. Overlaying gender quotas on top of a faction's exclusive pool of potential candidates significantly narrows the options of females who can be preselected.

Ultimately, gender quotas give party leaders greater control over candidate selection. Powerbrokers within a party are more likely to install candidates who are loyal to them rather than candidates who may better reflect community expectations. This is problematic on many levels - where candidates are installed, they would naturally feel beholden to the installer. It becomes easier to stack parliament with people with fixed loyalties to a group over integrity and commitment to their party's values or their local community. Quotas further invest the powerbrokers with control over the parliament, rather than the rank and file party members.

The rationale often given for introducing quotas is that women in politics have less capacity to attend branch functions, to serve on party committees, or to stand in unwinnable seats to win the respect of the party membership because they have jobs and families to attend to. This is an affront to the women in political parties who do give up their time in service of the party as well as to men who also have jobs and families themselves. Furthermore, installing someone untested by a party in terms of their commitment to the party's values and membership base can have dire consequences. There is no better example of this than Julia Banks.

Banks was a newcomer to the Liberal Party when she was preselected for the seat of Chisholm which she won in the 2016 federal election. Within one term she defected to become an independent and then ran against a sitting Liberal Minister in the seat of Flinders at the 2019 election. Banks should serve as a cautionary tale against preselecting women, or anyone for that matter, who are largely unknown to the party.

Quotas also assume that women cannot succeed on their own in the cutthroat preselection process, that they are weaker, more delicate or inferior, and that they need special protection. The problem is that if politics and the preselection system generates discriminatory or other unacceptable behaviour, the system itself needs to change. Just because someone is a man does not mean that he should have to put up with inappropriate preselection conduct. Installing women into parliament rather than allowing them to participate in preselections does not fix the process.

Discriminatory or improper behaviour would be unacceptable in any other job interview process. If we want our lawmakers to be exemplary citizens who uphold the law, and for party preselection processes to be fair, the same rules that apply to job interviews, which prevent baseless rumours being spread about a candidate or discriminatory conduct, should apply for all candidates seeking preselection, regardless of gender.

D. Inconsistencies

The 2019 federal election clearly showed that, even though Labor attacked the Liberal Party for having a so-called women problem on the basis that there are fewer female Liberal members of parliament than Labor ones, at the end of the day the vast majority of Australians vote on the policies of parties, not on identity politics concerns.

The difficulty for Labor will be trying to maintain this line of attack when Labor state governments around the country have introduced gender theory into schools and are teaching the next generation that gender is non-binary, gender identity is fluid and that there are multiple genders. If Labor is intellectually honest - and this is what those graduating from secondary school are currently being taught – then it is illogical for Labor to continue arguing that it is only more women who are needed or that there should be quotas for women only. What about trans, CIS, demi or the array of other defined genders? Should they not have quotas and be represented too?

Why is Labor's call for greater diversity limited to binary male/female genders only? And should there be quotas for those with other attributes such as disability, sexuality or race? The existence of party quotas for male and female parliamentarians opens the door to quotas for endless other attributes, from non-binary genders to other favoured traits. Essentially, a system like this would amount to socially engineering the composition of parliament.

The idea of having electorates is to ensure that voices from the local community can be represented in parliament. If quotas were to grow from just male/female, this would ultimately result in a socially engineered parliament based on attributes rather than on geographic electorates.

PART TWO

If the train has departed the station and the left and the media's combined efforts have successfully convinced the public that we must have more women in parliament, this does not mean that government should buy into the agenda of gender quotas. There are real solutions to increasing women's participation in politics as outlined in Part One. Furthermore, when it comes to discrimination against women, the real issue is not more women in parliament, but the portrayal of women across media which has profound impacts on our self-image and self-esteem. If government genuinely wishes to end discrimination against women, this is the issue that must be addressed.

A. The real discrimination

Talking about quotas is a diversion from addressing the real issue that keeps women down. Discrimination lies in the images across media that women see of themselves, which tell us that we are and always will be sexualised objects. Combating the sexualisation of girls and women is the genuine war against female discrimination. Television, the internet, teen magazines, billboards and shop front displays teach girls from a young age, consciously or unconsciously, that their worth is in their appearance and their value in the sexual gratification of men. The harm caused is significant.

According to the America Psychological Association:

> Self objectification has been shown to diminish cognitive ability and to cause shame. This cognitive diminishment, as well as the belief that physical appearance rather than academic or extracurricular achievement is the best path to power and acceptance, may influence girls' achievement levels and opportunities later in life.[73]

The sexualisation of females impacts girls and women across health domains, undermines confidence and causes emotional and self-image problems including shame and anxiety.[74]

Government is aware of this fundamental issue. Indeed, the Senate's Legal and Constitutional Affairs Reference Committee inquiry into the National Classification Scheme in 2011 made 30 recommendations which, if implemented today, would go a long

---

73 Task Force on the Sexualization of Girls, *Report of the APA Task Force on the Sexualization of Girls* (American Psychological Association, 2007) 34.

74 American Psychological Association, 'Sexualisation of Girls is Linked to Common Mental Health Problems in Girls and Women – Eating Disorders, Low Self-Esteem, and Depression; An APA Task Force Reports', (Press Release, 19 February 2007).

way to removing the impact of objectification of women through media.[75]

Instead, Australia's first research into the link between advertising and the objectification of women in 2018 found that sexualisaton and the objectification of women is increasing:

> Women are more likely than men to be shown wearing revealing clothing or
>
> simulating sex acts, being dominated or portrayed as objects or animals. Digital technology enables images of women's bodies to be altered, producing even narrower conceptualisations of female attractiveness and helping to facilitate the objectification of women.[76]

This research also cited links between representations of females and the influence of pornography.[77] The accessibility and acceptability of pornography in Australia compounds the objectification of women. Research from 2009 found that in Australia: 'It is not a matter of *whether* a young person will be exposed to pornography but *when*.'[78] Its proliferation means that its impact on our society is incredibly significant.

Research from 2012 on over 100 of the 250 most popular pornographic films found aggressive, abusive and coercive acts in almost every film. It also found that since the 1970s, pornographic films have become increasing more aggressive and humiliating.[79]

Once again, it is a mixed message for women. On the one hand

---

75 Senate Legal and Constitutional Affairs References Committee, Parliament of Australia, *Review of the National Classification Scheme: Achieving the Right Balance* (2011)

76 Women's Health Victoria, *Advertising (In)Equality: The Impacts of Sexist Advertising on Women's Health and Wellbeing*, Issue Paper No 14 (2018) 5.

77 Ibid 16.

78 Colleen Bryant, 'Adolescence, Pornography and Harm' (Issues Paper No 368, Australian Institute of Criminology, 2009) [2].

79 Natalie Purcell, *Violence and the Pornographic Imaginary: The Politics of Sex, Gender, and Aggression in Hardcore Pornography* (Routledge, 2012).

women are told they are equal to men; on the other they are viewed as sexual objects towards whom aggression and humiliation is acceptable. If the later message is not eliminated, then the former is inevitably intercepted.

The government has supported recommendations from the inquiry into the *Harm being done to Australian children through access to pornography on the Internet*, and has already established an Online Safety Consultative Working Group to advise on improving online safety for children. The government committed to ask this working group 'to consider the issue and report back on strategies to inform an effective policy response.'[80] However, it does not appear that this working group could possibly produce real outcomes to curb the harms of pornography given that they only meet twice a year and there is no transparency as to what, or if, advice is being given to Government.

These Senate inquiries demonstrate a recognition by government of the negative consequences of the objectification of women. Such objectification is so prolific that it is normalised in Australian society.

Taking the next step to actually combat the sexualisation of women will require genuine political will akin to the campaign against cigarette smoking which made smoking a public health issue and towards which significant tax-payer funds continue to be directed. If we truly want to eliminate modern discrimination against women, rather than jumping on quotas, government must do what it takes for all women to know that Australia sees us as worthy of protection against sexual objectification.

---

80 Senate References Committee on Environment and Communications, Parliament of Australia, *Australian Government Response to the Senate Report: Harm being done to Australian Children Through Access to Pornography on the Internet* (2017) 7-8.

Conclusion

No one disputes that there are fewer female parliamentarians than men. But filling seats through gender quotas does not address the real issues that the left either ignore or have never actually reflected upon. On this question there are deep divisions between the right and the left.

Politics is about the contest of ideas. The Australian people are not best served by tokenism but by the very best ideas rising to the top through rigorous interrogation in order to take our nation forward in the direction of increased peace and prosperity for all. If we want to enrich our parliament with the most qualified representatives, political parties ought to pursue a diversity of ideas generated through varied life experiences. This should also include encouraging more party supporters to become party members.

A lot of women in politics say that it was their families who inspired them to get involved by telling them that females could do and be anything they want. If girls do not have positive influences in their lives to help combat the negative messaging they receive about themselves through media, those negative messages resonate and take root.

Quotas represent tokenism at its height. Unless there is a commitment to combatting the sexual objectification of women, which brings with it shame and lack of self-esteem, genuine discrimination against women will continue on.

10

THE CHANGING FACE OF AUSTRALIAN MEDIA AND THE ABC

RICHARD ALSTON

It is only a generation ago since the Murdoch-Packer wars kept the commentariat and the political enthusiasts enthralled. Fairfax and News Ltd were the leviathans. The former was underwritten by its "rivers of gold" flowing from its effective monopoly over classified advertising of cars, jobs and real estate, while the latter was backed by its dominance in every state capital and its powerful international stable.

Alas, those days are long gone. After years of limping along, with regular downsizing of staff and quality content and the shrinking of the format to tabloid size, Fairfax finally succumbed to a takeover bid from Nine entertainment Co, allowable in the wake of cross media reform. There was little outcry as it was realized that the once venerable institution was on its last legs and at risk of going out of business altogether. The News Corp stable has done a lot better although even its flagship publication, *The Australian*, has mostly struggled to make a profit – in late 2017 it announced that it had returned to profit for the first time in nine years. This is despite transforming the business by growing paid subscribers - by 2018 its 135,000 digital subscribers exceeded the number of its print subscribers by some 50% - and focusing on building a strong online presence.

Unlike the Fairfax masthead, which lacked financial backers and had a constant struggle to survive, News Ltd was more fortunate. When Rupert Murdoch put his remaining print media interests into a separate vehicle, he made sure it had sufficient financial reserves to keep it going. *The Australian* was accordingly able to go for excellence in its choice of journalists. In addition to its already impressive lineup of political commentators, led by the doyen of political journalism Paul Kelly, ably assisted by Denis Shanahan, it recruited high quality journalists and opinion page experts in Professors Henry Ergas, Judith Sloane and Peter Van Onselen, as well as political commentators with high quality practical experience such as Chris Kenny and Troy Bramston.

But what has dramatically changed the media landscape is the emergence of powerful digital giants such as Google, Amazon, Facebook and Apple as life threatening competitors with vast cash, human and technology resources and the capacity to overwhelm almost any traditional media outlet.

The top four listed public companies in the US are all technology giants, with market caps hovering close to the $1 trillion mark. Microsoft is currently ranked the largest company in the world and Amazon and Alphabet (better known as Google) are close behind. Their extraordinary revenue streams and fabulous free cash balances enable them to invest in all manner of futuristic ventures and to increasingly move into the content space, hitherto the preserve of the media companies but who are now at serious risk of being swamped by the new entrants. Amazon, now the world's largest e-commerce marketplace, claims to have 647,000 employees. Google is now the world's second largest internet company by revenue. Facebook has nearly 2.5 billion monthly active users and Apple was the first company to reach $1 trillion in value. All of these have enormous market power which can easily enable them to drive competitors out of business.

These concerns led the Australian Federal Government in December 2017 to commission the ACCC to undertake the Digital Platforms Inquiry to consider the impact that digital platforms have had on the level of choice and quality of "news" and "journalistic content" to consumers. It was also required to consider the effect of online search engines, social media and digital content aggregators on competition in the media and advertising services markets, particularly in relation to the supply of news and journalistic content, and the implications for media content creators, advertisers and consumers. Its Digital Platforms (DP) Report, published in July 2019, provided a series of insights and recommendations to which the Federal Government responded in July 2020 by announcing that the ACCC had released a draft mandatory code of conduct to address bargaining power imbalances between digital platforms and media companies for a short period of public consultation. Watch this space.

The Media's Technology Future

But whilst the quality of print journalism remains high, its financial viability is another matter as the titans of yesteryear face an existential threat from new age international technology colossae. The DP Report does express deep concerns about the future of quality journalism in Australia, but it shies away from an exploration of the very real technological opportunities that are likely to emerge to satisfy our insatiable appetite for news in all its manifestations. Even if crystal ball gazing can be fraught it is not difficult to anticipate that quality journalism will survive but in very different forms, while the market for sensationalism will never have any shortage of commercial suppliers.

The Reuters Institute for the Study of Journalism at Oxford University observes that with the continuing development of artificial intelligence, voice operated systems and the integration of connected digital devices in everyday objects we are clearly only in the early phases of fundamental change. In the new environment independent professional and credible journalism will have a key role to play in meeting the public demand for ever more information. Television had to cope a decade ago with YouTube bypassing the networks to distribute content directly to consumers and more recently is having to adapt to the threat posed by playback and online subscription platforms such as Netflix. This has been accomplished with little government involvement, and journalism will also largely have to make its own way into the new era.

The ACCC agonises over the risk that public interest journalism may be "under-produced" but seems to ignore the prospect of market-based responses. If there is a sustainable demand for such products then it is hard to see why entrepreneurial players would ignore serious money-making opportunities. Paywalls, subscription services and the injection of micro advertisements into every available space are just a few of the new revenue-raising techniques. New forms of news presentation such as data journalism with sophisticated info-graphics are merely a taste of things to come.

The quality of the ACCC Report is variable. It bemoans the fact that "it can be difficult to exclude consumers who do not pay for news and journalism from accessing it." It also complains that newspapers can be passed on by paying customers to other non-payers such as libraries, airports and cafes. It deplores the fact that people are able to obtain information second hand. These "problems" have been around since forever and are unlikely to have been exacerbated by new technologies. It also worries about the "atomization" of journalism and the dilution of "brand value" and its possible impact on younger generations. These are little more than fancy terms for acknowledging the impact of the digital revolution on today's media, which already requires painful adjustment by all media participants. However, there is no reason why mere adaptation should require regulatory assistance. The ACCC's handwringing on this issue seems to ignore the weight of human experience. People have always exchanged information by word of mouth and will continue to do so. In Dickens' time, the coffee shop was a great source of information exchange where broadsheets were regularly handed around or left for the next customer. Even today, London's *Evening Standard* manages to prosper as a free daily tabloid thanks to advertising. Creativity in spreading the word, be it through specialist and trade magazines or news sheets, is impossible to suppress.

The Dangers of Unfettered Dominance by the Digital Platforms

None of the above is to ignore or downplay the awesome market power of the digital platforms. Existing media players such as News Corp understandably complain in loud terms about Google and others appropriating content produced by publishers without any proper regime to ensure adequate recompense. As Michael Miller, Executive Chairman of News Corp Australasia, wrote recently: "Their extraordinary profits are based on their unfair commercial exploitation of other people's content." His solution is for companies like Google to be required to negotiate a fair price for such use, as Facebook is reportedly interested in doing, in the face of governments around the world becoming increasingly frustrated with the nature and extent of the disruption. The media companies claim that they are being blocked from building subscription services to fund their journalism, forcing them to rely on a rapidly shrinking pool of advertising revenue, much of which has already been siphoned off by the digital platforms.

There does seem to be enough evidence to warrant government intervention to ensure that the digital companies are not able to unfairly exploit their overwhelming market dominance so as to constitute an abuse of market power. The DP Report indicates support for the creation of a specialist digital platforms branch to proactively monitor potentially unfair and anti-competitive practices. Another recommendation, which seems to have significant media industry support, is for codes of conduct, backed by legislated minimum standards, to ensure proper commercial arrangements operate in the market place. News has also called for amendments to the Copyright Act to make platforms liable for the misuse of copyrighted material.

The Impact of New Market Entrants

The private sector in Australia is clearly up for the challenge both in terms of commerce and philanthropy. Morry Schwartz, property developer and publisher, produces the *Quarterly Essay*, *The Monthly* and *The Saturday Paper*. Private Media CEO Eric Beecher's *Crikey* has recently announced plans to launch an investigative journalism team backed by two wealthy and experienced media philanthropists in John B Fairfax and Cameron O'Reilly. The DP Report finds that digital platforms have played an influential role in enabling the entrance of new competitors such, as BuzzFeed News Australia, social media posts extensively as a means of reaching audiences and has over 2.5 million Facebook "likes." Even Google has recently launched its News Initiative, a US$300 million global project to provide technical support and training to help publishers generate revenue in the online environment.

Meanwhile Australian billionaire and art gallery owner Judith Nielson acknowledges that "traditional forms of journalism are going through massive change and Australian journalism and intellectual life needs a shot in the arm." Accordingly, she has committed to spending $100m on establishing a new Institute for Journalism and Ideas.

The DP Report says that it is estimated that in the US between 2010 and 2015 philanthropy contributed around $100m a year to the production of news content. Crowdfunding is another readily available option for media companies. Both *The Guardian* and Wikipedia regularly solicit funds from their readers. All this suggests that there is little need for government subsidy or handouts.

The ACCC undertook its own survey of the total number of articles published by 12 selected publications between 2001 and 2018 and concluded that there had been fewer articles on four issues during the period: local government, local court matters, health and science. However, it made no attempt to analyse or explain these results. Government needs to be careful not to over-react to the fast-changing media environment and the resultant changes in consumer behaviour.

The first two issues of local government and local courts seem to have been lazily borrowed from the UK's Cairncross Review, *A Sustainable Future for Journalism*, published in February 2019. They could be the result of declining interest, fatigue, or availability from other sources. Whilst council proceedings, particularly the planning shenanigans which often bedevil such activities, are often of keen interest to ratepayers, the responsibility for making such information available surely lies at the local level.

It is not clear that the public has a need for ever more information of local court proceedings and if they do, beyond the titivating, there will always be a ready supplier. It is much harder to justify the public funded broadcasters needing to report routine police rounds. My television news viewing tells me that that SBS rarely intrudes into this space whereas for the ABC it is daily fare. No doubt it is much cheaper, as it only requires regular police contacts, but whether there is a genuine "public interest" justification is another matter.

A greater concentration on health and science is more difficult to justify. In my experience there is an absolute plethora of articles on these subjects, both scholarly and sensational and everything in between. The DP Report suggests that the declining provision of public interest journalism, particularly the reduction in sources providing local reporting, justifies "a degree of government intervention." It is hard to see how such a vague and non-specific recommendation can be of any assistance to policy makers.

The DP Report finds that there are 21 local government areas, including 16 in regional Australia, without any coverage from a single local newspaper. It does not endeavour to ascertain whether newspapers in adjoining areas provide coverage, as they would have every incentive to do, or whether residents are satisfied with the information they receive from other sources. Nevertheless, in recognition of the fact that in some areas local and regional media are struggling to survive the Federal Government has already established a Regional and Small Publishers Innovation Fund.

A Range of Views and Voices

There is no doubt that having access to a wide range of high quality news analysis and commentary is beneficial to both the nation and society. It follows that governments have some responsibility, consistent with the principle of non-interference, to ensure its continuing availability. Not all journalism, notably in the entertainment sector, provides a "public benefit".

The definition of "news" can be a vexed issue. Much of what the industry might regard as newsworthy can safely be left to the private sector, although the ABC often seems to see this as core business. Whilst journalism can play a valuable public role in exposing corruption, mismanagement or lesser peccadillos, providing a forum for ideas or campaigning on important policy issues, it does not follow that government has a subsidising role to play. Greeks bearing gifts usually expect some quid pro quo, thereby potentially compromising the integrity of the news provider.

Journalists have an important role, but not necessarily as paid employees of media organisations. The technology revolution now allows us to subscribe online to international stalwarts such as the *Wall Street Journal*, *The London Telegraph* and the *New York Times*. But increasingly top journalists are likely to become subscription bloggers, able to earn more than ever before, while many of their journalistic colleagues see their incomes and job opportunities diminish.

Plurality and Diversity

Plurality is a vague term. It can mean the number of players in a market, their geographical spread or their points of view. Similarly diversity in a media context is often confined to plurality of ownership which in turn seems to boil down to the politics of the proprietors. This is a very easy and fundamentally lazy game to play. Demonising Rupert Murdoch seems to have endless appeal to certain sections of the community. As the ACCC concedes, the term "diversity", as used in the Broadcasting Services Act 1992 relates only to quantitative analysis of media ownership and control and is not used to refer directly to diversity of perspectives, sources or any other factors. Why this should be so in an age of identity politics and obsessions with presenting only one side of important topics, such as climate change and asylum seekers, is hard to understand. A diversity of views is critical to the proper functioning of a democratic society, yet leading bodies such as universities and the ABC see nothing wrong with ignoring or banning views with which they disagree.

These characterisations conveniently ignore the commercial realities. No media outlet is likely to make a profit unless it caters to the broad interests of key segments of viewers, readers or listeners. Former editor-in-chief of *The Australian*, Chris Mitchell, has said that the editorial and op-ed pages of the newspaper are right of centre and its approach is much more focussed on economics and taxation and industrial relations. Some may choose to see these as right of centre issues, but they are nonetheless vital to the health of the economy and society. Such inclinations aside, this has not stopped News from endorsing left wing Labor leaders Gough Whitlam and Kevin Rudd, while in the UK the Murdoch press endorsed Labour's Tony Blair.

On the other hand Nine (formerly Fairfax) newspapers have a special attraction to left of centre readers, many of whom can't get enough of discrimination and racial vilification issues. This cannot simply be ascribed to the political hue of the proprietors themselves. It would be a commercially self-defeating strategy if all media outlets in a given market catered for only one side of politics. As commercial organisations they decide which demographic they can best appeal to and clearly there are readers in both major political camps. At the risk of over-generalisation, the world can be roughly divided into those who relate to the primacy of economics and those who prefer to focus on social issues. Families with children, small business operators, the military and older generations are crude examples of the former whilst students, environmentalists, social justice devotees and post materialists tend to populate the latter group.

It can be argued in broad terms that even if there were only News Ltd and Nine/ABC viewpoints the general public has a clear choice between competing viewpoints. The concept of "fake news" may have been popularised by Donald Trump but it has always been with us, be it the yellow journalism of the late 19th century, the propaganda of the wartime or the excesses of the gutter press, such as the late, unlamented *News of the World*. However the reality in today's online world is that the citizenry has access to a plethora of views across the spectrum and is able to do its own fact checking and site verification.

Trump has already led the way in demonstrating how to bypass traditional media outlets with his ingenious use of Twitter. His personal twitter account now has more than 60 million followers compared to the *New York Times* with around 45 million. The ACCC concedes that "digital platforms have also clearly had positive influences, including lowering certain costs for the production and distribution of journalism." Journalists have also taken advantage of these tools for both news gathering and reporting and will have no choice but to continue to adopt and adapt.

The Future of Journalism

The future of media companies is not as dire as the doomsayers predict. An estimated 90% of publishers' revenue still comes from print, with digital revenue only growing slowly. The Reuters Institute predicts that most of the existing forms of funding for professional journalism will decline as the move to a more digital environment continues apace and digital platforms such as Google and Facebook capture most of the advertising revenues. However, the Institute finds that not only is news more diverse, allowing hitherto marginalised voices to be heard and to access a far wider range of points of view, but the journalism is better than ever.

Whist the ACCC generally takes a pessimistic view of the future of journalism the Institute is more upbeat. Once media organisations were both content creators and access controllers. Now people can access content through platform channels like Facebook or via search engines, social media and news aggregators. As the ACCC reports, by 2018 a world wide survey across 37 different markets identified these new avenues as the main way of finding news online and for those under 35 years of age three quarters did so.

Instead of the negative concept of "atomisation" the Institute finds that these new access lines drive users to more and more diverse sources of information. Fears of "filter bubbles" causing highly motivated minorities to self-select insular news diets "currently seem misplaced." Indeed the great majority of the population surveyed did not access news sites more than once a day. This may be due to limited interest, low engagement, and distrust of news sites but it may also be that people have better things to do, like working for a living, than obsessing about the latest happening. People voting with their feet should not cause regulators to fret.

Perhaps the apparent discrepancy of views can best be explained by understanding that the ACCC has focussed more on the quantity of journalists – a traditional trade union concern – while the Institute takes a more holistic view and is rightly more concerned with preserving the quality of output. The latter is ultimately much more in the long term public interest than attempts to stave off job losses, which now occur in every sector.

In a healthy democracy like Australia there is a public interest in a free flow of accurate information. Quality journalism has a key role to play in the process by exposing wrongdoing or bad practices, risks to national security and personal privacy and the like. But this does not mean that as the number of journalists declines in the face of technological progress there is necessarily a case for government intervention or subsidisation.

The press can play a vital role in exposing scandals and corruption at all levels and it seems that the public appetite for such fare is never ending. If that is the case and the need for investigative journalism is demand-driven, then there is a compelling commercial incentive for a positive response from the news suppliers. This is not to let the big four off the hook, as they can no longer hide behind the shield that they are only purveyors and not carriers of false information. They have the technical capacity to take down offending material and they should be required to do so both speedily and effectively. Since 2014 Google has been required by the EU regulators to delete links from its European search results if it infringes on an individual's "right to be forgotten." Without debating the merits of this issue, it is clear that Google has the technical capacity to delete for it has already complied with more than 1.5m requests to do so.

The National Broadcasters, particularly the ABC

The ABC relies almost entirely on the taxpayer for funds and the Parliament has a duty to ensure that these monies are wisely spent. In the last 10 to 15 years, the commercial broadcasting sector has been under enormous pressure, having had to change formats, styles and charging regimes just to survive in the new, technology-driven world. But the ABC is under no such pressure. Its funding model is like a glorified defined benefit scheme, where performance and employer capacity to pay are irrelevant.

Its annual budget now exceeds $1 billion and can only go one way: up. It is never content with its lot, as evidenced by the extraordinary intervention during the last Federal election campaign of its newly installed managing director, David Anderson, who took it upon himself to go public to effectively argue for a vote for the opposition Labor Party, simply because he wanted more funds. The ABC acts as if it is a natural monopoly – there of right, to be respected and appreciated but never to be scrutinised or critically questioned. Perhaps it should take note of the impact on content of the technological winds of change from which it cannot be immune. In 2018 860,000 British viewers cancelled their TV licences – an 8% increase on the previous year – due to the "Netflix effect."

The ABCs statutory obligations under the *Australian Broadcasting Corporation Act 1983* include the provision of "innovative and comprehensive broadcasting of a high standard" and programs that inform, educate and entertain and which reflect the cultural diversity of the Australian community. It must also promote the arts in Australia, take account of the broadcasting services of the commercial sector and provide a balance between programs of wide and specialised appeal.

The generality of this wording gives the ABC an enormous amount of discretion, virtually *carte blanche*. A billion dollar budget should enable the ABC to commission or purchase high-quality content, be it Australian period drama, history, film remakes of classic or contemporary Australian literature or major political events. But it always seems to have other agendas – digital technology, the youth market or keeping the industrial peace with its large workforce. Despite claims that it does not chase ratings it manages to put on very many lowbrow programs, such as comedy and quiz shows, clearly designed to cater for the casual viewer in competition with the commercial sector.

Most of what is on offer on the ABC is not politically controversial. But Australians are entitled to expect that the great majority of its programs, especially news and current affairs, should be a cut above the commercials. I once suggested to Quentin Dempster, for many years a true in-house warrior, that the ABC should position itself as "the quality alternative to the commercials". He recoiled in horror, for reasons which I don't profess to understand.

The decline over recent years of ABC televisions news and its follow-up program the *7.30 Report* should be a matter of concern to management. In May 2018, faced with viewing numbers down by 100,000 or 12% over the preceding 12 months, the ABC simply proposed more journalist training. The answer should be to get out more and ask the public what it wants. Not so long ago Paul

Keating belled the cat with a typically withering blast that the ABC was failing as a news-gathering organisation and letting Australia down with too many tragic reports of no broader consequence and too many hard luck stories.

The DP Report is not particularly helpful in defining the nature and limits of the role of the national broadcasters, although it is unequivocally supportive of them. It simply asserts that they are the predominant means by which under-provision of journalism has been addressed. This implies that both have proactively responded to such a need whereas their performance is better described as self-interested business as usual. The Report is correct in applauding its contribution to investigative reporting, although it should also be acknowledged that its guaranteed funding makes it much easier for them to do so.

The Report makes no attempt to assess the appropriate level of the ABC budget, let alone suggest what might constitute its recommendation for "adequate" funding. Its concern for the sustainability of commercial news organisations is perfunctory – it simply recognises, in passing, that it is an "important" issue but otherwise offers no guidance or policy advice.

The Report also shows no interest in holding the ABC to account for its, at best, lip service to its Charter obligation to be impartial in its coverage rather than its relentless pursuit of only one side of the argument on big issues such as climate change and asylum seekers. The ACCC seems more interested in airing arguments for even greater protection against unidentified threats to its independence, despite noting that "stakeholders did not raise the independence of the national broadcasters as a significant issue in the context of this Inquiry."

No one I know wants to sell off the ABC, let alone close it down. We all want to be proud of our national broadcasters, not constantly frustrated by a one sided worldview. The ABC could do so much better. Its flagship news programmes are mediocre and not a patch on those of SBS, with its genuine interest in international news and serious commentary. If the ABC sought to cater for mainstream Australia instead of the special interest groups who prefer its relentless diet of soft social items it might regain the ground it once occupied as the journal of record.

But right now it is basically just another player in the media game. Perhaps the Government could consider the structural separation of its news and current affairs program from its other activities. This would enable proper judgments to be made about the quality of each offering, rather than allowing the ABC to conflate the totality of its programming by claiming "everyone loves the ABC." Another approach would be to established a high powered and balanced inquiry to decide the true role of the ABC and what its priorities should be. And, given its overwhelmingly Sydney centric character and values, the Government could follow the lead of the BBC by decentralising its operations.

11

A LIBERAL-CONSERVATIVE APPROACH TO AUSTRALIAN FOREIGN POLICY

JOHN LEE

The concern of international relations is the relationship between individuals, communities, nation-states and other entities such as international institutions. This is of high relevance at a time when there is a global pandemic which raises questions about the appropriate relationship between the individual, one's community, the nation-state, and bodies such as the World Health Organisation. As in domestic politics, there are profound and complex moral and practical questions to consider. On what basis is the obtaining and exercising of authority legitimate? Which entities are entitled to set binding policies and agendas? When are these entities entitled to deploy national resources and even use force?

A related issue is how political traditions such as liberalism and conservatism can be morally and practically applied to foreign affairs. If the alliance between liberals and conservatives in the centre-right Australian Liberal Party is perennially uneasy and their disagreements unresolved or unresolvable, one would expect that same discord be reflected in any purported centre-right approach to foreign policy.

Despite inevitable tensions, the discord need not be so great. The conduct of Australian foreign policy has, and continues to draw from, the foundations of liberalism and conservatism. These twin foundations continue to provide sensible moral and practical guidance for the way one ought to interact with other entities outside Australia.

Such guidance is important because much of the practice of foreign affairs is necessarily reactive and many decisions need to be made quickly. Admittedly poorly named movements also arise suddenly and cannot be ignored, for example populism or nativism versus internationalism. Without any political or moral framework for understanding what we ought to do, decision-makers are likely to lead Australia to adopt positions with consequences that were not intended and even in opposition to our fundamental principles.

Foreign policy and the purpose of government

Classical liberalism holds that the fundamental moral unit is the individual. This is diametrically opposed to collectivist approaches such as communism which holds that the interest of the collective ought to be the moral basis upon which society is organised and governed. Liberals are also deeply uncomfortable with the elevation of 'identity' such as race, religion, gender over that of the individual as they argue that an individual is far more complex and multi-dimensional than identity politics would suggest.

For liberals, protecting and enabling individuals to freely choose the purpose of their life, and how they lead their lives, overrides other principles. When applied to political science, the role of government is to protect and advance the freedom of the individual. This emphasis on the primacy of the individual leads to the liberal's insistence on the inextricable link between democratically elected governments and the legitimacy of that government. Except for the most extreme proponents, liberals accept that what 17th century political scientist Thomas Hobbes referred to as a 'Leviathan' is necessary to organise resources and activity in large communities. This includes the right of that elected 'Leviathan' or government to exercise coercion and impose other forms of punishments.

Unlike Hobbes, liberals do not accept that governments are given absolute and untrammelled rights to exercise power once established. Inextinguishable rights include processes to re-elect or remove governments, most practically through periodic 'free and fair' elections. Liberals also emphasise the importance of institutions such as an independent judiciary and the right to private property, without which the government would invariably descend into tyranny.

Furthermore, liberals are most exercised about protecting the rights of the individual or minority groups over that of the majority. For liberals, the tyrannical government often begins with a sovereign that gives voice to the arbitrary or unjust whims of the majority in that polity. Instead, governments must abide by agreed rules and laws regardless of the popular pressure placed on the former to behave differently.

Note that while liberals take an optimistic view of human beings, they recognise that different wants and needs – and therefore competition – are inevitable. From that competition will invariably arise inequality as there will be winners and losers. Rather than eliminate inequality, as communists attempt to do, liberals seek to regulate how individuals, entities, and in the case of foreign affairs, nations compete. It is for this reason that 'freedom' rather than 'equality' becomes the organising moral principle even if most liberals accept that measures to ensure more equal opportunity and measures to moderate levels of inequality are necessary.

The point remains that the primary interest for liberals when it comes to the purpose of government is to generate and sustain the conditions and institutions under which an individual can strive to lead the 'good life' (as that individual defines it) to the best of his or her abilities rather than to legislate for preconceived outcomes. When that principle is applied to international economic affairs, liberals will point out that the most successful nations with the highest levels of prosperity and achievement and the lowest levels of poverty and turmoil are those countries where economic and political freedoms are high and where there are institutions that place limits on the tenure of governments and the latter's capacity to exercise arbitrary or unfettered power over populations.

Liberals and conservatives: an uneasy alliance?

Prima facie, it might be difficult to see why liberals and conservatives share a political alliance at all. While liberals have an unchanging view of what good and legitimate government looks like – a constitutional liberal democracy that primarily enables the individual to strive and express themselves – conservatives do not inherently put forward any ideal abstraction. While liberals emphasise the fundamental virtue and worth of the individual, conservatives are interested in the value of established institutions and practices – some of which might be liberal in nature and others less so or not at all. Liberalism is premised on a fundamental optimism about human beings – even if they occasionally engage in folly – while conservatives believe institutions and conventions have tended to emerge and evolve to restrain irrational or unbridled inclinations towards various self-destructive vices.

In this country, conservatism is best reflected in the argument by the 18th century statesman and politician Edmund Burke that society is a 'contract' or 'partnership' not only 'between those who are living, but those who are dead, and those who are to be born.' Contrary to frequent caricature of the tradition, conservatism is not inherently opposed to change. But change must occur gradually and through evolution of existing institutions, conventions and practices. This is because such things have been cobbled and crafted together over generations to reflect what meets the preferences of Australians and as a response to what did not work so well and was subsequently altered. The fact that existing institutions, conventions and practices are sometimes seemingly at odds with each other, or have justifications based on myths, obsolete circumstances or even prejudices that are no longer held, does not mean one should quickly do away with them. Generations have adapted in a way which is beneficial or at least satisfactory to them. For conservatives, every successful society is built on a messy patchwork of institutions, conventions and practices. Destroying these to arrive at an elegant or preconceived destination is almost certain to bring disaster rather than progress.

Moreover, evolution or change should arise out of a relentless but gradual bargaining process between all stakeholders in a polity: individuals, communities, provincial and central governments etc. If laws and institutions change too quickly through insistence by any of these stakeholders – or the sidelining of the others – there is little prospect that the deleterious effects of unintended consequences can be mitigated or avoided.

In some countries, liberals would be the revolutionaries or at least disrupters. Given Australia's history and contemporary situation, it is possible to see why liberals – whose fundamental values have shaped the evolution of, and are reflected in the country's institutions and conservatives have become (uneasy) political allies. Australian liberals and conservatives are on the same side when it comes to warning against the overreach of governments, for example when it comes to expansive economic redistributive agendas or legislating for outcomes for which there is little consensus amongst stakeholders. Both approaches are suspicions of an over-emphasis on identity politics: for liberals, it perversely reduces the individual to only one subjectively defined identity; for conservatives, the rush to overturn established institutions and practices in advancing 'identity rights' or 'social justice' without considering the unintended consequences are of concern. Australian foreign policy and a rules-based order

With justification, both major political parties laud the bipartisanship across many issues in foreign affairs. It is true that the most caustic debates are reserved for domestic rather than foreign policy. Even so, liberal and conservative principles discussed above do provide a framework for Australia to respond to major contemporary issues, with enormous ramifications for the country. These include the United States–China relationship and how Australia is positioning itself in this context, attitudes to the US alliance and the growing backlash against globalisation.

In the broadest terms, *the liberal tradition provides a moral and policy compass for the conduct of foreign policy while the conservative tradition offers prudence and pragmatism.* The former offers purpose and the latter wisdom about temperament and when it is important to exercise restraint. Both traditions can co-exist to provide plausible foundations for the ethical exercise of coercion and force over the will of another nation or other entity. Indeed, a strong case can be made that Australian foreign policy is at its finest and most effective when these two traditions are concordant.

Consider the basic direction of Australian strategic policy for the past one hundred years. We have allied ourselves with the leading naval power in the region: first the United Kingdom up to the Second World War and then the US after that. With the emergence of the Chinese People's Liberation Army Navy (PLA Navy) as a challenger to American sea power pre-eminence in the Indo-Pacific, there are increasing calls to reposition ourselves strategically and assume a more equidistant or even neutral stance between the US and China. Although this is not the formal position of the current or recent Labor Party, it is nevertheless true that these calls have largely come from the left-of-centre or progressive side of politics (with the most notable exception being Malcolm Fraser.)

Why have the fiercest resistance to such calls come from liberal-conservative thinkers even if it means taking a far more robust stance against an economic partner such as China? Consider the remarks of General Douglas MacArthur in a broadcast to the American people after the conclusion of the Japanese Surrender Ceremony on 2nd September 1945:

> Various methods through the ages have attempted to devise an international process to prevent or settle disputes between nations... If we do not now devise some greater and more equitable system, Armageddon will be at our door...
>
> To the Pacific basin has come the vista of a new emancipated world. Today, freedom is on the offensive, democracy on the march. Today in Asia as well as in Europe, unshackled peoples are tasting the full sweetness of liberty...

MacArthur's remarks were to prove relevant and prescient for the next seven decades. The post-war period was marked by dramatic transformation in East Asia. The United States established a series of bilateral alliances, most notably with Japan, South Korea and Australia. Security alliances or else arrangements were gradually cobbled together with many of the major maritime states including the Philippines, Thailand, Singapore and Malaysia in addition to a de facto military partnership with Taiwan.

A messy but integrated political and economic system developed around this hub-and-spokes security architecture. America offered capital, know-how and access to its immense consumer market to help East Asian economies back on their feet, or in some cases, to embark on the pathway to modernisation for the first time in their history. East Asian states enjoyed protection, stability and economic access to the US economy in return for supporting the US's geo-strategic presence in the region.

This so-called rules-based order was essentially a liberal hegemonic rules-based order: a system of rules, laws, institutions and treaties underpinned by a liberal superpower offering protection and public goods for all nations agreeing to play by its (the superpower's) rules. The argument that a region dominated by an authoritarian China will fundamentally alter the rules and norms in the region in a manner that will be deeply uncomfortable for liberal-democratic nations is primarily a liberal claim. Just as the post-war order made existence safer for democracies and allowed them to thrive, an order led by an authoritarian power will reset arrangements in a manner which will benefit autocratic regimes and related approaches.

It is also a liberal insight – now appropriated by other political traditions – that habits of cooperation, consultation and compromise are best developed in liberal-democratic systems. Moreover, it is a liberal framework which best articulates the reality of competition and how entities ought to compete in a rule-of-law system. Fairness is not defined in terms of regional or international equality. The US-led rules-based order is fair because that order does not permanently privilege previous winners nor constrain opportunity for newcomers but merely establishes fair rules for how nations compete. Its basic principle is the rule of law where governments, firms and individuals enjoy rights and fulfil obligations regardless of wealth or power. In any competitive environment, it becomes more important that countries abide by and compete according to rules rather than break them.

International politics is an anarchic or self-help system. Importantly, both liberals and conservatives agree that the resilience and success of the post-World War Two order depends on two propositions: first, it must be immensely costly, even prohibitive, for any country to seek to challenge and overturn that order; and second, the benefits to one's national interests of preserving the existing order far exceed the purported benefits of undermining it.

These two propositions can never be taken as granted and the conditions for them to prevail must be constantly attended to and reinforced. To that end, liberal conservatives have emerged as the strongest advocates of Japanese Prime Minister Shinzo Abe's desire to take a more expansive view of Japan's strategic role in the region and are moving ever closer to a quasi-alliance with Tokyo. Liberals are comfortable with the pluralistic values and transparent nature of Japan while conservatives believe that the quasi-alliance with Japan strengthens the existing security architecture and institutions in the region, thereby enhancing stability and resilience of the preferred existing order.

While Australia might have common strategic interests with countries such as Vietnam when it comes to balancing China, liberals will maintain there are inherent limits to the extent to which cooperation and trust is possible with non-liberal democratic nations. Indeed, in the recent *2017 Foreign Policy White Paper*, a striking passage was inserted which had liberal fingerprints all over it: To support a balance in the Indo–Pacific favourable to our interests and promote an open, inclusive and rules-based region, Australia will… work more closely with the region's major democracies. The US, Japan, South Korea, India and India were nominated as the primary candidates.

Moreover, both liberals and conservatives point out that our alliance with the US is a living security relationship which is evolving and adapting as the strategic environment changes. The rise of China and the increase in uncertainty more generally have led both countries to further integrate their militaries and align strategic perspectives and objectives. The US and Australia are doing the same with Japan while countries such as India and Indonesia are moving in similar directions even if they are not committing to the strong balancing and countering postures of Washington, Tokyo and Canberra. In contemporary times, it makes sense to increase rather than lower the costs and risks for a China seeking to revise the existing order.

For conservatives, urgent calls to fundamentally reorder our strategic affairs are viewed with great suspicion and wariness regardless of whether there are any liberal principles or values in play. In particular, the unintended consequences of both placing too much faith in multilateral institutions with broad and aspirational aims that nevertheless lack the power to enforce their own principles and also of resetting our relations with the US in favour of China carry enormous risks for Australia in exchange for highly uncertain or even non-existent rewards.

Fundamental realignment would lead to mostly negative unintended consequences. Our military, strategic and intelligence capabilities would be immediately degraded were we to place less emphasis on the alliance. This means we would begin in this brave new world in a weaker position. Given that almost all maritime countries in the Indo-Pacific want the US to be more, rather than less engaged, the enhanced standing and position Australia enjoys as an American ally of prime importance would be diminished.

Moreover, there is no reason to believe that China's policies towards Australia would become more favourable were we to reorient our strategic bearings. Is China more likely to consider Australian interests in the South China Sea? Would Beijing tone down its export of authoritarian principles and protection for other authoritarian regimes to appease Australian liberal sensibilities? Would the

Communist Party cease its foreign interference and influence operations in Australia or shelve threats of economic punishment and coercion against Australia when disagreements invariably occur in the future? One does not jeopardise a relationship of such unique and immense value with the world's only superpower for such unlikely or unknown benefits.

Conservatives would also remind us that despite rises and falls in the popularity of American Presidents, polls over time consistently show an abiding appreciation and support for our alliance with the US, for the American role in the region, and for developing more intimate relationships with other liberal democracies in the region. That perspective – both informed and the result of received prejudices – forms the basis of a country's strategic and national culture and preferences. That which is the result of trial and error, observation, and practice spanning generations cannot be so easily ignored or dismissed and overturned.

Foreign policy and the sovereignty of the nation state

The newer, and probably more furious debate will be about globalisation, the benefits or otherwise of economic interdependence and lowering obstacles to trade and investment, and multinational or transnational organisations and entities. Even at this early stage, there seems to be a far greater prospect of a serious rift between the liberal-conservative approach on these issues and the so-called progressive approach. This was evident in the 2019 Lowy Lecture delivered by Prime Minister Scott Morrison in October when he referenced the need to avoid a 'negative globalism that coercively seeks to impose a mandate from an often ill-defined borderless global community. And worse still, an unaccountable internationalist bureaucracy.'[81] That speech

---

81 https://www.lowyinstitute.org/publications/2019-lowy-lecture-prime-minis-ter-scott-morrison

was ridiculed by Labor foreign affairs spokesperson Penny Wong as 'disturbingly lightweight' and reminiscent of the 'right-wing nationalism' she attributed to the Donald Trump administration.[82]

It is not an issue that can be dismissed as being raised for 'short-term political gain' as Wong suggests. While one might ultimately disagree with the sentiments expressed by Morrison, he is articulating a perspective on profound and consequential developments that pertain to perennial questions of legitimacy, obligation and governance, and will be of growing interest and pertinence to liberals and conservatives.

At the heart of the debate is the role and purpose of the nation-state. A useful framing of the issue was previously provided by Samuel Huntington, a political scientist seen by many Americans as the greatest of his generation. In 2004, he published an essay introducing a dilemma about globalisation.[83] Huntington observed a growing discord between the views of intellectual and economic elites on the one hand – academics, civil servants, executives in global companies etc. – and the views held by the majority of the American population on the other.

The former – who stood to gain most (but not exclusively) from a globalised world given their education, exposure, connections and superior resources – viewed national boundaries as largely obsolete and in need of further erosion. The latter – sometimes accurately and other times misguidedly so – felt like they were being denied the benefits and were suspicious of promises by elites that they would help governments moderate the malign side-effects of globalisation. Whereas the elites felt the nature and exercise of authority and power was becoming more transnational for the benefit of the world, much of the national population simply felt

---

82 See Paul Karp, "'Disturbingly lightweight': Penny Wong targets Morrison over China and 'negative globalism'," *The Guardian*, 13 October 2019.

83 Samuel Huntington, "Dead Souls: The Denationalization of the American Elite," *The National Interest* March/April 2004.

powerless and left behind.

The COVID-19 pandemic has brought these issues into sharp relief. For liberals and conservatives, the nation-state and related barriers are not simply a historical construct that should waste away just as traditions and older technologies lose their usefulness and fall out of favour. Nations encapsulate, protect and promote a bundle of interests, values and institutions broadly supported by that population. Democracy is the process through which a government earns the right to legitimately represent and advance those interests, values and institutions. If a sovereign democratically elected government gives up its right or capacity to make decisions to that effect, the basis for its legitimacy is diminished.

Some might argue this discussion is a red herring because there is no 'world government' but only global institutions and agreements which sovereign nations freely sign on to. There are few genuinely trans-national entities in the world. Even the Security Council of the United Nations which can authorise the use of force against another state under certain conditions is made up of five permanent member nation-states with a veto and is therefore an exclusive grouping of powerful nations rather than a transnational body.

However, the present concern is not world government but the increasing assertiveness of international entities, bureaucracies and elites that do not bear the responsibility or costs of the policies they advocate. Every policy has direct costs and opportunity costs that might impact on national security and wealth, social cohesion or the existing way of life for segments of one's polity. Consider which entities have the right to make decisions about how societies manage the pandemic: the appropriate balance between social isolation and a lock-down on one hand and keeping the economy going on the other; whether one ought to put an economic 'price' on the life of an individual when it comes to public policy and spending and how that 'price' is calculated; the extent to which individuals can be forced to abide by agreed policies to limit the spread of the virus and by which entities, etc. If those most affected are excluded from voicing their approval or objections, then discord between the two groups Huntington identifies (in admittedly stylised fashion) will grow.

For liberals, the purpose and process of elected government will have been undermined. As far as conservatives are concerned, such external elites are usually unconnected to or disinterested in the institutional and social fabric of the nation-state and community which is best placed to decide through a process of trial and error what is desirable and feasible. The worst errors in governance and policy are those that propose a top-down elegant solution to complex problems. The liberal conservative approach is not to abandon globalisation or internationalism, which is impossible in functional terms, but to preserve the right and ability of sovereign governments to determine the nature and pace of any change through consultation with their own populations and to tailor any prescription to suit the circumstances of particular countries.

Bear in mind that many agendas pursued by international organisations and entities might be well aligned with liberal and/ or conservative perspectives in substance. It is the tendency for such organisations and entities to reject examination by elected governments and their populations as being superfluous or to dismiss the latter's concerns as ignorant, or even worse, wicked which is problematic. For liberals and conservatives, the attitude of international bodies and spokespeople on issues such as border protection and climate change policy are not only gallingly arrogant and intellectually intolerant but contemptuous of political principles of accountability, legitimacy and empirical wisdom.

Policy, consistency, and hierarchy or priorities

Finally, the argument for there being a liberal-conservative approach to foreign policy is not the same as demanding there is always consistency or coherence when it is applied to any concrete issue. As Owen Harries pointed out, a country pursues many goals, many of which have moral and practical worth: justice, peace, freedom, security, prosperity, stability etc.[84] Unless one falsely believes that all these ends are necessarily and always in harmony with each other, choices must be made with respect to priorities. The order of that necessary hierarchy of priorities will vary from occasion to occasion as circumstances change. In the US, that fissure was brought into sharp relief in the debates between liberals (who were really 'muscular' liberals referred to confusingly as neo-conservatives) and conservatives about the desirability and wisdom of whether to launch an invasion of Iraq in 2003 – a disagreement from which the two sides have yet to fully forgive each other.

In the Australian context, there is no such civil war. Liberals might argue that a democratic China with liberal institutions would be far less of a challenge, but conservatives would caution against the folly of any regime change agenda. Democracy promotion can be advanced through our foreign affairs and aid, but conservatives warn that the histories and institutions of countries are *sui generis* and reform driven from without is almost always a fool's errand.

The unpredictability of events means the conduct of foreign policy can never be left on autopilot. The purpose of appealing to liberal and conservative traditions is to provide a framework and mindset for both moral and practical action that will continue to serve Australia well.

---

84 Owen Harries, "Morality and Foreign Policy," *Policy* 21:1 2005, p. 29.

12

THE PUBLIC SERVICE
A SERVICE TO AUSTRALIA?

Scott Prasser

Introduction

A competent, corrupt-free, merit-based and, as much as possible, apolitical and independent public service is the cornerstone of any successful government and society. It is the bedrock of a modern democracy. It is what ultimately distinguishes civilised societies from those still run on the whim of an all-too powerful leader, or from those governed by vested interests and patronage that dispense public goods unfairly depending on who you know or what group you belong to rather than on clearly identified needs and due process.

An effective public service is as much a guardian of taxpayers' resources as parliament. A public service that is able to give 'frank and fearless' advice to elected governments, based on expertise, experience, and a concern with the public interest, rather than just partisan hegemony by the government of the day, will contribute significantly to good government, governance and policy. Dictatorial governments can succeed for a time, but without an independent competent public service they ultimately fail as they succumb to the mistakes caused by leaders's hubris and whims. A sycophantic public service, no matter how competent administratively, will eventually find itself implementing, without an opportunity to voice any warnings, wasteful and even harmful programs.

This brief chapter reviews the Australian public service and its place in the functioning of our democracy. By public service we mean both the Commonwealth Public Service (now called the Australian Public Service – APS) and those serving the six states and two territories. By 'public service' we include the core government departments under direct ministerial direction and responsibility that are funded from government budgets. This also includes many other government agencies and advisory and regulatory bodies that are also so funded. In addition, there are semi-autonomous statutory agencies and corporations or government business enterprises (GBEs), many of which generate their own income from sales of services. Although at arm's length from day-to-day government direction, GBEs are managed by government appointed chairs, councils and boards, and have to meet government service and financial targets.

This chapter argues that Australia, with a few exceptions, has been served well by its public services, both Commonwealth and State. Services ranging from health, education, social welfare, communications, transport, and other areas have been delivered over a vast country with a small population relatively efficiently and effectively, and with better outcomes than in many other developed countries. This has been achieved under a regime of relatively low government spending and taxation[85] which makes it an even more impressive success story. It reflects what has been described as Australian 'exceptionalism.'[86] While acknowledging

---

85 OECD, *Government at a Glance*, OECD, Paris, 2015 and 2019
86 Willian Coleman, "The Australian Exception," in William Coleman (ed), *Only in Australia. The History, Politics and Economics of Australian Exceptionalism*, Oxford University Press, Oxford, 2016, pp. 1-16.

influences from the United Kingdom, United States and Canada, Australia has forged its own successful forms of government, economic development, and civil society. Our public services have been an integral and essential part of this success; they too have been 'exceptional' in many ways.

The focus of this chapter is to highlight the key features of our public services and to consider whether changes that have occurred in the last few decades will diminish its contribution to Australia's ongoing success. For instance, has the drive for managerialism, neoliberalism, and New Public Management (NPM)[87] made our public services too thin and under-resourced? Have the never-ending demands for more and more accountability and external mechanisms, like anti-corruption bodies and the growth in administrative law and courts, made the public service even more cautious and robbed it of any risk-taking and entrepreneurial abilities? Have these, and the demands for ever more consultation in an increasingly fragmented society, made it just so much harder for the public service to implement programs in a timely and economical fashion? Have demands that the public service be 'responsive' to the elected governments of the day undermined the public service's ability to give 'frank and fearless' advice? While organisational change, review, and 'reform' have been important in keeping the public service up to the mark, have they become too frequent, losing sight of core objectives, thereby becoming an end in itself? Has the massive expansion of politically appointed ministerial staff to assist ministers undermined ministerial-public servant relationships and confused accountability? Have the demands for a more representative bureaucracy in the 1970s – and now for an 'inclusive' public service – undermined the merit principle that was once regarded as the cornerstone of our political

---

87 For an excellent summary see: Isi Unikowski and John Wanna, "The Public Sector," in Peter Chen *et al* (eds), *Australian Politics and Policy*, University of Sydney Press, Sydney, 2019, pp. 124-141.

neutral, anonymous and independent Westminster public service that had the competence and the wherewithal to give what used to be called 'frank and fearless' advice to politicians?

Of course, there is an alternative view that many of these changes have been for the better. The public service is doing more with less. Technology is being harnessed as never thought possible in delivering services. New organisational forms outside the traditional public services structures are ensuring citizens receive faster and better support than ever before. Government is now more 'joined-up' and less territorial than previously. Reviews and reorganisations have kept the public service in sync with its external environment. External review bodies have removed the corrupt, improved accountability, reduced waste, and increased community trust. Lateral recruitment and less permanency for senior staff have improved access to more talent. Increased policy centralisation in prime ministers' and premiers' departments has allowed better whole-of-government coordination and ended the departmental fiefdoms and demarcation wars of the past. Policies aimed at 'inclusion' have made the public service more representative of the society it seeks to serve and thereby made it easier to implement policies. And, after all, why shouldn't the public service be more responsive to a democratically elected government's policy priorities and have its ideas questioned by politically appointed ministerial staff committed to a government's policy goals? [88]

These are the issues this chapter will consider. However, before proceeding it is important to understand the nature of Australian government and its federal structure, and how Australia's history, geography, and demography have affected the shape, focus, and role of the public service in this country.

---

[88] Many of these views can be seen in an excellent summary by Patrick Weller, "Policy Professionals in Context: Advisors and Ministers," in Brian Head and Kate Crowley (eds), *Policy Analysis in Australia*, Policy Press, Bristol, 2015, pp. 23-36.

Some key influences

Australia, unlike the United States or Canada, was essentially established by government. Historically, Australia was an administered state run by civil servants from the Colonial Office in London who appointed the governors to oversee each colony, and who were assisted by clerks, police, and other officials to administer, establish order, and develop each colony. They were all essentially career public servants. The 'state' was here from the beginning of Western settlement. State ownership and the exercise of responsibilities occurred on a far greater scale than in Britain or elsewhere. This, combined with Australia's geography, vast size, and distance, small population, and lack of private capital, meant the 'state' initiated, owned, and operated a vast number of enterprises. Private enterprise either failed or had to be supported by government subsidies or the granting of monopoly standing.

This was called "colonial socialism". It was partly ideologically driven, given the growth of trade unionism and Labour parties, but it was a more pragmatic necessity given Australia's geography. In 1930, historian Keith Hancock described Australia as a "vast public utility"[89] with some state governments owning butcher shops, jam factories (hence *State* jam in Queensland), quarries, and timber mills. As Jonathan Pincus says, "Australian colonists looked to government more keenly than elsewhere in the Empire"[90] and consequently by "1890 the Australian colonies collectively operated by far the largest government-built, government-owned and government operated railway system in the world".[91] The involvement of Australian governments in running so many public enterprises provoked political scientist Alan Davies to remark that:

---

89   Keith Hancock, *Australia*, Benn, London, 1930.
90   Jonathan Pincus, "Socialism in Six Colonies: The Aftermath," in Coleman, *Only in Australia*, p. 168.
91   Pincus, "Socialism in Six Colonies," p. 166.

The characteristic talent of Australians is not for improvisation, nor even for republican manners; it is for bureaucracy. We take a somewhat hesitant pride in this, since it runs counter not only to the archaic and cherished image of ourselves as an ungovernable, if not actually lawless people; but more importantly because, we have been trained in the modern period to see our politics in terms of liberalism which accords to bureaucracy only a small and rather shady place. Being a good bureaucrat is, we feel, a bit like being a good forger.[92]

Australia's colonies developed at a time when the major reforms flowing from the Northcote-Trevelyan Report (1854) were only just starting to be absorbed in Westminster and hence were not fully transmitted to Australia. Consequently, colonial public services, like the pre-reformed British civil service, were more prone to patronage and corruption – a feature that was to continue despite a number of royal commissions across the different colonies during the 1890s.[93]

The Commonwealth Public Service (CPS) came into being in January 1903 with the passing of the *Commonwealth Public Service Act 1902*. While imbued with the principles of the reformed Westminster civil service, the new CPS had some important variations. Its all-encompassing legislation was influenced by North American practice and reflected "the spirit of scientific management".[94] There was no UK legislative counterpart. Nor did the British Civil Service have a powerful statutory Public Service Commissioner (under the formidable Duncan McLachlan), like the Commonwealth's, to oversee personnel matters. Early access by public servants to conciliation and arbitration in Australia's unique industrial relations system also set Australia apart from Westminster.

---

92 Alan Davies, *Australian Democracy*, Longmans, Melbourne,1958, p. 3.
93 Habib Zafarullah, *Public Service Inquiries and Administrative Reforms in Australia, 1895-1905*, PhD Thesis, Department of Government, University of Sydney, 1986.
94 John Nethercote, "Australia's Distinctive Governance," in Coleman, *Only in Australia*, p. 283.

Influenced more by the United States and Canada than Westminster, Australia adopted a federal system bound together by a written Constitution with responsibilities divided between the national government (the Commonwealth) and the six states (the two territories of the ACT and NT came much later). Local government is not provided for in the Constitution[95] and remains firmly under the control of the States.

The result of the new federation was not just two public services – the Commonwealth and the States – but seven (now nine). Each state public service developed at a different time with its own particular interpretations of the British model. Moreover, despite the original constitutional division of powers and responsibilities, there quickly followed from federation some necessary interactions between the Commonwealth and the States with numerous intergovernmental processes, agreements, and institutions.[96] Indeed, the Constitution (Section 101) envisaged there would be an Interstate Commission to cover trade issues, but it hardly operated and soon became defunct.[97]

The Premiers' Conference, started by the States prior to federation, became increasingly important from the 1920s given increasing Commonwealth domination of finances. It was chaired by the prime minister and, during the 1930s, was pivotal in co-ordinating Australia's response to the Great Depression (the Premiers' Plan).[98] By 1992, the Premiers' Conference had become the Council of Australian Governments (COAG) with over a dozen standing ministerial councils, and even a Reform Council to monitor agreements (abolished by the Abbott Government in 2014).

---

95 The federal Hawke Labor Government's 1988 referendum to give constitutional recognition to local government failed dismally.

96 Jack Richardson, *Patterns of Australian Federalism*, Research Monograph No 1, Centre for Research on Federal Financial Relations, ANU, Canberra, pp. 114-122.

97 Richardson, *Patterns of Australian Federalism*, pp. 71-82

98 Campbell Sharman, *The Premiers' Conference: An Essay in Federal – State Interaction*, Occasional Paper No 13, ANU, Canberra, 1977.

In the wake of the recent pandemic crisis, COAG is now being transformed again with Prime Minister Scott Morrison wanting a more direct, streamlined intergovernmental process.

However, one of the consequences of the federal system has been the increasing duplication of agencies and services between the levels of government. For a combination of political, financial, policy and legal reasons, the Commonwealth has increasingly intruded into areas that were previously the sole constitutional responsibility of the States (such as education and health). The Commonwealth's larger financial resources (it collects 80 per cent of all taxes), and its ability to use Section 96 to fund the states on any area of policy, have been key drivers. As a result, there are now Commonwealth *and* State departments of education, transport, agriculture, health, natural resources, environment, and even local government. Attempts to rectify this, by transferring functions and tackling the imbalance in federal-state taxes, never make much progress, as the failure of the most recent effort, the Abbott Government's 2015 *Reform of the Federation Green Paper*, clearly shows.

A further consequence of the federal system is that government functions, and therefore public sector employment, are distributed across the three levels of government. Contrary to popular perceptions, the Commonwealth is not the major public sector employer: the states and territories are. Indeed, as **Table 1** shows, the Commonwealth only employs about 12 per cent of all government employees (in 1988 it was 25 per cent)[99] compared to the States' 79 per cent and local government's 9.4 per cent.[100] The figures cover all public sector employees, including those

---

99   This decline reflected the considerable privatisation that has occurred since then by successive Labor and Coalition governments eg Commonwealth Bank, Qantas, and Telstra.

100   See Australian Bureau of Statistics (ABS), *6248.0.55.002: Employment and Earnings, Public Sector*, Australia, 2018-19.

from government departments, public corporations, universities, non-profit institutions controlled by the government, government marketing boards, legislative courts, municipal authorities and other statutory authorities. However, if considering only employment in the Commonwealth's current 18 departments and 80 agencies, employee numbers are just over 147,000 in 2018-19[101] - considerably less than the 242,000 in **Table 1**.

Despite the Commonwealth's financial dominance, and dependence by the States for about 50 per cent of their revenue from that source, the States are not totally subservient to Commonwealth demands. The States do have the ability to make important policy initiatives of their own and have varied spending priorities.[102] After all, the States have primary responsibility for resource development, environment and conservation, education (except universities), health (especially hospitals), law and order, and social services delivery. Their GBEs cover key areas of infrastructure: roads, rail, ports, much electricity generation, gas, and water supply. Many of the problems with public sector performance in Australia are primarily the responsibility of the States, but the public and the media remain confused about which tier of government is responsible for what.

Table 1: Public Sector employees June 2019

	'000
Commonwealth	242.1
States	1,610.6
Local government	194.0
Total	2,046.7

Source: ABS-6248.0.55.002 - Employment and Earnings, Public Sector, Australia, 2018-19

---

101   Australian Public Service Commission, *State of the Service Report 2018-19*, Commonwealth of Australia, Canberra, 2019, 'APS at a Glance,' p. vi

102   Nicholas Aroney, Scott Prasser and Alison Taylor, "Federal Diversity in Australia: A Counter Narrative," in Gabriel Appleby, Nicholas Aroney, and T John (eds), *The Future of Australian Federalism*, Cambridge University Press: Cambridge, 2012, pp. 272-299.

Issues

At the outset, this chapter outlined a number of issues concerning the public service in Australia. Some of the issues concerning the impact and problems of federalism and intergovernmental coordination have already been addressed. However, some key issues, in particular, are now examined in more detail.

Size and growth of the public sector in Australia

One of the complaints about the federal system is that the overlap of functions has led to an overly large public sector characterised by excessive growth. Again, the Commonwealth is usually the target of this criticism. Related to this is that total Australian government spending and taxation is too high. Overall however, Australia does not have a large public sector compared to other developed countries in the OECD. Indeed, despite our federal system, total Australian public sector employment is below the OECD average.

Certainly, depending on particular situations (such as war) and particular governments, (usually – but not only – Labor administrations), Commonwealth public service growth has, at times, been high. The last decade highlights this. Numbers grew annually under the Rudd-Gillard-Rudd governments (2007-2013). However, from 2014-2017 under Coalition governments, direct public service employment fell by 9 per cent.[103] From 2017-18 there was a decline by 0.9 per cent and a further fall of 2.1 per cent from 2018-2019. The trend is clear: the Commonwealth Public Service is getting smaller.

However, for a variety of reasons, the record of the states and territories, in terms of containment of public sector growth, has long been less impressive. One reason is that many of the states

---

103 Australian Public Service Commission, *State of the Service Report 2016-17*, Commonwealth of Australia, Canberra, p. 5.

have resisted privatisation and the efficiencies and improved personnel practices this can afford. Because the states are very much in direct service delivery, such as in education and health where they employ large numbers of teachers and nurses, there is ongoing public pressure for more staff. Further, in these areas, and in many GBEs, they remain the last bastions of unionism; and if Labor is in office, these unions are integral to the party's structure.

Retention and expansion of staff, rather than cutting numbers, is the name of the game. This is exemplified by recent developments in Queensland. After 14 years of Labor administrations in Queensland, the incoming Newman LNP Government appointed a Commission of Audit which found runaway public debt, unsustainable public service growth, and considerable inefficiencies in state GBEs.[104] The Newman Government initiated spending cuts and extensive public servant redundancies, and attempted privatisation. In a state where the Queensland Government is the single largest employer, with many regional branches, these efforts were seen as going too far, too quickly. The electorate backlash resulted in the Newman Government losing office after only one term. Since then, Labor has embarked on expansion of the public service across a range of areas regardless of the state's financial situation, and without any attempt to achieve other efficiencies.[105] Public service growth in Queensland currently accounts for 40 per cent of the total states' growth in this sector. Privatisation remains off the agenda.

Unrelenting change – the coming of New Public Management

Anyone who thinks the public services are still havens of stability and glacier-like change should think again. They used to be; and

---

104   Queensland Commission of Audit, Report, Queensland Government Printer, Brisbane 2013.

105   Sarah Elks, "Queensland Treasurer breaks own rules on public service jobs," *The Australian*, 9 June 2017.

a more stable political environment supported this slower pace. Governments nationally and across the States held office for long periods and changes in governments were less frequent.[106] This is not to say there were not many challenges, crises, or issues to manage. There were. However, public service change was more incremental, largely internally driven and no less important.

The long-standing Coalition federal government (1949-72) rejected suggestions for a major royal commission to review the Commonwealth Public Service despite similar developments in New Zealand, UK, Canada, Ireland, and the United States. Perhaps Patrick Weller was correct when he observed that "the rhythm of government was different"[107] in those times. Economic and social pressures were less urgent, expectations of government were lower, media coverage was more limited, and thus there was a reduced need for more government policies with accompanying administrative support.

The watershed for widespread public service change in Australia occurred with the election of the federal Whitlam Labor Government in December 1972. Whitlam came to office with an ambitious program for social change and institutional renovation – and for constitutional reform too. It appointed over 70 public inquiries and 13 royal commissions, that extended Commonwealth involvement into more and more new areas, including many where the States had the prime constitutional responsibility (such as in education, urban affairs, environment, local government).

One royal commission that had a major impact on the public service was the *Australian Post Office Commission of Inquiry*. Its

---

106 Nationally the Coalition held office from 1949-1972; Across the States: Coalition in Queensland 1957-1989; Victoria, Liberals 1955-1982; Liberals in NSW 1965-1976; South Australia Liberal and Country League, 1938-1965; WA Liberals 1959-1971; Labor dominated Tasmanian politics since the 1930s with only intermittent Liberal incursions.

107 Weller, "Policy professionals in context," p. 25.

recommendations led to the abolition of the Post Master General's Department (PMG) that had been one of the seven original departments at federation and the largest employer (over half). Its functions were transferred to two statutory authorities (now Australia Post and Telstra). These staff were no longer employed under the *Public Service Act*. The Commonwealth Public Service was reduced by 120,000 overnight and as one commentator said, its character altered forever.[108]

The second review was the more traditional, all-encompassing *Royal Commission on Australian Government Administration* that many had wanted since the late 1950s. Chaired by long-term public servant, by now retired, Dr HC Coombs, it reported to Whitlam's successor – the Fraser Government. Its value has been hotly contested by both adherents and critics, but the overall assessment is that its impact was greater than first appears, less because of its specific recommendations that were accepted, than as a result of the information it released and the debates it started.[109]

The real long-term impact of the Whitlam Government was that it let the genie out of the bottle and inaugurated a new era – an era of ongoing change, peppered by numerous external and internal reviews – one characterised by bureaucratic reconfigurations, restructuring and reorganisations, and which marked the beginning of the fragmentation of the Commonwealth Public Service. Departments became impermanent led by heads who were themselves no longer permanent (see below). Never-ending change, too readily labelled 'reform', became the norm. It was what 'good' governments were supposed to do – left and right, federal and state.

---

108   Paddy Gourley, "Inquiring into government administration," in Scott Prasser and Helen Tracey, *Royal Commissions and Public Inquiries: Practice and Potential,* (Connor Court:: Ballarat, 2014) , pp. 205-6.

109   Gourley, "Inquiring into government administration," pp. 216-221.

After the Whitlam Government, successive Commonwealth administrations each held their own public reviews and made further changes. The Fraser Coalition Government appointed the non-public Administrative Review Committee under Sir Henry Bland[110] and then the more open Reid Review.[111] The Hawke-Keating Labor Government released a public service reform policy paper[112], re-vamped the Public Service Act, and initiated, in 1987, a major amalgamation of departments. The Howard Coalition Government appointed the National Commission of Audit[113] and released a major paper on public service reform[114] and made ruthless cuts during the first half of its time in office. The Rudd Labor Government appointed the Moran Review.[115] The Abbott Coalition Government established the Commission of Audit, while Abbott's successor, Malcolm Turnbull, ordered the Thodey Review[116] that reported in 2019 to the Morrison Government. The obsession with public service change and reform continues unabated. The latest Commonwealth Public Service Commission *State of Service* report babbles excruciatingly and enthusiastically about how "hard work on public service reform is ... taking place to ensure the Australian Public Service can meet the challenges ahead, with strong momentum for change across the service".[117] But will my Newstart payment arrive on time?

There were also, at this time, parallel changes at the state level with

---

110 Roger Wettenhall and Paddy Goruley, "Sir Henry Bland and the Fraser Government's Administrative Review Committee: Another Chapter in the Statutory Wars? *Australian Journal of Public Administration*, Vol 68, No 3, September 2009, pp. 351-69.

111 *Review of Commonwealth Administration*, AGPS, Canberra, 1983.

112 John Dawkins MP, *Reforming the Australian Service: A Statement of the Government's Intentions*, AGPS, Canberra, 1983

113 Kate Jones and Scott Prasser, *Audit Commissions: Reviewing the Reviewers*, Connor Court: Ballarat, 2013.

114 Peter Reith, *Towards a Best Practice Australian Public Service*, AGPS, Canberra, 1996.

115 *Ahead of the Game: Blueprint for the Reform of Australian Government Administration* (Moran Review)

116 *Independent Review of the Australian Public Service* (Thodey Review)

117 Australian Public Service Commission, *State of the Service Report 2018-19*, p. 2.

many reviews, some mimicking the Commonwealth initiatives, others leading the Commonwealth. State administrative reform was to get a particular boost from the 1980s, not experienced at the federal level, by a series of financial, administrative, and corruption scandals which were exposed by high profile royal commissions and inquiries. These caused new institutional arrangements that had a large impact on the public service and included new permanent anti-corruption bodies and integrity arrangements; expanded freedom of information laws; whistleblower protection legislation; public servant and ministerial codes of conducts; and tighter pecuniary interest requirements. The importance of these developments in reshaping state public administrations cannot be underestimated.[118]

These developments also gave further impetus to expansion of the 'new administrative law' that had been under gradual development since the Gorton Government appointed in 1969 the *Commonwealth Administrative Review* under Sir John Kerr, later Governor-General.[119] That Review was concerned with the wide-ranging statutory discretions of public officials. Federally, it led to the development of the ombudsman, administrative appeals tribunals, and freedom of information laws. While these changes enhanced the rights of citizens in dealing with government, they have also placed public servants under greater scrutiny, spawned a host of new bodies, slowed decision making, and added to administrative costs. These issues have been further exacerbated across the states by the aforementioned anti-corruption bodies which have strong coercive powers and, while in a few cases have exposed high level corruption, have inevitably been tied with investigating minor complaints of no worth. A independent review of one State's anti-

---

118   See – Janet Ransley, "Public Inquiries into political wrongdoing,", pp, 43-54; Charles Stamford, "Royal Commission into integrity systems," in Prasser and Tracy, pp. 55-76.

119   John Kerr, Chairman, Commonwealth Administrative Review Committee, *Report*, Commonwealth Government Printer, Canberra, 1971.

corruption body found that:

> A substantial proportion of complaints typically do not call for any substantive response, being frivolous or vexatious or containing minor, repetitive, or incoherent matter. Many others contain allegations which, upon further scrutiny are simply not substantiated or for other reasons do not warrant any further action.[120]

The review believed there had developed a "burgeoning and excessive 'integrity industry'"[121] in the state tying up too many resources for little value. The Commonwealth should be wary of establishing a similar anti-corruption regime as now encompassing all the states. The evidence for such a body has yet to be established.

Overall, at the Commonwealth level, there has been considerable bipartisan support for the reorganisations, consolidations, commercialisations, outsourcing, hiving off, privatisation, focus on outputs and performance measures, and on other private sector techniques that have been categorised as 'managerialism' and which form part of the new public management (NPM) driven by the neoliberal policy agenda of smaller, more accountable government.[122]

While many of these changes have been of value, the constancy of change, the sometimes haphazard and destructive manner way in which it has been implemented, and the drama surrounding each incarnation of the 'reform' agenda, has not been without costs. Organisation change takes time. Work is disrupted. Benefits take considerable time to show – if at all. Careers go on hold. As March observed, "Most change ...results from ... relatively stable routine processes that relate organisations to their environments".[123] Smith

---

120 Review of the Crime and Misconduct Act 2001 (Qld), *Report*, Queensland Government, Brisbane, March 2013, p. 114.
121 Review of the Crime and Misconduct Act, p. 204.
122 Unikowski and John Wanna, "The Public Sector," pp. 124-141.
123 James March, "Footnotes to Organisational Change," *Administrative Science Quarterly*, Vol 26, No 4, December, 1981, p. 564.

and Weller might have been correct to conclude that in the 1950s and 1960s "there was too little analysis of the institutions and processes of government".[124] Now we have too much.

Perhaps the worst aspect of all this change, this restructuring, this beheading of department heads, is that it has undermined the one key value of any bureaucracy: experience, records, and organisational memory. That has now been lost. The public service is no longer good at being a good bureaucracy. Organisational amnesia[125] has become endemic across the public services. It has forgotten what works, and what doesn't.

Politicisation of the public service

The essence of the Westminster system, as it applies to the public service, came from the aforementioned the 1854 Northcote-Trevelyan Report. Its purpose was to:

> ... obtain full security for the public that none but qualified persons will be appointed to [all the public establishments], and that they will afterwards have every practicable inducement to the discharge their duties.[126]

Northcote-Trevelyan brought an end to patronage in the British Civil Service where positions were treated like pieces of property to be bought and sold, or to be used by governments as favours to their supporters whom the Report described as those who were "unambitious ...indolent or incapable." It wanted the Civil Service to be filled with an "efficient body of permanent officers" – selected on merit by an entrance exam and working to high

---

124   Robert Smith and Patrick Weller, "The Bureaucracy Royal Commission – A Chance for Change," *Contemporary Australian Management*, July, 1975, p. 26.

125   Christopher Pollitt, "Institutional Amnesia: A Paradox in the 'Information Age'?" *Promethus*, Vol 18, No 1, 2000, pp. 5-16

126   S. Northcote and C.E. Trevelyan, *Report on the Organisation of the Permanent Civil Service*, Her Majesty's Stationery Office, London, 1854, p1

standards of independence, probity and non-political alignment. This meant public servants could serve whatever government was in power with equal dedication and efficiency.

It was adopted in Australia with some variations – some already mentioned. At the Commonwealth level the Public Service Commissioner, later the Public Service Board, ensured integrity of recruitment practices and handled all personnel matters like promotion, dismissal, and pay. As Wiltshire wrote, in Australia "great pains [were] taken to remove any hint of political interference with recruitment and promotion of public servants".[127] The aim was to ensure the public service "should be in the position to provide fearless and impartial advice to the government of the day".[128]

There are criticisms of this approach. Recruitment was from too narrow a background. It prevented lateral recruitment from industry and university. There were issues of trust when governments changed. This problem confronted the Menzies Coalition Government when it won office in 1949 after nearly a decade in the political wilderness. It had to decide if it would keep many of Labor's appointees – it did.[129] The same issue faced the Whitlam Government when it came to office after 23 years in opposition, but its reactions were different and would set the pattern for all subsequent governments: it wanted a 'responsive' public servant attuned to its social reform agenda, and new blood.

The result is that these days notions of permanency for senior staff are gone. They have been replaced by fixed term contracts, performance targets and incentives. Governments directly make senor appointments. Incoming governments frequently dismiss

---

127 Ken Wiltshire, *An Introduction to Australian Public Administration*, Cassell, North Melbourne, 1973, p. 170.

128 Wiltshire, *An Introduction*, p. 171.

129 See Elaine Thompson's "Menzies and the Public Service," paper presented to, *Menzies Era Conference*, ANU and USQ, ANU, Canberra, 10-11 November 1994 – quoted with permission.

the senior staff appointed by the previous regime. Sometimes they do this immediately – as John Howard did when he sacked 40 per cent of the departmental secretaries within his first 100 days. Others act more cautiously. And as we have seen, even when the same government remains in office, succeeding leaders also make changes reflecting their assessment of senior public servant in terms of their political agenda. Turnbull made changes to Abbott's selections, and Morrison, likewise, initiated further alterations to public servant appointments on becoming prime minister.

So, Australia has moved from Westminster notions of limited government involvement in senior appointments to a more direct Washington style hands on control – 'Washminster', but without the checks and balances provided by the American Senate confirmation process. These new arrangements are now an accepted part of both Federal and State public sectors. Whether the quality of advice has declined because of these developments is a matter for debate. However, Professor Gary Banks, formerly head of the Productivity Commission and the Australian New Zealand School of Government, argues that public service policy and analytical capabilities have declined.[130]

Added to these long-standing, politically driven appointments, there is a need to consider how current trends about gender quotas will affect the competency and perceived trust in the public service in the future. This is a debate too few are willing to have. It seems we are moving backwards to a new form of patronage. It will only get worse. It will have the same adverse effects on the quality of public administration as the one the Northcote-Trevelyan report sought to end over 160 years ago.

---

130   Gary Banks, "Public Inquiries, Public Policy and the Public Interest," *Inaugural Peter Karmel Lecture in Public Policy*, ANU, Canberra, 3 July 2012,

Conclusions

Perhaps we should conclude with what Robert Menzies, Australia's longest serving prime minister, had to say about the public service after leaving office:

> If you were to ask me what I thought the most deep-seated fault in Australia I would unhesitatingly reply that the old notion of disinterested public service has almost disappeared and that politics has come to be merely regarded as a war of interests in which much loot is to be won from the defeated.[131]

Menzies practised what he preached. He kept most of the senior public servants inherited from Labor and adhered to strict Westminster principles of an apolitical public service throughout his term in office. Australia prospered. Respect held.

Overall, our public services have served us well. They have evolved, improved, and become part of the Australian success story. Their flaws are rarely of their own making but, inevitably, are ones imposed on them by our political leaders and an ever-demanding society. Gerald Caiden summed it up, thus:

> Administrative reform deals with the administrative side of government, of the public sector ... While it can improve political decision making, it cannot reverse political decisions. And it is political decisions which are largely responsible for poor government performance, many public sector deficiencies, and much public maladministration. Political leaders make dumb decisions which are administratively disastrous. No amount of administrative reform can remedy such errors, although innocent public administrators will be blamed and will be expected miraculously to produce good out of bad.[132]

---

131 Quoted in Hon Matthew Mason-Cox, Legislative Council, NSW Parliament, 14 November 2006.
132 Gerald Caiden, *Administrative Reform Comes of Age*, Walter de Gruyter, Berlin, 1991, p. 11.

13

RELIGIOUS FREEDOM

Denis Dragovic

Israel who? It seems a lifetime ago that the rugby great was in the courts and on the news fighting for his right to preach the Bible in the age of social media. The debates over religious freedom seem to also occupy some distant past. Yet it wasn't that long ago that the issue preoccupied the minds of many around the country. Now it's largely forgotten. The left did say that it was an unnecessary indulgence. Maybe they were right. Maybe for some, religious freedom was a plaything that a society coddled by wealth and security could afford to tinker with. Then the pandemic hit, and religious freedom is no longer on the agenda. But is there something in protecting religious freedom that would serve us all even during crises?

The answer to this question is yes and it's a largely untold story. The religious freedom debate was centred on the law. Its proponents wanted to rewrite the law. Its detractors spoke of how the law would threaten them. Getting the law right is important, but it's just a small part of what needs to be done for society to benefit from the universal human right of freedom of religion. The more important and difficult part, is outlined in this chapter.

There is today a growing hostility to religious voices being heard in the public square. The lawfare against the powerful is daunting to the average parishioner. He or she finds the indecipherable codes of conduct intimidating. The passionate and powerful can take the risk and wait for the inevitable backlash as they are well prepared to weather the storm. For the worshipper with a mortgage and three kids every step is a tentative one. Can I post a meme about the merits of traditional marriage? Can I ask for time off in the middle of the day to pray? What if I don't want to wear a rainbow lanyard?

It's for these people that religious freedom needs to be protected and it is with these people that the protection of religious freedom begins. To secure a place for religious freedom in our society Australians will need to be convinced that it is worth protecting. As the Prime Minister rightly recognized, 'it's not the laws that make freedom of religion work, it's the culture that accepts it.'[133] Freedoms need to be wanted and valued by the people. The human right to religious freedom is only secure if people recognize the important positive role religious belief has played and continues to play in our society.

In this chapter I will outline what needs to be done by explaining first, why religious freedom is important, followed by how religious freedom is being threatened and finally, what should be done about it.

Why is religious freedom important?

There are three arguments on which advocates of religious freedom base their position. Firstly, that religious freedom is a right given by God inherent to all humans, secondly, that it is a fundamental right in international human rights law and lastly, that it is necessary for a liberal society.

---

133 Matt Coughlan and Rebecca Gredley, 'Keep religious freedom law simple: senator' *The Canberra Times*, 10 July 2019

These are either circular arguments or obscure to most people. How does it impact me if Australia doesn't adhere to an international human right? Why does it matter if someone's concept of a liberal society isn't fully met? For most people these are academic debates leaving them no less convinced of the value of religious freedom. They may have sympathy for tradition or some semblance of faith, but these arguments don't change people's minds, nor will they mobilise people to protect the right to practice a faith.

There is a simpler argument, one that is relevant to everyone especially when times are tough: a strong religious community is good for everyone including non-believers and society more broadly.

The *Handbook on Religion and Health*, an Oxford University Press publication, finds that religious commitment:

> ... (is) often related to a healthier diet, greater physical activity and exercise, less severe alcohol abuse/dependence, less cigarette smoking, less psychological stress, lower anxiety, less depression, more positive emotions ... greater social support and integration, and positive personality traits.[134]

Religious people are also more likely to be happy. In the book *Gross National Happiness*, Arthur Brooks writes, 'There is an immense amount of data on this subject, and it indicates conclusively that religious people really are happier and better off emotionally than their secular counterparts.'[135] Rodney Stark, a professor of sociology, explains that religious people are less likely to get a divorce or drop out of school, and more likely to contribute to charities and have superior mental health.[136]

---

134 Harold G. Koenig, Dana E. King, Verna Benner Carson, *Handbook of religion and health*, Oxford: Oxford University Press, 2012

135 Arthur C. Brooks, *Gross national happiness: why happiness matters for America--and how we can get more of it*, Basic Books, New York, 2008

136 Rodney Stark, *America's Blessings: How Religion Benefits Everyone Including Atheists*, Templeton Press, West Conshohocken, 2012

It is not just individual believers who benefit but nonbelievers and society as a whole. In *More God, Less Crime: Why Faith Matters and How It Could Matter More* Byron Johnson surveys the research and finds that regular church attendance among youth lessens the risk of illicit drug use and parental religious devotion lessens youth delinquency.[137] His research sheds light on the under studied field of religion and criminology. It isn't that God acts in mysterious ways. It's much simpler than that. Through church networks that offer support and teach self-control while condemning inappropriate behaviour, young people are less likely to stray. In a 2015 analysis of all published studies relating religion to crime among adolescents there was found to be a well-documented inverse relationship.[138] Among adult prisoners a 2018 research paper found religiosity was related to a sense of meaning and purpose in life, which in turn tended to be inversely associated with the offenders' negative emotional states and intended aggression. It concluded by saying, 'Unless offenders find self-transcendent reasons for being hopeful and optimistic about their future (e.g., God still loves them and has purpose for their lives) and become self-motivated for change, rehabilitation efforts will remain an ongoing challenge for correctional authorities.'[139]

Beyond social factors, a study by academics Ilan Alon, Shaomin Li and Jun Wu found that religious freedom itself has a positive impact on economic performance. They conclude that, 'Tolerance, including toward religion, is a cultural value with an economic advantage. The absence of social hostility toward religion is a

---

137 Byron Johnson, *More God, Less Crime: Why Faith Matters and How It Could Matter More,* Templeton Press, West Conshohocken, 2012

138 Kelly, P. E. et al. (2015) 'Religion, Delinquency, and Drug Use: A Meta-Analysis', *Criminal Justice Review,* 40(4), pp. 505–523

139 Jang, SJ, Johnson, BR, Hays, J, Hallett, M & Duwe, G n.d., 'Existential and Virtuous Effects of Religiosity on Mental Health and Aggressiveness among Offenders', *Religions,* 2018 vol. 9, no. 6

valuable social (and economic) asset.'[140] Supporting this, a recent report in Australia revealed that those who found religion later in life became more generous, giving 1.5 times more to charities and volunteering 1.7 times more often.[141] This type of activity is a major contributor to strengthening the ties that bind society together, something known as social capital. None of this is new to most Australians. Hugh McKay notes that 88 percent of non-Church going Australians believe the presence of a church is good for a community.[142]

Despite these benefits public shaming by progressive elites, a lack of legal protection and a sense of exclusion from society push believers into self-censorship and out of the public sphere. If this is to continue the outcome will be that religious individuals will reap the health and happiness benefits, but society will lose. In a rough appraisal Rodney Stark estimates that the United States economy saves a total of US$2.6 trillion per year due to its religiosity, driven in large part by lower crime rates.[143]

Beyond the benefits to individuals and communities there are certain prerequisites for nations to function. One of them is a higher order set of values which reach across generations and against which right is distinguished from wrong. Why is gender equality important in Australia but not in Saudi Arabia? Why do some societies accept capital punishment and others don't? Is looking after elderly parents a responsibility of their children or the government? Overarching values that distinguish right from wrong give us the parameters from which we build consensus on

---

140 Alon, I., Li, S., & Wu, J. (2017). An Institutional Perspective on Religious Freedom and Economic Growth. Politics and Religion, 10(3), 689-716

141 Deloitte Access Economics, 'Donating and volunteering behaviour associated with religiosity', 2017.

142 Hugh Mackay, *Beyond Belief: How we find meaning with or without religion*, Macmillan Publishers, 2016

143 Rodney Stark, *America's Blessings: How Religion Benefits Everyone, Including Atheists*, Templeton Press, West Conshohocken, 2012 p168

how society should be structured and the country governed.

In Australia, millennia old Christian values are being rapidly forced from the public square, replaced by a menagerie of passing fads and on-trend philosophies. The firm foundation stone of religion is being replaced by a circular argument of right and wrong – first it is defined through the law, and those who write the law then rely upon that same law to define right and wrong. The risk is that the law becomes a football between different groups and across generations, each trying to dictate their own version of goodness in legal garb. Not unique to Australia, this situation is replicated around the world and is contributing to the emergence of populists on the left and the right.

Is Religious Freedom Under Attack?

While it may be clear that religion is good for us all, is religious freedom under threat? There is a long list of examples of believers being victims because of their faith. Vocal commentators and cultural progressives often argue that the high-profile cases of Archbishop Porteous and Israel Folau are aberrations, proving that there isn't a problem with religious freedom. They are wrong. These cases are high profile because the individuals are high profile. That, of course, is why the media reports on them. For this same reason the media aren't reporting on the many low-profile parishioners who have to choose between their faith and their job and who are withdrawing from society or censoring their beliefs.

A two-year-old Australian law firm specialising in religious freedom cases, the Human Rights Law Alliance, has already had over 60 cases including ones where:

- During a conversation with a classmate struggling with anxiety a Christian university student offered to pray for him with his permission. Permission was granted. Shortly afterward the

Christian student was asked, 'What would you do if your friend was gay?' to which he responded that he'd show love to them but would not necessarily agree with what they were doing. The Christian student was suspended from university and had official disciplinary action recorded on his transcript.

- A teacher in a government school who posted on social media news articles about gay marriage with comments in support of traditional marriage was placed under investigation by the Department because of complaints that he was 'homophobic'

- An employee who raised concerns about being pressured to march in a 'pride' parade and subscribe to 'pride' newsletters was warned and then placed under investigation by an employer

- A General Manager who had hired LGBTIQ personnel was asked about his views on the Safe Schools Coalition. He explained that he disagreed with the concept of gender fluidity and the promotion of sexual diversity. He was terminated from his employment.

These examples are a brief representation of the many under-reported instances of religious believers being inhibited. In each case it took the intervention of the Human Rights Law Alliance to seek a remedy. Without their intervention these people would most likely have been cowed out of their job or university.

Those who believe that freedom of religion is a fundamental human right are a favourite target of progressive elites for all the wrong reasons – reasons that matter and need to be understood because they represent a bigger battle that is currently being fought.

Firstly, there's a common line of commentary that associates religious belief with institutional religion's complicity in past wrongs, from the Crusades against Muslims through to more recent institutional child sex abuse cases. It is a lazy idea but one that has taken root. The problem though is that human rights including freedom of religion are individual rights. Such rights shouldn't be withheld to right wrongs committed against groups in the past or present.

Secondly, freedom of religion is also despised because it buttresses free speech. By limiting what you think or believe, people can control what is said and heard. That is why freedom of religion is one of the most important freedoms in our society. By its very nature it facilitates thought and debate on some of the most difficult questions (such as the purpose of life, and how others ought to be treated), which in turn informs the critical questions that shape the society we aim to become.

These two motivations for the attacks upon religious freedom are indicative of the direction our society is headed. Caving in on religious freedom amounts to giving ground on those other cornerstones of our society. That is why we can't be complacent by simply settling for a few amendments to the law. That is why more needs to be done.

What needs to be done?

Below I outline individual strategies that the federal government might initiate targeting three groups who will play important roles in the coming years—the cultural elites, religious believers and medical practitioners.

Cultural Elites

The cultural elites in the media, boardrooms and universities of Australia hold considerable sway over the way religion is perceived by and presented to Australians. Convincing them of the importance of religion will require a tailored approach.

The first step is to research the role religion plays in our society. Nearly all of the research on individual benefits and the social value of religion and religious belief, such as the work referenced earlier, has been done in the United States. While useful as a guide and most likely indicative of an overall similarly positive effect in Australia, we live in a different social context. The results could be skewed in one direction or the other. In addition, the academics who are leaders in their field are based in the US and appear regularly in public debates on US radio and television helping to spread knowledge, but their insights and research rarely reach our shores in a publicly accessible way. Funding domestic research would create new and powerful voices who could advocate for the social benefits of religion.

> Recommendation #1: The Australian government should provide funding through the Special Research Initiatives funding stream for research on religion and society. At a cost of approximately $1m for one researcher for four years the government could fund 3-5 researchers to begin the process of collating relevant research and initiating new research on how religion impacts Australia.

The second action needed is to educate a religiously illiterate cultural elite on the basic foundations of major religions and the findings on the benefits of religion. The Freedom of Religion Commissioner, if the enacting legislation is passed, should draw upon the prestige among progressive elites of the Australian Human Rights Commission and take a leading role in this effort.

The actions of Rugby Australia provide an example of how early intervention could have prevented unnecessary confrontation. Rugby Australia repeatedly misunderstood Israel Folau's Instagram post in which he wrote that 'drunks, homosexuals, adulterers, liars, fornicators, thieves, atheists and idolaters,' would go to hell. This was then reported in newspapers and spoken of by corporate and social leaders as homophobic and hate speech.

Had we a Freedom of Religion Commissioner at that time that person could have explained the nuances and complexities of religion: I know a lot of people who would tick one or more of those boxes. Do I hate them? No. Do I fear them? Of course not. Folau's Christianity teaches people to love all of God's creation. That Folau appeared on the cover of *Star Observer*, a gay magazine promoting a gay rugby club is evidence of this.[144] Believing that someone is destined for hell because God determined it to be so while you, as a mere human, love him or her as you love every human are not incompatible positions, as difficult as it may be for many non-Christians to understand.

Similarly, consider news sites such as *The Age* (which on Christmas day of last year labelled Barnaby Joyce's call to respect a greater authority that is beyond our comprehension as 'bizarre')[145] or *The Conversation* (that headed an email on the Monday before Christmas with 'How Mary's virginity still damages women'). These sorts of examples illustrate a media elite that is out of touch with the majority of Australians and ignorant of the harm they do.

Explaining to Qantas, *The Age*, *The Conversation* or other companies how they and society would benefit from approaching similar situations differently, namely, in a way that better understands religious sensitivities is an important task of the Commissioner. Engaging early with the community, media and corporate leaders, including leaders of the LGBTI community, will help avoid fractious and unnecessary confrontation.

> Recommendation #2: Appoint a Freedom of Religion Commissioner who can engage with the cultural elite and explain the value of religion to individuals and society and stand up to the anti-religious narrative dominating that segment of society.

---

144 Laurence Barber, 'Throwback: In 2014, The Star Observer Celebrated Its 35th Anniversary – With Israel Folau', July 19, 2019.

145 Latika Bourke, 'Barnaby Joyce suggests God is the solution to climate change in bizarre Christmas video,' *The Age* (App) 25 December 2019 (The title was changed some time later deleting the adjective 'bizarre')

Religious believers

There's a large group of Australians who declare themselves religious but are not regular worshippers. These are the Australians who mightn't go to synagogue every Saturday, wear a yarmulke or send their kids to a Jewish school but who still embrace the values and tradition of their faith. They include Australians who attend Christmas and Easter mass but choose to cheer their favourite football team on Sunday. They mightn't contribute *zakat*, wear a hijab or fast during Ramadan but they still see God's hand at work in this world.

These are the Australians who will be most at risk when their religious freedoms are threatened yet they are unaware of this threat or unwilling to contribute and make a stand now. They need to be informed and mobilized to stand up and be heard. But by whom and how?

This cohort is most likely to be engaged with religion through religious service providers—private schools, aged care homes or charities. Collectively religious service providers are very trusted with deep connections to the community. Over 60% of all aged care services are provided by religious groups, approximately 30% of all schools in Australia are religiously affiliated and nearly a quarter of all charities are religious.

Establishing an 'advisory group' to government in a similar form to multicultural, business and social advisory groups already in existence would give purpose and legitimacy to a group united by their appreciation of the unique role religious groups play in society. Bringing them together under a single body with specific terms of reference would strengthen their voice and give them a common platform.

The advisory group should be composed of a diverse group including, for example, religious school principals, directors of religious charities, doctors and CEOs from religious hospitals,

Vice Chancellors of faith-based universities and leaders of aged care facilities.

This group should be tasked with the role of advising the federal government and opposition and where appropriate state governments on the impact any legislative changes will have to the operation of religious service delivery organisations. Their secondary role would be commissioning and being advocates for reports showcasing the important role the religious services sector plays in Australian society. Such a group will provide a platform to each member to advocate on behalf of the religious services sector and in turn mobilise religious believers. In this instance, the whole would be far stronger than the sum of the parts. The voice of religious service providers is the strongest and most trusted in the community. It needs to be given a platform and channelled for this purpose.

> Recommendation #3: Establish an advisory council of religious service providers under the Prime Minister with a small secretariat and a modest budget. The advisory council would include CEOs of charities and aged care facilities and hospitals, principals of schools and Vice-Chancellors of faith-based universities. The primary purpose could be to advise on the impact legislative changes would have on religious service delivery organizations along with an important secondary role of advocating to the public the important role the religious services sector plays.

Religious Discrimination Act

Recommendation 17 of the Ruddock Review was that the government commission the collection and analysis of data on the experience of freedom of religion in Australia including incidents of violence and threats, unreasonable restrictions on the ability of people to express, manifest or change their faith, and the extent to which religious diversity is accepted and promoted in Australian society.

The Second Draft Exposure Bill envisages the Freedom of Religion Commissioner be tasked with collating research on the objects of the Act which include, 'to ensure that people can, consistently with Australia's obligations with respect to freedom of religion and freedom of expression, and subject to specified limits, make statements of belief.' But depending upon the progress of the Bill, the Commissioner won't be appointed until early 2021 if at all in this post-COVID world.

But the Australian Law Reform Commission (ALRC) will report on 'whether religious exemptions (not resolved by the Religious Discrimination Bill) could be removed from anti-discrimination laws while also guaranteeing the rights of religious institutions to conduct their affairs in accordance with their ethos,' in December 2020. It is important that Parliament and the public have a better insight into the lived experience of religious Australians before finalizing a response to the ALRC report.

> Recommendation #4: The government should initiate as soon as possible Recommendation 17 of the Ruddock Religious Freedom Review and commission the collection of data on the lived experience of religious believers and institutions.

Medical Profession

The medical profession will, in the future, be on the front lines of the debate over religious freedom through conscientious objection. With late term abortion, assisted suicide and euthanasia now legal in parts of Australia the new frontline for religious medical practitioners will move to medical procedures such as gender reassignment, body modification and genetic enhancements. There has been a raging debate among ethicists on the scope and extent of acceptable conscientious objection. The so-called *Consensus Statement on Conscientious Objection in Healthcare* is one example of where some ethicists would want the profession to go. It is an Orwellian construct that requires healthcare practitioners to make their case before a tribunal to 'test the sincerity' and 'reasonability' of their moral objections and requires healthcare practitioners who are exempted 'to compensate society and the health system for their failure to fulfil their professional obligations by providing public-benefitting services.' Were this to be adopted in codes of conduct it would mean putting someone's faith on trial. It would lead to punishment of those who put their faith first.

It's not just doctors and nurses who will have to face this ethical dilemma. Interviewed for an article, Laura Gonzales, a young disability support worker, was unsure how she'd respond to a disabled client requesting the services of a sex worker. She said, 'As a Christian, that is against my beliefs. Do I just submit to it? If I raise it with my supervisor, will they understand my objections? That would be the best-case scenario; worst-case, you might get fired.'[146]

Will medical students be required to sign the so-called *Consensus Statement*? Will religious doctors be screened out of jobs in public hospitals if they don't sign? These are likely dilemmas society will be facing soon.

The Second Exposure Draft Bill provides a robust defence of conscientious objections for certain health practitioners (doctors, nurses, psychologists, midwives and pharmacists but not social workers like Laura or importantly clergy who engage in counselling) though, not without considerable criticism within the public arena. At the time of writing this chapter the Bill remained in draft form. In the instance that the protections are withdrawn then the Freedom of Religion Commissioner should engage with health practitioners as a priority to find alternative mechanisms to buttress protections for health practitioners of faith.

---

146 Phoebe Moloney, 'Emily's Voice anti-abortion advertising removed from Newcastle bus,' *Newcastle Herald*, 21 June 2019.

Conclusion

When religious freedom is treated like a gift granted by the state and enforced by law it is likely to fall short of expectations because there will be few willing to defend it. We should aspire to create a society where religious beliefs are a matter of respect between neighbours and strangers and valued for the contribution it makes to society.

Robust research, discussed in this article, has found that religious people are happier and less likely to commit crime, get divorced or drop out of school and are more likely to contribute to charities and have better mental health. If there was a drug that could deliver those results every investor would be calling their broker, every government would be subsidising it and every community would be distributing it. Yet when it comes to religion and the prerequisite freedoms, we not only don't seem to see the benefit but appear willing to inflict self-harm by limiting the very freedom that has contributed to our success.

Overt displays of religiosity and the use of religious reasoning to justify public policy has become a taboo. The consequences of this social own goal are extensive and costly but it's not too late to stop. As we emerge from the COVID-19 lockdowns the Morrison government has an opportunity to strengthen society, uphold international human rights, empower the broader community and push back against the forced moral conformity of today's age by adopting the above recommendations and moving ahead to protect religious freedom..

14

APPOINTMENTS AND COURAGE

James Allan

In February of this year British commentator and author Douglas Murray argued forcefully that the newly re-elected Conservative government there must be far more courageous in how it makes its appointments to all the key positions across government. In order to go any distance at all in a democracy towards reclaiming the culture which shapes future citizens and ultimately policy choices any conservative government needs, said Murray, 'to make appointments that *demoralise* the opposition'[147] – it needs to make them to top positions in the public broadcaster, the various commissions and tribunals, the leading educational institutions, the courts, everything. Murray's idea is that conservative governments need to start appointing actual conservatives to these key positions, not liberal-leftists. And his remarks came closely after release of research by the Taxpayers' Alliance in Britain that found that after ten years – a whole decade – of supposedly right-of-centre Conservative governments

---

147   James Delingpole Podcast with Douglas Murray, Podcast 56, February 2020.

the vast preponderance of public appointments still went to avowed left-liberals, the sort of appointees who are, perhaps, a smidgen of a fraction of a *soupçon* to the right of the sort of person that the left-wing party would have appointed. Or perhaps not even a smidgen. Either way, such left-liberal Conservative Party appointees are not committed conservatives, not even close.

In fact, and this is bracing, the Taxpayers' Alliance in its search through the past decade of Conservative Party appointments to all the key positions ultimately in the hands of the government could find only two (yes, two!) public appointments that had been given to known conservatives. One was to William Shawcross to head up the Charities Commission and the other to the late Sir Roger Scruton as an unpaid advisor to the government's Building Better, Building Beautiful Commission. And as some will know Scruton was for a time driven from that position by supposed past assertions later proved doctored that were aired by a left-wing activist journalist in the *New Statesman*. Initially various prominent Conservative MPs did not support Scruton, a well-known conservative philosopher. It took a year for Scruton to be subsequently, and fully, vindicated and get his post re-instated which happened just before his death. Such was the plight of the man who was the second of only two instances in ten years of an actual 'obvious to all' conservative being appointed by a United Kingdom Conservative government to anything remotely important.

So Murray's advice boils down to a plea to conservative governments to jettison the status of invertebrates, grow a backbone, and make appointments of people who will infuriate the left-wing activists. Murray said 'The far left will rail and rage. To which the Conservatives can respond: "If you don't like it, you ought to have won an 80-seat majority in Parliament at the last election."'[148]

An underlying premise of Murray's, one with which I wholly agree,

---

148   Ibid.

is that the left/far-left outrage mob will be indignant about such appointments. (I would add to that this further gloss, that the outrage mob would be indignant about *any* appointee at all who was more than a smidgen of a fraction of a *soupçon* to the right of the sort of person that the left-wing party would have appointed. It follows, in my view, that a certain amount of courage or bravery is needed in the face of that outrage. Alas, amongst right-of-centre politicians this is a trait sadly not anywhere in evidence in the Anglosphere right now outside of Trump's America.) Going back to Douglas Murray, his plea in the face of such a core premise is that: 'This kind of surrender to the left has got to stop'.[149] Indeed Murray, in a similar vein, wrote in the British newspaper, *The Telegraph* that '[w]hen you see the BBC pump out another unadulterated piece of left-wing grudge-whisking … it is certainly because [left-leaning appointees] so dominate our cultural institutions that their now dated values and worldview are believed to be the norm even when they have been rejected at the ballot box…Well here is a thought. I would think that the present [Tory] government has no more than three to six months to enact it. Flood the public sector with Right-of-centre cultural and political figures. Change the weather. Re-centre the culture. If they don't do it now they never will, and the frit-ness of the last decade will remain the default position of this one.'[150]

In the rest of this very brief chapter I want to canvass, through this prism of courage, the Australian Coalition government's record on

---

149   Ibid.
150   Douglas Murray, 'Where are all the conservative thinkers who should be rebalancing public life?', *The London Telegraph*, Feb.9ᵗʰ, 2020. In this same article Murray's take on the Scruton affair is that the conservative philosopher 'ha[d] been treated as disgracefully as it is possible to be treated by the government of the day', remembering that it was treatment by a Conservative government of a Conservative appointee, *their appointee*. This, and the almost as bad treatment of Toby Young, go some way to answering those conservative party faithful who throw up their hands and cry 'we just can't find people willing to be put forward'. 'If that's true', responds Murray, 'it isn't exactly difficult to work out why Right-wing, or even just vaguely conservative people, might not find the whole appointments thing attractive'.

the appointments front – a Coalition government, remember, that has been in office Down Under for seven consecutive years now. Then, after that bleak and depressing exercise, I will have a few words to say about the question of 'what's to be done?', especially in the light of the corona virus outbreak and resulting lockdown and economic damage that will ensue.

Starting, then, with the record of the past seven years of Coalition government appointments in Australia let me give readers the expedited account of that record. Across the board the appointments have been at least as bad as in Britain; they have displayed no courage whatsoever; with one, maybe two, possible exceptions it is near on impossible to think of appointees who were committed, 'obvious to all' conservatives; High Court of Australia judicial appointments, in some ways the most important appointments a government on the right-of-centre can make, have been woefully awful (with one appointee to that top court – and I am not making this up I assure you – establishing a world first, literally, when the Coalition appointed the wife of a retiring High Court judge to take her husband's place on the country's top court, and take it from me this appointee is anything but a constitutional conservative); appointments to the upper echelons of the public broadcaster, a body that receives over one billion dollars a year in taxpayer monies and that has not got a single, solitary identifiable conservative – not one – as a presenter or producer on any of its main current affairs television shows, have ranged from the weak (a smidgen of a fraction of a *soupcon* to the right of the sort of person that the left-wing party would have appointed) to a good deal to the left of that; likewise appointments to the Human Rights Commission, which amongst other things oversees parts of the s.18C hate speech laws that only a few years ago the Coalition government was committed to repealing (and of course did not), have ranged from soft-left 'safe' choices to one that was so far to the political left that the Green Party could easily be imagined as having made it.

If we were to move into appointments that the government has only an indirect say over, such as university Vice-Chancellors, again the record is abysmal. Across three dozen or so universities in this country not more than one or two (and these are debatable given the institutional 'capture' once in office) are led by an 'obvious to all' conservative. The same goes for the myriad of ever multiplying Deputy Vice Chancellors overseeing such 'important to conservatives' things as 'Diversity and Equity'. Show me a self-confessed conservative here and I'll show you someone who has difficulties with the truth. And this, recall, at a time when the numbers and percentages of self-identifying conservative academics is low, really low, and getting lower. Again, no one could accuse these past seven years of Coalition governments in Australia of having displayed courage in their appointments. Appeasement, arguably so. Courage, none whatsoever. Put differently, Douglas Murray's pleas as to needed future actions apply at least as much to today's conservative government in Australia as they do to Britain's. The difference is that at present there would seem to be some scintilla of hope for, some glimmerings of a change of direction in, the United Kingdom's Boris Johnson government. Indeed optimists up there might say they sense a trace element of governmental courage what with, for instance, a few recent signs of a willingness potentially to take on the BBC and make the subscription fee voluntary rather than compulsory as at present (though, truth be told, the corona virus scare has probably undercut this 'bravery' in Boris Johnson's Tories). In Australia, by contrast, one can scan the whole appointments horizon without spotting any evidence of courage, or of a desire 'to make appointments that *demoralise* the opposition', or of a newfound urge to end 'this kind of surrender to the left'.

To put this claim in context turn for a moment to the United States and to President Donald Trump's administration. Say what you will about the man – and unlike virtually all Australian academics I like the man and really like his record as President – he is courageous when it comes to appointments. Indeed, 'courageous' may well understate things. When Supreme Court nominee Brett Kavanaugh was being pilloried and attacked in an attempt to have his nomination withdrawn (with accusations that were decades old – actually, they would have been more credible had they been decades old, they were in fact freshly minted accusations alleging something decades old – and could not be independently confirmed by anyone and so were of a sort that could be brought to bear against literally anyone) President Trump and his administration stood by their nominee until he was eventually confirmed. I do not believe that another conservative leader in the entire democratic world would have remained steadfast in the way President Trump did with this crucial judicial nominee. Moreover, this was both the right thing to do as well as being a strategically wise thing to do – it showed that on such appointments this right-of-centre administration would not surrender to left-wing outrage mobs and was prepared to attempt to 'change the weather and re-centre the culture'. (Notice, too, that this Kavanaugh attitude by some on the Left that we should 'believe all women' is hypocritically gainsaid by many of those same people when it is one of their political own in the cross-hairs, someone like Joe Biden, the allegations against whom are considerably stronger and more supported by circumstantial evidence than was true of those against Kavanaugh.) The same attitude has been on display with all of President Trump's judicial appointees, not just on the Supreme Court but on the federal Circuit Courts as well. Indeed the President is on the verge of 'flipping' the Ninth Circuit, the country's largest and the one from which emanate many of the nationwide injunctions blocking various of his immigration and other Executive Orders. This Ninth Circuit has been in Democrat hands since President Carter. President Trump has been single-minded in appointing only known conservative judges to this court, not obsessing over identity politics factors of the sort that (disgracefully in my view) seemed to drive many Coalition appointments in this country.

Compare that US experience to Australia's by considering one of the High Court's most recent constitutional decisions, *Love v Commonwealth*. This case, on the question of deporting plaintiffs who were born outside Australia, who are foreign citizens and who have not been naturalised or made Australian citizens, but who claim to be Aborigines, was in my view a disgrace. By 4-3 it effectively constitutionalised identity politics; in a weird sort of way it elevated the common law – judge made law to be clear – above the Constitution itself; it introduced a race-based limit on the Parliament's power; it looked very much to be a clear case of outcome oriented judging, meaning you start with the conclusion you want and then struggle to find rationales to get you there; amusingly, sort of, the case more or less ignored or abandoned the established heads of powers interpretive methods – the ones that to my mind have unfortunately been used by our top court to deliver the most pro-centre federalism case law in the world, but did so out of the blue in a case, this case, where no Australian State actually benefitted from that abandonment; oh, and given the tools the judges had to work with it is now fair to say that this *Love* case means our top judges are vying for the title of the most activist judges in the common law world.

But here's the remarkable thing. Of the four judges in the majority, three of them were appointed by the Coalition government. In fact these were the three most recently appointed top judges, all in the last few years, two by Attorney-General Brandis under the Abbott government and one by Attorney-General Brandis under the Turnbull government. Let me say that again. In one of the most activist decisions ever as far as Australian constitutional law is concerned, three of the four majority Justices were appointed by the present 2013-now Coalition government. This is astounding. It would seem that we now have to rely on the left-wing Labor Party to give us remotely constitutionally conservative judges, because two of the three judges in dissent (the sensible ones) were in fact appointed by Labor – the left-wing party in Australia.

Worse, consider some of the lunatic, post-modernist, steeped-in-identity-politics, blatantly activism-enhancing comments of these three recent Coalition appointed High Court judges. All three, Justices Nettle, Gordon and Edelman, indulged in all sorts of politically correct nostrums and observations that sound far more political and activist than legal and constitutional – all basically leveraging or bootstrapping off the common law decision in *Mabo* to end up with a constitutional outcome that amounts to a just-discovered limit on the elected Parliament's power. And so the first, Justice Nettle, talks of how 'different considerations apply … to … a person of Aboriginal descent' and that the Commonwealth's claims to the contrary 'intuitively … appear at odds with the growing recognition of Aboriginal peoples as "the original inhabitants of Australia"' and of their 'essentially spiritual connection with "country"'. The second, Justice Gordon, talks of 'the deeper truth', of a 'connection [that] is spiritual and metaphysical', of how this 'is fundamentally a question of otherness' [I kid you not!] and then tells us that judge-made law now recognises 'that Indigenous peoples can and do possess certain rights and duties that are not possessed by, and cannot be possessed by non-Indigenous peoples of Australia.' She then tries to rely on the fact that 'the Constitution does not prohibit special treatment of a race', without going on to note that the Constitution's lack of prohibition is aimed at Parliament – not at four unelected top judges remaking the Constitution in their own image. As for the third of the recent Coalition appointees, Justice Edelman, he talks of 'essential meaning[s]', 'metaphysical construct[s]', 'powerful personal attachment[s] to land' and then, remarkably I think, says 'To treat differences as though they were alike is not equality. It is denial of community. Any tolerant view of community must recognise that community is based on difference'. I have no clear idea of what that means by the way but neither it, nor any of the other political ramblings have anything to do with the judges' assigned task, which is to interpret a Constitution.

After that brief recital of what the sort of judges being appointed by our supposedly right-of-centre government are doing in this country is there any conservative voter in Australia who wouldn't prefer President Trump's approach? And courage? And resolve? And willingness 'to make appointments that *demoralise* the opposition' and move away from what amounts to a 'kind of surrender to the left'?

Readers can repeat for themselves this sort of analysis of Coalition appointments to the public broadcaster ABC, to the overbearing (and in my view needing to be completely shut down but don't hold your breath waiting for that from this conservative government) Human Rights Commission, to the Administrative Appeals Tribunal, indirectly to the top university positions, the list goes on and on and on. Nowhere is the quality of courage anywhere in evidence. Nowhere is Douglas Murray's advice being heeded.

So what to do? The question is infinitely easier to pose than to answer. Still, a few notions do spring to mind. First off, every Minister in a Coalition government must realise that most of the top bureaucrats and many of the advisors have political views that are left-leaning. The Attorney-General's department will give what the staff see as independent advice; but it will also be what most conservatives see as left-leaning advice; and that is patently true when it comes to appointments. The same goes for the Minister of Health or the Treasurer or anyone making appointments. This may not be a happy fact; its long-term reversal may require action to fix our schools and universities (another area, it almost goes without saying, over which this seven-year Coalition government has been completely pusillanimous, gutless and wholly without courage); but till that is done Ministers must be wary to avoid capture by their departments. This is doubly true as regards appointments.

Related to that bracketed concern is the need to do something about Australian school results. Any self-respecting conservative government must do something about teacher training – trying to reduce the volume of politically correct nostrums being force-fed to would-be teachers while also, somehow, improving the calibre of those who are today willing to go into the profession (and I speak in terms of averages here, clearly there are n=1 exceptional individuals scattered throughout teaching).

Here's another 'what to do?' suggestion. This is for the State Coalition governments. Be more careful with whom you pick to fill top police leadership positions. Our police forces seem to me to be in dire need of sensible conservative leadership that stops kowtowing to the various politically correct nostrums of the day and has its officers single-mindedly focus on stopping crime. I come from a middle class Toronto family where it went without saying that one would always support the police. Now, what with the promiscuous virtue-signalling and over-reach on matters of offence-giving and the like I'm more sceptical of the police. Not the officers on the beat, the lousy leadership. And the behaviour of more than a few of the police forces in this country through the corona virus scare, its heavy-handedness and lack of common sense, has only magnified my concerns on this front. (And for what it's worth, here's a different, but telling State example sent to me: the State Library of NSW recently awarded a literary prize and funding to a young lady who, in her acceptance speech, announced that her next book would be on "abolishing the family". This was funded by a NSW Coalition government and overseen by a former National Party Minister, George Souris. You can't make it up.)

Here's a last 'what to do?' suggestion, though I wish I had more proposals. Given the track record of right-of-centre governments vis-à-vis appointing hopelessly weak, a smidgen of a fraction of a *soupçon* to the right of the sort of person that the left-wing party would have appointed, now is the time to copy the Trump approach. Namely, produce a list of possible appointees (to the top court, to the Human Rights Commission, whatever) and promise to appoint from that list come what may. This delivers transparency from the start; it binds the hands of spineless Ministers and others who would otherwise go to water; it delivers a mandate for change of the personnel occupying key appointed positions. Best of all, it allows the voting public (the Coalition's supporters) to see the mooted appointees and to react to obviously weak or poor choices – and believe me some of the Coalition appointees to the High Court of Australia, and likewise to the Human Rights Commission, would have been laughed out of consideration had they been made public, in advance, as possibilities. Of course this sort of Trump-like course of action is very much a second-best option. The best option would be to have a right-of-centre government that made 'no surrender to the left by us' choices all on its own. But that is now patently a pie-in-the-sky scenario. So this 'publish a list and promise to pick from it' alternative, albeit a second-best option, is clearly better than what we have at present. It is miles better in fact.

Here's what is now obvious. Conservatives know how to preserve institutions, at least in theory, but experience shows that they are hopelessly incompetent when it comes to recapturing them from the Left. They can argue for the *status quo*, but not for recapture of the surrendered culture. President Trump's insight, the manner in which he differs from predecessors, is that his goals and values are broadly conservative but his methods are much more similar to those of his opponents – to fight and scrap and play to win, which is in part why they hate him so much. Or put in the terms with which I started this short chapter, appointments matter. They matter in the sense of conservative governments having the courage to make appointments that demoralise the opposition matters. Starting down the path suggested by Douglas Murray matters. Moving away from appointments that amount to a 'kind of surrender to the left' matters. And to be clear, it matters not just as a route to getting 'our' people onto the relevant institutions, it matters in a larger sense as a recognition that those institutions shape and protect the culture. These institutions can be understood as a standing body of opposition often times not in synch with political developments, and so institutions that can be expected to attempt to frustrate the democratic mandate of any right-of-centre elected government seen by them as a threat to their worldview.

In the wake of the corona virus lockdowns, with the attendant (and to my mind considerably over-done) economy-jarring steps that have been taken to combat that virus, there is an opportunity immediately to take all future appointments across the board far more seriously and to start behaving in the way Douglas Murray suggests. No, the way Murray begs any committed right-of-centre government to do if it is to have any long-term influence on the culture and the society. There is no time like the present for this Morrison government to start heeding this advice. Alas, perhaps the best (and saved for last) example of the Coalition appointing left-wingers is the example of the partyroom making Malcolm Turnbull leader in 2015. The pusillanimity problem, in other words, starts at the top and appears to go down from there. Hence, and sadly, it's a lot easier to be a Cassandra rather than a Pollyanna as far as betting on the likelihood of better future appointments emanating from the right side of Australian politics is concerned.

15

CAN THE MORRISON GOVERNMENT 'KEEP AUSTRALIA RIGHT'?

Peter Kurti

In the midst of events there is no perspective[151]

Scott Morrison's summer season began badly in December 2019. Snapped chillaxing on vacation with his family in Hawaii while much of southern Australia was engulfed by bushfires, the Prime Minister was slow to dispel mounting feelings back home that our leader had abandoned us to the blazing inferno. By the time his plane touched down in Sydney one Saturday evening shortly before Christmas, dusk also appeared to be falling on his premiership.

Six months later, and Morrison has never looked more prime ministerial. As global cases reached 10 million at the time of writing (late June) – with over 2.5 million of those in the USA – and global deaths have tipped over the half million mark, Morrison can

---

151   Barbara Tuchman, *A Distant Mirror: The Calamitous 14ᵗʰ Century*, (London: Penguin, 2017), 483.

look back with some satisfaction at his government's response to the covid pandemic: just 104 deaths by 30 June, and around 7,800 cases. In an essential poll conducted at the end of June, 71 per cent of those surveyed thought the government's response to covid was good; just 12 per cent thought it was poor.[152] However, Morrison didn't succeed in his suppression strategy alone, of course.

State and territory leaders played an important part although with varying degrees of competence. Borders were closed, lockdowns rigorously imposed across the country, and people settled down to what was quickly dubbed 'the new normal'. But it was the *Ruby Princess* fiasco in NSW that introduced many of the cases to Australia in the first place; and Victorian premier, Daniel Andrews's blunders led to a worrying mid-year resurgence of cases in his state and so earned the rebuke they deserved. The message from the public was clear: health restrictions imposed on all – especially about social distancing – must be observed by all, without exception.

Even so, Australia has come through the first wave of coronavirus infections well. But a second – and possibly third – wave will almost certainly follow. Since it cannot afford further costly shutdowns, the country is going to have to learn to live with covid, maintaining altered social practices and taking appropriate precautions against an extremely infectious virus. This may only change if – and when – a vaccine becomes available; but that is unlikely to happen much before 2021-22. And even the arrival of a vaccine may not be enough to prevent the country sliding into a deepening economic crisis.

When coronavirus first began to spread, efforts to meet the health challenge facing Australia were of paramount importance. Flattened and suppressed, rather than eliminated altogether, the threat to public health has been mitigated. Now, however, the Morrison government faces a monumental task to rebuild the

---

152   "Government response to Covid-19", *Essential Report* (23 June 2020).

country's economic prosperity while at the same time acting to support those in low-wage jobs and those who work in what is called 'customer-experience' roles such as tourism, hospitality, and travel.

By mid-2020, it was estimated that 40 per cent of the Australian workforce was on some form of government assistance provided under federal JobKeeper and JobSeeker schemes. That kind of assistance cannot continue indefinitely, however, and might not even be available to the same extent – if at all – during bouts of covid-19 that are yet to come.

Closed international borders mean that the higher education sector will take a serious hit because of the absence of overseas students. Nor are prospects for economic recovery likely to improve while internal state and territory borders remain closed thereby restricting interstate economic activity. Free and unhindered movement across internal borders is essential for the overall wealth and well-being of the country. The costs of covid-19 – both financial and personal – will continue to mount even as restrictions are eased, travel resumes, and commercial life around the country revives.

As the country came to terms with the lockdown in the first half of the year, opinion concerning both the effectiveness and the appropriateness of Scott Morrison's response divided sharply. Concern about the extent of government assistance (or "bailouts", as some described them); about the civic and social cost of confining people to their homes; about the economic cost of forcing businesses to close (some never to re-open); and about unprecedented restrictions on freedom of movement and association fuelled criticism that was, at times, intense. After all, as the government sought quickly to strike the right balance between liberty and the need to safeguard public health, it became apparent, just as quickly, that the state can muster very extensive powers when needed.

With one eye to the catastrophe unfolding in the Great Britain and another to the likelihood of a returning wave of covid-19 once social restrictions were eased, most Australian business leaders were satisfied with government action to protect public health. By June 2020, however, they also issued calls for the economy to be re-opened, for children to return to schools, (thereby freeing up parents to return to the workplace), and for urgent review (and repeal) of regulations that threatened to hinder a return to prosperity.

Contributors to this collection of essays formulated their initial views about the action they wanted to see from the Morrison government towards the end of 2019 – long before the advent of covid-19. By the middle of 2020, however, the challenge facing the Coalition government in its efforts to 'Keep Australia Right' looked very different. Each contributor was invited to review their advice to Scott Morrison, taking into account the impact of covid-19.

As the Morrison Government responded to the pandemic, advocates of small government were faced with a sudden and extensive expansion of the size of government; those arguing for fiscal restraint had to reckon with the impact of massive state expenditure on the national budget; defenders of individual liberty witnessed restrictions on freedom that would have been hard to countenance just a few months previously; and those committed to upholding capitalism and the free market faced calls to admit that capitalism had failed and that socialism had, in the end, prevailed. "The centre right", warned one commentator, "will need to craft a new narrative on [sic] the role of government."[153]

Predictions about eras ending have rained down upon us in recent months, all inspired by the impact covid-19 is supposedly having on societies around the world. In Australia, for instance, we have

---

153　Greg Sheridan, "Coronavirus: Centre-right in need of new narrative", *The Australian* (1 April 2020).

been warned that we are witnessing the end of globalisation; the end of capitalism; the end of individualism; the end of liberty; and the end of personal autonomy. In place of these fallen heroes, we are told, expect to see: the rise of nationalism; the rise of socialism; the rise (or return) of big government; the rise of a police state; and the rise of excessive and expensive state-funded welfare.

Given that the very ways people go about their lives and conduct their affairs have changed – in some respects, quite possibly, for good – there are grains of truth blended into this pudding mix of prophecies. It is almost certainly true, as the country begins to recover from the first wave of covid-19 and begins the long (and painful) process of economic repair, that social, political, and commercial arrangements will be different. Qantas, for example, which announced in late June 2020 that 6000 or so jobs were going to be cut, will be a very different corporation for a very long time; and industries related to travel, such as tourism and hospitality, are going to be very different, too. Each of the essays in this collection considers the kinds of change we might expect to see across every aspect of Australian society.

In broad terms, however, if we can expect to see the end (or hibernation) of anything, it is likely to be the end (or hibernation) of ideology. The best response the Morrison Government can make to circumstances that are especially covid-volatile is one marked by pragmatism rather than ideology. Of course, if *ideology* is understood as a system of ideas framing one's world outlook, then pragmatism, itself, is an ideology because it, too, represents a particular way of seeing how things are in the world.

Whilst that may be true, for present purposes the term *pragmatism* is used to emphasise the *practical* application of policy to immediate or short-term problems, so as to distinguish it from policies framed with the intention of realising long-term objectives and goals. The approach to policy formation which characterises the progressive

Green-Left, for example, is to revise, reform, and replace existing institutions in an effort to align the way things *are* with a conception of the way things *ought* to be. A time of national crisis might seem the opportune moment to move things "forward" and to make "progress" towards some ideologically informed notion of the "future" – whether it is coal-free, fossil-free, or wealth-free. But policies intended to re-align, and which are made to conform to outlines provided by an ideological cookie cutter will fail, and for two related reasons.

First, pursuit of an ideological objective will often fail to take into account the circumstances of the *really real* as they are today. Whether the policy objective is to soak the rich, rid us of coal, or peg all workers to a minimum wage, the direction to be followed and the terrain to be covered in pursuit of that objective must involve taking a bearing from where things are *now*. But where are things now? How do matters stand today? And how can one take a bearing when covid-chaos prevails?

A second reason that policy fuelled by ideology (in the sense in which it is being used here) is likely to fail is related to its disregard for how the "really real" is today. Pre-occupied with how things *ought* to be and reckless as to how things *are*, ideology runs a grave risk of being insensitive to the importance of maintaining economic and social cohesion. The progressive wants to disrupt, dismantle, and "improve" without regard to the impact such action is likely to have on people and communities today. The conservative wants to maintain, and, where necessary, to adapt and adjust. The progressive ideologue says, pointing to fertile, utopian uplands: *that's where we need to be*; the pragmatic conservative says: *this is where we are and from where we must begin*. But genuine conservatism, as the public policy expert, Oren Cass, has remarked, "seeks to maintain social conditions that encourage the good decisions that help individuals, families, and communities thrive. For most decisions that matter, both economics and culture play a role."[154] The challenge of Keeping Australia Right for recovery in a post-covid world, therefore, requires government to encourage the making of good decisions; it calls, in other words, for the pragmatism of conservatism and not the ideological recklessness of progressivism.

Opinion is divided, often sharply, concerning the response made by the Morrison Government to coronavirus. As case numbers began to abate in mid-May 2020, some felt justified in their earlier warnings that government was overreacting and had imposed an unwarranted debt-laden economic burden. Countries, such as Sweden, which had not imposed strict lockdowns appeared to have suffered little damage from the virus and this added weight to claims that the response of the Australian government was unwarranted.

But then, in late May 2020, case numbers, and the number of deaths, in Sweden began to rise steadily; perhaps things were not so good in Sweden after all. Meanwhile, the situation in the United Kingdom and the United States got steadily worse. Even in Australia, with a relatively small number of cases (and deaths), spikes began to occur in Melbourne. And all this while economists, bankers, and business leaders were bracing for the full impact of covid-19 to make itself felt in the final quarter of 2020.

Scott Morrison, throughout the covid crisis, has exercised calm and decisive leadership even amidst efforts to reign in the wayward and zealous posturing of some state premiers. Morrison, himself, has been nothing if not prime ministerial throughout. Mind you, after his disastrous smokey start to the year, no one should be surprised. There never was going to be another 'Hawaiian shirt' moment; nor was he ever going to delegate responsibility entirely to premiers and argue that primary responsibility for managing the pandemic rested with the States.

---

154   Oren Cass, "The Problem with the Culture Problem", *First Things* (January 2020).

Criticised by some for not having any apparent ideological compass, Morrison has, nonetheless, demonstrated a considerable capacity to govern with much-needed conservative pragmatism. Government has intervened as needed: financial support was forthcoming to avert ruin; restrictions were imposed to avert contagion; and the country was re-opened as soon as practicable. Opportunities for structural reform of the economy – particularly for deregulation and other supply-side reform – now present themselves. It remains to be seen whether Morrison will shrug off the mantel of pragmatic conservatism and opt for a gaudy ideological robe as the impact of hardship makes itself felt.

To date, however, Morrison has neither underplayed the crisis nor sought to minimise the challenge he and his government face to deliver prosperity once again to the 'lucky country'. Voters will deliver their verdict on Morrison at the ballot box in 2022 and only then will we know, for certain, what Australians made of efforts by their prime minister to manage the catastrophic impact of an unforeseen pandemic. Can the Morrison Government keep Australia right? Time, as they say, will tell. But the need for it to do so has never been more pressing.

CONTRIBUTORS

James Allan is Garrick Professor of Law at the University of Queensland and a regular columnist for The Spectator Australia.

Richard Alston has worked variously as a barrister, politician and diplomat and currently earns a living as a company director.

Terry Barnes is a public policy consultant who has had senior ministerial advisory roles in federal and Victorian governments. He was senior personal adviser to two federal health ministers, Michael Wooldridge (1993-97) and Tony Abbott (2003-07).

Morgan Begg is a research fellow with the Institute of Public Affairs.

Robert Carling is an economist with a background in federal and state Treasuries, the IMF and the World Bank, and currently a Senior Fellow at The Centre for Independent Studies.

Denis Dragovic is a practitioner and scholar of religion and society, and is an Honorary Senior Fellow at the University of Melbourne

Peter Kurti is Director of the Culture, Prosperity & Civil Society program at the Centre for Independent Studies and also Adjunct Associate Professor of Law at the University of Notre Dame Australia.

John Lee is a non-resident senior fellow at the US Studies Centre and Hudson Institute in Washington. From 2016 to 2018 he was a senior adviser to the Australian foreign minister.

Alan Moran is an economist, and formerly Deputy Secretary, Energy in the Victorian Government. He has written extensively on energy and the environment, including chapters in four international compilations. His latest book was *Climate Change: Treaties and Policies in the Trump Era*. His work can be seen at www. regulationeconomics.com

Karina Okotel is a mother, lawyer, lecturer, past Senate candidate, former Liberal Party vice president, and former previous councillor and deputy mayor.

Hugh Puttenham is a consultant psychiatrist

Scott Prasser is a public policy analyst and commentator

John Ruddick is a writer and political activist.

John Slater is a solicitor based in Brisbane and the former Policy Director at the Menzies Research Centre.

Andrew Stone was chief economist to prime minister Tony Abbott and is the author of *Restoring Hope: Practical Policies to Revitalise the Australian Economy*.